The
Buddha's Ancient Path

菩提寺
LOS ANGELES BUDDHIST UNION
7833 Emerson Place
Rosemead, CA 91770
Tel: (626) 280-1213

Piyadassi Thera

The Buddha's Ancient Path

First published in the United Kingdom
by Rider & Company 1964
Reprinted 1964

This Sri Lankan edition 1974
Second impression 1979
Third impression 1987

ISBN 955-24-0024-4

To

My Teacher, the late

Venerable Pelene VAJIRAÑĀNA (sanghanāyaka),

Founding-Superior of the Vajirārāma, Colombo

and

The Venerable Madihe PAÑÑĀSĪHA (sanghanāyaka),

the present Superior,

in respectful admiration

Ujumaggamhi akkhāte gacchatha mā nivattatha:
Attanā codayattānaṁ nibbanaṁ abhihāraye

Theragāthā, 637

'Declared is the straight path,
Walk along, falter not;
Let each admonish himself,
And by stages reach Nibbāna.'

CONTENTS

PREFACE

Two thousand five hundred years ago, in the Deer Park at Sarnath, India, close to the ancient city of Vārānasī, was heard the Message of the Buddha which was to revolutionize the thoughts and life of the human race. Though this Message was first heard by just five ascetics, it has now penetrated peaceably to the remotest corners of the world, and the demand for better and deeper understanding of its meaning is great.

Many expositions of the Buddha's Teaching in English have appeared in recent years, but a great number of them lack authenticity and do not represent the Buddha-word correctly. I have in all humility undertaken to set out as accurately as possible the Teaching of the Buddha as it is found in the Pāli Canon, the Tipiṭaka, of the Theravāda which has preserved the oldest and most faithful tradition. This book, therefore, gives a comprehensive account of the central conception of Buddhism—the Four Noble Truths—with special emphasis on the Noble Eightfold Path which is Buddhism in practice. I have named the book *The Ancient Path* (*purāṇamaggaṁ*), the very words used by the Buddha in reference to the Eightfold Path.

As an introduction the first chapter gives a concise account of the life of the Buddha, while the second sets out the correct standpoint of Buddhism. The Four Noble Truths and the Eightfold Path are discussed at full length in the following chapters. A good deal of space is devoted to Buddhist meditation, as found in the *suttas* or discourses of the Buddha, in chapters 12, 13 and 14.

I now express my sense of gratitude first to Nyanaponika Thera, who invited and encouraged me to write this book while I was staying at the Senanayaka (Forest) Hermitage, Kandy, Ceylon, for the many interesting discussions I had with him on the subject and for information on special points, and to Mr. Francis Story, the Anagārika Sugatananda, who with much kindliness read through the type-script and made useful and valuable suggestions. To Bhikkhu Jinaputta, Messrs. V. F. Gunaratna, the Public Trustee of Ceylon, R. Abeysekara and D. Munidasa, also, I am grateful for much help and encouragement. I would also like to record here my deep gratitude to four distinguished members of the Order, the Theras: Metteyya, Soma, Kassapa and Ñāṇamoli with whom I have been associated for more than a decade. Many a lively discussion that I have had with them on the *Dhamma* has inspired me. They are no more. Meetings end in partings (*saṁyogā viyogantā*). Last but far from least to Mr. K. G. Abeysingha, who so tirelessly typed the whole script, I am grateful.

PIYADASSI

Vajirārāma,
Colombo 5,
Ceylon

I

THE BUDDHA

THE Buddha, the founder of the great religion[1] Buddhism, lived in North India over 2500 years ago and is known as Siddhattha (Skt. Siddhārtha, one whose purpose has been achieved). Gotama (Skt. Gautama) was his family name. His father, Suddhodana, ruled over the land of the Sākyans at Kapilavatthu on the Nepalese frontier. Mahāmāyā, princess of the Koliyas, was Suddhodana's queen.

On a full-moon day of May—vasanta-tide, when in India the trees were laden with leaf, flower and fruit, and man, bird and beast were in joyous mood, Queen Mahāmāyā was travelling in state from Kapilavatthu to Devadaha, her parental home, according to the custom of the times, to give birth to her child. But that was not to be, for halfway between the two cities, in the Lumbini grove, under the shade of a flowering Sal tree, she brought forth a son.

Lumbini or Rummindei, the name by which it is now known, is 100 miles north of Vārānasi[2] and within sight of the snow-capped Himālayas. At this memorable spot where Prince Siddhattha, the future Buddha, was born, Emperor Asoka, 316 years after the event, erected a mighty stone pillar to mark the holy spot. The inscription engraved on the pillar in five lines consists of ninety-three Asokan (*brāhmi*) characters, amongst which occurs the following: '*Hida Budhe jāte Sākyamuni*', 'Here was born the Buddha, the sage of the Sākyans'. The mighty column is still to be seen. The pillar, 'as crisp as the day it was cut', had been struck by lightning even when Hiuen Tsiang, the Chinese pilgrim, saw it towards the middle of the seventh century after Christ. The discovery and identification of the Lumbini park in 1896 is attributed to the renowned archaeologist, General Cunningham.

1. The term religion is used here in the sense of a 'Way of Life' and not in the sense in which it is commonly understood. See p. 31.

2. The name for Benares used by the Indian Government after independence.

Queen Mahāmāyā, the mother, passed away on the seventh day after the birth of her child, and the babe was nursed by his mother's sister, Pajāpati Gotami. Though the child was nurtured till manhood in refinement amidst an abundance of material luxury, the father did not fail to give his son the education that a prince ought to receive. He became skilled in many a branch of knowledge, and in the arts of war easily excelled all others.

Nevertheless, from his childhood the prince was given to serious contemplation. When the prince grew up the father's fervent wish was that his son should marry, bring up a family and be his worthy successor; but he feared that the prince would one day give up home for the homeless life of an ascetic.

According to the custom of the time, at the early age of sixteen the prince was married to his cousin Yasodharā, the only daughter of King Suppabuddha and Queen Pamitā of the Koliyas. The princess was of the same age as the prince. Lacking nothing of the earthly joys of life, he lived knowing naught of sorrow. Yet all the efforts of the father to hold his son a prisoner to the senses and make him worldly-minded were of no avail. King Suddhodana's endeavours to keep life's miseries from his son's inquiring eyes only heightened Prince Siddhattha's curiosity and his resolute search for Truth and Enlightenment.

With the advance of age and maturity the prince began to glimpse the woes of the world. As the books say, he saw four visions: the first was a man weakened with age, utterly helpless; the second was the sight of a man mere skin and bones, supremely unhappy and forlorn, smitten with some pest; the third was the sight of a band of lamenting kinsmen bearing on their shoulders the corpse of one beloved for cremation. These woeful signs deeply moved him. The fourth vision, however, made a lasting impression. He saw a recluse, calm and serene, aloof and independent, and learnt that he was one who had abandoned his home to live a life of purity, to seek Truth and solve the riddle of life. Thoughts of renunciation flashed through the prince's mind and in deep contemplation he turned homeward. The heart-throb of an agonized and ailing humanity found a responsive echo in his own heart. The more he came in contact with the world outside his palace walls, the more convinced he became that the world was lacking in true happiness.

In the silence of that moonlit night (it was the full moon of July) such thoughts as these arose in him:

'Youth, the prime of life, ends in old age and man's senses fail him when they are most needed. The hale and hearty lose their vigour and health when disease suddenly creeps in. Finally death comes, sudden perhaps and unexpected, and puts an end to this brief span of life. Surely there must be an escape from this unsatisfactoriness, from ageing and death.'

Thus the great intoxication of youth, of health, and of life left him.[1] Having seen the vanity and the danger of the three intoxications, he was overcome by a powerful urge to seek and win the Deathless, to strive for deliverance from old age, illness, misery and death,[2] to seek it for himself and for all beings that suffer. It was his deep compassion that led him to the quest ending in Enlightenment, in Buddhahood. It was compassion that now moved his heart towards the Great Renunciation and opened for him the doors of the golden cage of his home life. It was compassion that made his determination unshakable even by the last parting glance at his beloved wife asleep with their babe in her arms.

Now at the age of twenty-nine, in the flower of youthful manhood, on the day his beautiful Yasodharā, giving birth to his only son, Rāhula, made the parting more sorrowful and heart-rending, he tore himself away—the prince with a superhuman effort of will renounced wife, child, father and a crown that held the promise of power and glory, and in the guise of an indigent ascetic retreated into forest solitude to seek the eternal verities of life. 'In quest of the supreme security from bondage—*Nibbāna*'.[3] This was the great renunciation.

Dedicating himself to the noble task of discovering a remedy for life's universal ill, he sought guidance from two famous sages, Ālāra Kālāma and Uddaka Rāmaputta, hoping that they, being masters of meditation, would show him the way to deliverance. He practised concentration and reached the highest meditative attainments possible thereby, but was not satisfied with anything short of supreme enlightenment. Their range of knowledge, their ambit of mystical experience, however, was insufficient to grant him what he earnestly sought. He left them in turn in search of the still unknown.

In his wanderings he finally reached Uruvela, by the river Nerañjarā at Gayā. He was attracted by its quiet and dense groves and the clear waters of the river. Finding that this was a suitable

1. *Yobbanamada, ārogyamada, jīvitamada.*
2. See *A.* i. 146, *sutta* 38.
3. *M.* i. 163, *sutta* 26.

place to continue his quest for enlightenment, he decided to stay. Five other ascetics who admired his determined effort waited on him. They were Kondañña, Bhaddiya, Vappa, Mahānāma and Assaji.

There was, and still is, a belief in India among many of her ascetics that purification and final deliverance from ill can be achieved by rigorous self-mortification, and the ascetic Gotama decided to test the truth of it. And so there at Uruvela he began a determined struggle to subdue his body, in the hope that his mind, set free from the shackles of the body, might be able to soar to the heights of liberation. Most zealous was he in these practices. He lived on leaves and roots, on a steadily reduced pittance of food, he wore rags from dust-heaps; he slept among corpses or on beds of thorns. The utter paucity of nourishment left him a physical wreck.

'Rigorous have I been in my ascetic discipline. Rigorous have I been beyond all others. Like wasted, withered reeds became all my limbs. . . .' In such words as these, in later years, having attained to full enlightenment, did the Buddha give his disciples an awe-inspiring description of his early penances.[1]

Struggling thus for six long years, he came to death's very door, but he found himself no nearer to his goal. The utter futility of self-mortification became abundantly clear to him by his own experience; his experiment for enlightenment had failed. But undiscouraged, his still active mind searched for new paths to the aspired-for goal. Then it happened that he remembered the peace of his meditation in childhood under a rose-apple tree, and confidently felt: 'This is the path to enlightenment'. He knew, however, that, with a body so utterly weakened as his, he could not follow that path with any chance of success. Thus he abandoned self-mortification and extreme fasting and took normal food. His emaciated body recovered its former health and his exhausted vigour soon returned. Now his five companions left him in their disappointment; for they thought that he had given up the effort to live a life of abundance.

Nevertheless with firm determination and complete faith in his own purity and strength, unaided by any teacher, accompanied by none, the Bodhisatta[2] (as he is known before he attained enlighten-

1. For a detailed account see *M.* 36, translation by I. B. Horner in *The Middle Length Sayings*, Vol. I (Pāli Text Society, London).

2. A Bodhisatta (Skt. Bodhisattva) is one who adheres to or is bent on (*satta*) the ideal of enlightenment, or knowledge of the four noble truths (*bodhi*). In this

ment) resolved to make his final search in complete solitude. Cross-legged he sat under a tree, which later became known as the Bodhi tree, the 'Tree of Enlightenment' or 'Tree of Wisdom',[1] on the Bank of the river Nerañjarā, at Gayā (now known as Buddha-Gayā)—'a pleasant spot soothing to the senses and stimulating to the mind'—making the final effort with the inflexible resolution: 'Though only my skin, sinews and bones remain, and my blood and flesh dry up and wither away, yet will I never stir from this seat until I have attained full enlightenment (*sammā-saṁ-bodhi*).' So indefatigable in effort, so unflagging in his devotion was he, and so resolute to realize Truth and attain full enlightenment.

Applying himself to the 'Mindfulness on in-and-out Breathing' (*āna + apāna sati*), the meditation he had developed in his childhood,[2]

sense, the term may be applied to any one who is bent on enlightenment. But it is specially applied to an aspirant for full enlightenment (*sammā-saṁ-bodhi*). A Bodhisatta fully cultivates ten perfections or *pārami* which are essential qualities of extremely high standard initiated by compassion, and ever tinged with understanding or quick wit, free from craving, pride and false views (*taṇhā, diṭṭhi* and *māna*) that qualify an aspirant for Buddhahood. They are: generosity, morality, renunciation, wisdom, effort, forbearance, truthfulness, determination, loving-kindness and equanimity (*dāna, sīla, nekkhamma, paññā, viriya, khanti, sacca, adhiṭṭhāna, mettā* and *upekkhā*).

1. It appears to be rather strange that no mention of the Bodhi tree is made in the two discourses (nos. 26 and 36 of the *Majjhima Nikāya*) which graphically describe the Bodhisatta's struggle and search for enlightenment.

The Account given in the two discourses is as follows:

'Then I, monks, seeking for whatever is good, searching for the incomparable, matchless path to peace, walking on tour through Magadha in due course arrived at Uruvela, the camp township. There I saw a delightful stretch of land and a lovely woodland grove, and a clear flowing river (the Nerañjarā) with a delightful ford, and a village for support nearby. It occurred to me monks: "Indeed, it is a delightful stretch of land. . . ." "Indeed this does well for the striving of a young man set on striving." So I, monks, sat down just there, thinking: "Indeed this does well for striving."' (Miss I. B. Horner's translation *The Middle Length Sayings*, i, 210.)

Perhaps the Buddha felt it was not necessary for him to mention that he sat under a tree as it was well known then that recluses and ascetics sat cross-legged in the open under trees for their meditation.

In the *Mahāpadhāna-sutta* (*D.* ii. 4), however, the tree is mentioned. It is an *Assattha*, the sacred fig tree, *ficus religiosa*. Mention of the tree was made by the Buddha Gotama when he referred to the lives of the previous six Buddhas, his predecessors. Addressing the monks he said: 'I, now, monks, am an Accomplished One (*arahaṁ*), a Supremely Enlightened One (*sammā-saṁ-buddho*). I attained supreme enlightenment under the fig tree (*assatthassa mūle abhisambuddho*).'

2. Read *M.* 36 with the *Com. MA.* ii. 291 and *Ānāpāna Saṁyutta* no. 8 (*S.* v. 317).

the Bodhisatta entered upon and dwelt in the first meditative absorbtion (*jhāna* skt. *dhyāna*,[1] a term difficult to translate). By gradual stages he entered upon and dwelt in the second, third and the fourth *jhānas*. Thus cleansing his mind of impurities; with the mind thus composed, he directed it to the knowledge of recollecting past births (*pubbenivāsānussatiñāṇa*). This was the first knowledge attained by him in the first watch of the night (6 p.m. to 10 p.m.). Then the Bodhisatta directed his mind to the knowledge of the disappearing and reappearing of beings of varied forms, in good states of existence, and in states of woe, each faring according to his deeds (*cuti* + *upapāta ñāṇa*). This was the second knowledge attained by him in the middle watch of the night (10 p.m. to 2 a.m.). Next he directed his mind to the knowledge of the destruction of the taints (*āsavakkhayañāṇa*).

He understood as it really is: This is suffering (*dukkha*), this is the arising of suffering, this is the cessation of suffering, this is the path leading to the cessation of suffering.[2] He understood as it really is: These are the taints (*āsavas*), this is the arising of the taints, this is the cessation of the taints, this is the path leading to the cessation of the taints.

Knowing thus, seeing thus, his mind was liberated from the taints: of sense-pleasures (*kāmāsava*), of becoming (*bhavāsava*), and of ignorance (*avijjāsava*).[3] When his mind was thus liberated, there came the knowledge: 'liberated' and he understood:

Destroyed is birth, the noble life (*brahma cariyaṁ*) has been lived, done is what was to be done, there is no more of this to come (meaning, there is no more continuity of the mind and body, that is, no more becoming, rebirth). This was the third knowledge attained by him in the last watch of the night (2 a.m. to 6 a.m.).[4]

Thereon he spoke these words of victory:

'Being myself subject to birth, ageing, disease, death, sorrow and defilement; seeing danger in what is subject to these things; seeking the unborn, unageing, diseaseless, deathless, sorrowless, undefiled, supreme security from bondage—Nibbāna, I attained it (literally I experienced it). Knowledge and vision arose in me; unshakable

1. See chapter 14, Right Concentration (*sammā-samādhi*).
2. For details see chapter 3 on The First Noble Truth, *dukkha*.
3. Elsewhere we see taint of false view (*diṭṭhāsava*) added to these as the fourth taint (*āsava*).
4. *M.* 36.

is my deliverance of mind. This is the last birth, now there is no more becoming, no more rebirth.'[1]

Thus did the Bodhisatta Gotama on another full moon of May, at the age of thirty-five, attain Supreme Enlightenment, by comprehending in all their fullness the Four Noble Truths, the Eternal Verities, and become the Buddha, the great Healer and Consummate Master-Physician (*bhisakko*) who can cure the ills of beings.

For a week, immediately after this enlightenment, the Buddha sat at the foot of the Bodhi tree experiencing the bliss of deliverance. Then he thought over the Dependent Arising (*paṭicca samuppāda*).[2] The Blessed One then spent six more weeks in lonely retreat at six different places in the vicinity of the Bodhi tree.[3] At the end of the seven weeks, he made up his mind to communicate the *Dhamma*, his discovery of the Ancient Path (*purānaṁ maggaṁ*), to his former friends, the five ascetics.

Knowing that they were living at Vārānasī in the deer park at Isipatana, the Resort of Seers (modern Sarnath), still steeped in the unmeaning rigours of extreme asceticism, the Buddha left Gayā for distant Vārānasī, India's holy city, walking by stages some 150 miles. There at the deer park (*migadāya*) he rejoined them.

Now on a full moon day of July, at eventide, when the moon was rising in a glowing Eastern sky, the Blessed One addressed the five ascetics:

'Monks, these two extremes ought not to be cultivated by the recluse, by one gone forth from the house-life. What two? Sensual indulgence and self-mortification which lead to no good. The middle way, understood by the Tathāgata,[4] the Perfect One, after he had avoided the extremes, gives vision, and knowledge, and leads to calm, realization, enlightenment, Nibbāna. And what, monks, is that middle way? It is this Noble Eightfold Path, namely:

1. *M.* 26.
2. This deeply profound doctrine is discussed in chapter 4, The Arising of Suffering.
3. Vinaya, Mahāvagga.
4. Even before the advent of the Buddha the word *Tathāgata* was used, but in the sense of 'being' (*satta*) as in the saying '*hoti tathāgato parammaraṇā*—will there be a being after death?'. The Venerable Sāriputta used it in this sense when explaining a point to the Venerable Yamaka. See *S.* iii. 111 and commentary. After the advent of the Buddha, however, it was used as an epithet for the Buddha, and the Master frequently used it when referring to himself. The commentary to the *Anguttara Nikāya* (P.T.S. i. 103) gives the following meanings to the word. 'One attained to Truth.' 'One who understands things as they are and not otherwise.' 'Thus gone' (*Tathā* + *gata*).

right understanding, right thought, right speech, right action, right livelihood, right effort, right mindfulness, right concentration.'[1]

Then the Buddha explained to them the Four Noble Truths.[2]

Thus did the Enlightened One proclaim the *Dhamma* and set in motion the matchless 'Wheel of Truth' (*anuttaraṁ dhammacakkaṁ*).

With the proclamation of the *Dhamma*, for the first time, and with the conversion of the five ascetics, the deer park at Isipatana (Sarnath) became the birth place of the Buddha's Dispensation (*Buddha-sāsana*), and of the *Saṅgha*, the community of monks, the ordained disciples.[3]

Before long fifty-five others headed by Yasa, a young man of wealth, joined the Order of the Sangha. When the Rains (*vassāna*, July–October) ended, the Buddha addressed his disciples, the Accomplished Ones (*arahats*), now sixty in number and said:

'Released am I, monks, from all ties whether human or divine. You also are delivered from fetters whether human or divine. Go now and wander for the welfare and happiness of many out of compassion for the world, for the gain, welfare and happiness of gods and men. Let not two of you proceed in the same direction. Proclaim the *Dhamma* (doctrine) that is excellent in the beginning, excellent in the middle, excellent in the end, possessed of meaning and the letter and utterly perfect. Proclaim the life of purity, the holy life consummate and pure. There are beings with little dust in their eyes who will be lost through not hearing the *Dhamma*. There are beings who will understand the *Dhamma*. I also shall go to Uruvela, to Senānigāma to teach the *Dhamma*.'[4]

1. *Vinaya*. i. 10, *S*. v. 420.
2. The path and the Four Noble Truths which outline the basis of the entire teaching will be discussed in later chapters.
3. The Emperor Asoka came on pilgrimage to this holy spot and caused a series of monuments and a commemorative pillar with the lion capital to be erected. This capital with its four magnificent lions upholding the '*Dharma-Cakra*', 'the Wheel of *Dharma*', now stands in the museum of Sarnath, and is today the official crest of India. The '*Dharma-Cakra*' festival is still kept in Ceylon.

Jawaharlal Nehru writes: 'At Sarnath near Benares, I would almost see the Buddha preaching his first sermon, and some of his recorded words would come like a distant echo to me through two thousand five hundred years. Asoka's pillars of stone with their inscriptions would speak to me in their magnificent language and tell me of a man who, though an emperor, was greater than any king or emperor.'

The Discovery of India (The Signet Press, Calcutta), p. 44.

4. *Vinaya Mahāvagga*.

Thus did the Buddha commence his sublime mission which lasted to the end of his life. With his disciples he walked the highways and byways of Jambudīpa, Land of the rose apple (another name for India), enfolding all within the aura of his boundless compassion and wisdom.

The Buddha made no distinction of caste, clan or class when communicating the *Dhamma*. Men and women from different walks of life—the poor and the needy, the lowliest and the lost, the literate and the illiterate, brahmins and outcasts, princes and paupers, saints and criminals—listened to the Buddha, took refuge in him, and followed him who showed the path to peace and enlightenment.

Caste, which was a matter of vital importance to the brahmins of India, was one of utter indifference to the Buddha, who strongly condemned so debasing a system. The Buddha freely admitted into the Order people from all castes and classes, when he knew that they were fit to live the holy life, and some of them later distinguished themselves in the Order. The Buddha was the only contemporary teacher who endeavoured to blend in mutual tolerance and concord those who hitherto had been rent asunder by differences of caste and class.

The Buddha also raised the status of women in India. Generally speaking, during the time of the Buddha, owing to brahminical influence, women were not given much recognition. Sometimes they were held in contempt, although there were solitary cases of their showing erudition in matters of philosophy, and so on. In his large-heartedness and magnanimity, the Buddha treated women with consideration and civility, and pointed out to them, too, the path to peace, purity and sanctity. The Buddha established the Order of Nuns (*Bhikkhunī Sāsana*) for the first time in history; for never before this had there been an Order where women could lead a celibate life of renunciation. Women from all walks of life joined the Order. The lives of quite a number of these noble nuns, their strenuous endeavours to win the goal of freedom, and their paeans of joy at deliverance of mind are graphically described in the 'Psalms of the Sisters' (*Theri-gāthā*).[1]

While journeying from village to village, from town to town, instructing, enlightening and gladdening the many, the Buddha saw how superstitious folk, steeped in ignorance, slaughtered animals in worship of their gods. He spoke to them:

1. *Psalms of the Early Buddhists—The Sisters,* translated by C. A. F. Rhys Davids. P.T.S. Translation Series.

'Of life, which all can take but none can give,
Life which all creatures love and strive to keep,
Wonderful, dear, and pleasant unto each,
Even to the meanest. . . .'[1]

Thus when people who prayed to the gods for mercy, were merciless, and India was blood-stained with the morbid sacrifices of innocent animals at the desecrated altars of imaginary deities, and the harmful rites and rituals of ascetics and brahmins brought disaster and untold agony, the Buddha, the Master of merciful wisdom, pointed out the Ancient Path, the path of the Enlightened Ones, of righteousness, love and understanding. Being one who acted in constant conformity with what he preached, the Four Sublime States (*brahma-vihāra*)[2] always dominated his acts.

The Buddha never encouraged wrangling and animosity. Addressing the monks he once said: 'I quarrel not with the world, monks, it is the world that quarrels with me. An exponent of the *Dhamma* quarrels not with anyone in the world.'[3]

Though the Order of the *Saṅgha* began its career with only sixty disciples, it expanded into thousands, and in those early days an adherent sought entry into it by pronouncing the threefold formula known as the 'Three Refuges' (*ti-saraṇa*):

'*Buddhaṁ saraṇaṁ gacchāmi*
Dhammaṁ saraṇaṁ gacchāmi
Sanghaṁ saraṇaṁ gacchāmi

Dutiyampi Buddhaṁ saraṇaṁ gacchāmi
Dutiyampi Dhammaṁ saraṇaṁ gacchāmi
Dutiyampi Sanghaṁ saraṇaṁ gacchāmi

Tatiyampi Buddhaṁ saraṇaṁ gacchāmi
Tatiyaṁpi Dhammaṁ saraṇaṁ gacchāmi
Tatiyaṁpi Sanghaṁ saraṇaṁ gacchāmi'

'I go for refuge to the Buddha (the Teacher)
I go for refuge to the Dhamma (the Teaching)
I go for refuge to the Sangha (the Taught)

1. Sir Edwin Arnold, *The Light of Asia*.
2. The Four Sublime States are: unbounded lovingkindness (*mettā*), compassion (*karuṇā*), sympathetic joy (*muditā*), equanimity (*upekkhā*), see chapter 8.
3. *S.* iii. 138.

For the second time I go for refuge to the Buddha
For the second time I go for refuge to the Dhamma
For the second time I go for refuge to the Sangha

For the third time I go for refuge to the Buddha
For the third time I go for refuge to the Dhamma
For the third time I go for refuge to the Sangha.'[1]

As a result of the increasing number of monks, monasteries came into being, and in later times monastic Indian universities like Nālandā, Vikramaśilā and Odantapuri became cultural centres which gradually influenced the whole of Asia, and, through it, the mental life of mankind.

After a successful ministry of forty-five years the Buddha passed away at the age of eighty at the Sala Grove[2] of the Mallas at Kusinārā (in modern Uttara Pradesh about 120 miles north-east of Vārānasī), with a final admonition to his followers:

'*Vayadhammā saṁkhārā, appamādena sampādetha*'[3]

'Subject to change are all component things. Strive on with heedfulness.'

With only a few followers at the beginning, Buddhism penetrated into many a land,[4] and is today the 'religion' of over 500,000,000, more than one-fifth of the world's population.

Buddhism made such rapid strides chiefly due to its intrinsic

1. *Vinaya Mahāvagga.*

2. In a way it is interesting to note that this greatest of Indian Rishis (seers) was born under a tree in a park, attained enlightenment under the Bodhi tree (a cutting from the south branch of which brought by Sanghamittā, the Arahat Theri, daughter of Emperor Asoka of India, third century B.C., still flourishes at Anurādhapura in Ceylon, and is the oldest recorded tree in the world), set in motion the 'Wheel of Truth' (*Dhammacakka*, Skt. *Dharma-cakra*) at the deer park under trees, and finally passed away under the twin sāla trees. He spent most of his time in the open, in the forests and villages of India.

3. *D.* 16. The discourse on the passing away of the Buddha (*Parinibbāna-sutta*), wherein are recorded in moving detail all the events that occurred during the last months and days of the Master's life.

4. Today Buddhism is found in Ceylon, Burma, Thailand, Cambodia, Laos, Vietnam, Nepal, Tibet, China, Japan, Mongolia, Korea, Formosa, in some parts of India, Chittagong in Pakistan, Malaya and in some parts of Indonesia. Several Western countries with Buddhist Saṅgha are now qualifying to be included in this list.

worth and its appeal to the reasoning mind, but there were other factors that aided its progress: never did the messengers of the *Dhamma* (*Dhammadūta*) use any iniquitous methods in spreading the doctrine. The only weapon they wielded was that of universal love and compassion. Furthermore Buddhism penetrated to these countries peaceably without disturbing the creeds that were already there.

Buddhist missions to which the annals of religious history scarcely afforded a parallel were carried on neither by force of arms nor by the use of any coercive or reprehensible methods. Conversion by compulsion was unknown and repugnant to the Buddha and his disciples.

'There is no record known to me,' wrote Professor T. W. Rhys Davids, 'in the whole of the long history of Buddhism throughout the many centuries where its followers have been for such lengthened periods supreme, of any persecution by the Buddhists of the followers of any other faith'.

Buddhism was thus able to diffuse itself through a great variety of cultures throughout the world.

2

THE BUDDHIST STANDPOINT

ONE of the noteworthy characteristics that distinguish the Buddha from all other religious teachers is that he was a human being with no connection whatsoever with a God or any other 'Supernatural' Being. He was neither God nor an incarnation of God, nor any mythological figure. He was a man, but a super-man, an extraordinary man (*accariya manussa*). He was beyond the human state inwardly though living the life of a human being outwardly. Just as he is for this reason called a unique being, man par excellence (*purisuttama*).

The Buddha says: 'Even as, monks, a lotus born and grown in water, stands above, unsmeared by water, so the Tathāgata, monks, born and grown up in the world, yet lives lord over the world without coming together with the world.'[1]

Depending on his own unremitting energy, unaided by any teacher, human or divine, he achieved the highest mental and intellectual attainments; reached the acme of purity, and was perfect in the best qualities of human nature. He was an embodiment of compassion and wisdom, which became the two guiding principles in his dispensation (*sāsana*).

Through personal experience he understood the supremacy of man, and the concept of a 'supernatural' being who rules over the destinies of beings below, he found to be a mere illusion. The Buddha never claimed to be a saviour who tried to save 'souls' by means of a revealed religion. Through his own perseverance and understanding he proved that infinite possibilities are latent in man and that it must be man's endeavour to develop and unfold these possibilities. He proved by his own experience that enlightenment and deliverance lie absolutely and entirely in man's hand. Being an exponent of the strenuous life by precept and example, the Buddha

1. *S.* iii. 138.

encouraged his disciples to cultivate self-reliance, thus: 'You are your own refuge, who else could refuge be?'[1]

It was also the Buddha who for the first time in the world's history taught that deliverance could be attained independently of an external agency, that deliverance from suffering must be wrought and fashioned by each one for himself upon the anvil of his own actions.

None can grant deliverance to another who merely begs for it. Others may lend us a helping hand indirectly; but nevertheless the highest freedom is attained only through self-realization and self-awakening to Truth. Self-realization can come only to one who is free to think out his own problems without let or hindrance. Each individual should make the appropriate effort and break the shackles that have kept him in bondage, winning freedom from the shackles of existence by perseverance, self-exertion and insight, and not through prayers and petitions to a Supreme Being. The Buddha warns his disciples against shifting the burden to an external agency, a saviour, a God or Brahma, directs them to the ways of discrimination and research, and urges them to get busy with the real task of developing their inner forces and qualities. He says: 'I have directed you towards deliverance. The *Dhamma*, the Truth, is to be self-realized[2].

Buddhist monks are not priests who perform rites of sacrifice. They do not administer sacraments and pronounce absolution. An ideal Buddhist monk cannot and does not stand as an intermediary between men and 'supernatural' powers; for Buddhism teaches that each individual is solely responsible for his own liberation. Hence there is no need to win the favour of a mediating priest. 'You yourselves should strive on; the Tathāgatas only show the path.'[3]

The path is the same Ancient Path trodden and pointed out by the Enlightened Ones of all ages. It is the Noble Eightfold Path leading to enlightenment and highest security.

Another distinguishing characteristic is that the Buddha never preserved his supreme knowledge for himself alone. To the Buddha such a wish is utterly inconceivable. Perfect enlightenment, the discovery and realization of the Four Noble Truths (Buddhahood), is not the prerogative of a single being chosen by Divine Providence; nor is it a unique and unrepeatable event in human history. It is an achievement open to anyone who earnestly strives for perfect

1. *Dhp.* 160. 2. *M.* 38. 3. *Dhp.* 276.

purity and true wisdom, and with inflexible will cultivates the Noble Eightfold Path.

Those who cultivate the path and reach the highest stage of realization (*arahatta*), the final liberation from suffering, have been solemnly declared by the Buddha to be his equals as far as the emancipation from defilements and ultimate deliverance is concerned:

'Victors like me are they, indeed,
They who have won defilements' end.'[1]

The Buddha, however, also made clear to his disciples the difference between a fully Enlightened One and the Arahats, the Accomplished Saints:

'The Tathāgata, O disciples, while being an Arahat,[2] is fully Enlightened. It is he who proclaims a path not proclaimed before, he is the knower of a path, who understands a path, who is skilled in a path.[3] And now his disciples are way-farers who follow in his footsteps. That, disciples, is the distinction, the specific feature which distinguishes the Tathāgata, who being an Arahat, is Fully Enlightened, from the disciple who is freed by insight.'[4]

When communicating the *Dhamma* to his disciples the Master made no distinction whatsoever amongst them; for there were

1. *M.* 26.

2. Sanskrit *arhat* 'the consummate one', 'The Worthy One'. One of the titles applied exclusively to the Buddha and the perfected disciples. As the books reveal, the first application of the term to the Buddha was by himself. That was when the Buddha was journeying from Gayā to Vārānasī to deliver his first sermon to the five ascetics. On the way, not far from Gayā, the Buddha was met by Upaka, an ascetic, who, struck by the serene appearance of the Master, inquired: 'Who is thy teacher? Whose teaching do you profess?'

Replying in verse, the Buddha said:

'I, verily, am the *Arahat* in the world,
A teacher peerless am I.'

He used the word for the second time when addressing the five ascetics thus: 'I am an *Arahat*, a Tathāgata, fully enlightened.'

The word is applied only to those who have fully destroyed the taints. In this sense, the Buddha was the first *Arahat* in the world as he himself revealed to Upaka.

3. *Maggaññu, maggavidū, maggakovido.*

4. *S.* iii. 66.

no specially chosen favourite disciples. Amongst his adherents all those who were Arahats, who were passion-free, and had shed the fetters binding them to renewed existence, had equally perfected themselves in purity. But there were some outstanding ones who were skilled in different branches of knowledge and practice, and because of their mental endowments gained positions of distinction, but special favours were never granted to anyone by the Master. Upāli, for instance, who came from a barber's family, was made the chief in matters of discipline (*vinaya*) in preference to many Arahats who belonged to the class of the nobles and warriors.

There is not even an indication that the Master entrusted the dispensa tion (*sāsana*) to any particular disciple before he passed away; not even to his two chief disciples, Sāriputta and Mahā Moggallāna. He did not appoint anyone as his successor. In this connection it is interesting to note that the Buddha made clear to his disciples, before he passed away, that he never thought of controlling the Order. Addressing the monks round his death-bed the Master said:

'The doctrine and the discipline (*Dhamma-vinaya*) which I have set forth and laid down for you let them after I am gone be the teacher to you.'[1]

Even during his life time it was the *Dhamma-vinaya* that controlled and guided the monks. He was no potentate. The Buddha's Ancient Path, the Eightfold Path, is the teaching for free men.

The Buddha appeared at a time when autocracy was prevalent in India. But his teaching was somewhat of a threat to such autocratic government. He did not, however, interfere with the politics and the government of the country; for he was never a meddler in things where interference was useless, but that did not deter him from giving voice to his democratic thoughts and views. The Buddha's teaching definitely encourages democratic ideas and institutions. Though the Buddha wisely refrained from interfering with the then existing governments, he made the *saṅgha*, the community of monks, an absolutely democratic institution.

As the Marquess of Zetland, a former Viceroy of India, said:

'It is probable that the tendency towards self-government evidenced by these various forms of corporate activity received fresh impetus from the Buddhist rejection of the authority of the

1. *D.* 16, *Parinibbāna-sutta.*

priesthood and further by its doctrine of equality as exemplified by its repudiation of caste. It is indeed to the Buddhist books that we have to turn for an account of the manner in which the affairs of these early examples of representative self-governing institutions were conducted. And it may come as a surprise to many to learn that in the assemblies of Buddhists in India two thousand years and more ago are to be found the rudiments of our own parliamentary practice of the present day. The dignity of the assembly was preserved by the appointment of a special officer—the embryo of "Mr. Speaker" in our House of Commons. A second officer was appointed to see that when necessary a quorum was secured—the prototype of the Parliamentary Chief Whip, in our own system. A member initiating business did so in the form of a motion which was then open to discussion. In some cases, this was done once only, in others three times, thus anticipating the practice of Parliament in requiring that a Bill be read a third time before it becomes law. If discussion disclosed a difference of opinion the matter was decided by the vote of the majority, the voting being by ballot.'[1]

Characteristic, again, is the Buddha's method of teaching the *Dhamma*. The Buddha disapproved of those who professed to have 'secret doctrines'; saying: 'Secrecy is the hall-mark of false doctrine.' Addressing the Venerable Ānanda, the personal attendant of the Master, the Buddha said: 'I have taught the *Dhamma*, Ānanda, without making any distinction between exoteric and esoteric doctrine, for in respect of the Truth, Ānanda, the Tathāgata has no such thing as the "closed fist" of a teacher, who hides some essential knowledge from the pupil.'[2] He declared the *Dhamma* freely and equally to all. He kept nothing back, and never wished to extract from his disciples blind and submissive faith in him and his teaching. He insisted on discriminative examination and intelligent inquiry. In no uncertain terms did he urge critical investigation when he addressed the inquiring Kālāmas in a discourse that has been rightly called 'the first charter of free thought'.

A summary of the Kālāma sutta is as follows:

Kesaputta was a small town in the kingdom of Kosala. The inhabitants of this town were known as Kālāmas. When they heard that the Buddha had entered their town, they came to him for guidance and said:

1. *Legacy of India*, Ed. by G. T. Garratt (Oxford, 1937), pp. x, xi.
2. *D.* 16.

'Venerable sir, there are some recluses and brahmins who visit Kesaputta. As to their own view they expound it in full, but as to the view of others, they condemn, revile and cripple it. Other recluses and brahmins, on coming to Kesaputta, do likewise. Venerable Sir, we doubt and waver as to which of these worthies speak truth and which falsehood.'

'Yes, Kālāmas, right it is for you to doubt, doubt has arisen in a doubtful matter. Come, O Kālāmas, be ye not led by reports or tradition, or hearsay, nor by what is in a religious text, nor by mere logic or inference, nor by considering appearances, nor after reflection on an approval of some theory, nor by seeming possibilities, nor upon the consideration "this recluse is our teacher". But, O Kālāmas, when you know for yourselves: "these things are unwholesome, these things are blameable and unprofitable," then indeed, do ye reject them. . . .

'And when you know for yourselves: "these things are wholesome, blameless and profitable", then do you, having undertaken them, abide therein.' Then the Buddha questioned them thus: 'Now, what think ye O Kālāmas, when greed, hate and delusion arise in a man do they arise to his profit or to his loss? Are they blameable or not?'

– To his loss, Venerable Sir, they are blameable.
– Now, what think ye, Kālāmas, when freedom from greed, hate and delusion arise in a man, do they arise to his profit or loss? Are they blameable or not?
– To his profit, Lord. They are blameless.
– So then, Kālāmas, as to my words to you just now: 'Be ye not led by reports . . . abide therein.' Such was my reason for saying them.[1]

To take anything on trust is not in the spirit of Buddhism, so we find this dialogue between the Master and his disciples:

– If, now, knowing this and preserving this, would you say: 'We honour our Master and through respect for him we respect what he teaches?'
– No, Lord?
– That which you affirm, O disciples, is it not only that which you yourselves have recognized, seen and grasped?
– Yes, Lord.[2]

1. *A.* i. 188, *sutta* 65. Cf. *A.* i. *sutta* 66 and *A.* ii. *Bhaddiya sutta* 193.
2. *M.* 47.

And in conformity with this thoroughly correct attitude of true inquiry, it is said, in a Buddhist treatise on logic: 'As the wise test gold by burning, by cutting it and rubbing it (on a touchstone), so are you to accept my words after examining them and not merely out of regard for me.'[1]

Buddhism is free from compulsion and coercion and does not demand of the follower blind faith. At the very outset the sceptic will be pleased to hear of its call for investigation. Buddhism, from beginning to end, is open to all those who have eyes to see and mind to understand.

Once, when the Buddha was dwelling in a mango grove at Nālandā, Upāli, a fervent follower of Nigaṇṭha Nātaputta (Jaina Mahāvīra),[2] approached the Master with the sole intention of debating with him and defeating him in argument. The subject was the theory of *karma* which both the Buddha and Mahāvīra professed, although their views on it differed. At the end of the very friendly discussion, Upāli being convinced by the arguments of the Buddha, agreed with his views, and was ready to become a follower, a lay disciple (*upāsaka*). Nevertheless cautioning him, the Buddha said: 'Of a truth, householder, make a thorough investigation. It is good for well-known men like yourself to make a thorough investigation'. Upāli, however, became more satisfied and delighted with the Buddha for thus cautioning him, and took refuge in the Buddha, the *Dhamma* and the *Sangha* (the Order).[3]

This episode clearly explains that the Blessed One was not anxious to gain followers except through their own conviction—a lesson this that missionaries should learn.

The Buddha never interfered with another man's freedom of thought; for freedom of thought is the birthright of every individual. It is wrong to force someone out of the way of life which accords with his outlook and character, spiritual inclination and tendencies. Compulsion in every form is bad. It is coercion of the blackest kind to make a man swallow beliefs for which he has no relish; such forced feeding cannot be good for anybody, anywhere.

The Buddha's sole intention was to make clear to others that seeing things as they are is not the result of mere belief in, and fear of, some external power, either human, superhuman or even

1. *Jñānasāra-samuccaya*, 31.
2. One of the so called six 'heretics' or teachers, contemporaries of the Buddha. For accounts of these teachers read *Sāmaññaphala sutta*, *D.*2, or its translation in *Dialogues of the Buddha*, Part I.
3. *Upāli sutta*, *M.* 56.

infra-human. In the understanding of things, belief and fear do not play any role in Buddhist thought. The truth of the *Dhamma* can be grasped only through insight, never through blind faith, or through fear of some known or unknown being. The history of religions reveals that it is fear in man, enmeshed in ignorance, which creates the idea of an omnipotent external agency; and once that idea is created, men move in awe of the child of their own fear, and work untold harm to themselves, and, at times, to others, too.

Instructing the monks the Buddha says: 'Those who have mere faith in me, mere affection in me, they are bound for a good state of existence (but they do not attain the highest, *arahatta*, final emancipation). Those who are striving for *Dhamma*, who are bent on the path, they are bound for awakening, for *arahatta*.'[1]

These are clear indications that the Buddha did not want his followers to recognize anything indiscriminately and without reason.

Not only did the Buddha discourage blind belief, and fear of the omnipotent as unsuitable approaches for understanding the truth, but he also denounced adherence to unprofitable rites and rituals, because the mere abandoning of outward things, such as fasting, bathing in rivers, animal sacrifice and similar acts, do not tend to purify a man, do not make a man holy and noble.

We find this dialogue between the Buddha and the Brahmin Sundarīka Bhāradvāja. Once the Buddha addressing the monks explained in detail how a seeker after deliverance should train himself, and further added that a man whose mind is free from taints, whose life of purity is perfected, and the task done, could be called one who bathes inwardly.

Then Bhāradvāja seated near the Buddha heard these words and asked him:

– Does the Venerable Gotama go to bathe in the river Bāhuka?
– Brahmin, what good is the river Bāhuka?
– Indeed, Venerable Gotama, the river Bāhuka is believed by many to be holy. Many people have their evil deeds (*pāpa*) washed away in the river Bāhuka.

Then the Buddha made him understand that bathing in rivers would not cleanse a man of his dirt of evil, and instructed him thus:

1. *M.* 22.

'Bathe just here (in this Doctrine and Discipline—*Dhamma-vinaya*), Brahmin, give security to all beings. If you do not speak falsehood, or kill or steal, if you are confident, and are not mean, what does it avail you to go to Gayā (the name of a river in India during the time of the Buddha)? Your well at home is also a Gayā.'[1]

The Buddha proclaimed a path free from all superstition and cruelty, that is, he made it impossible for his followers to behave in any way detrimental to the welfare of living beings, by outlawing all oppression, spoliation and plunder.

What then is Buddhism?

Some prefer to call the teaching of the Buddha a religion, others call it a philosophy, still others think of it as both religion and philosophy. It may, however, be more correct to call it a '*Way of Life*'. But that does not mean that Buddhism is nothing more than an ethical code. Far from it, it is a way of moral, spiritual and intellectual training leading to complete freedom of mind. The Buddha himself called his teaching '*Dhamma-vinaya*', the Doctrine and the Discipline. But Buddhism, in the strictest sense of the word, cannot be called a religion, for if by religion is meant 'action or conduct indicating belief in, reverence for, and desire to please, a divine ruling power; the exercise or practice of rites or observances implying this . . .; recognition on the part of man of some higher unseen power as having control of his destiny, and as being entitled to obedience, reverence, and worship.'[2] Buddhism certainly is not such a religion.

In Buddhist thought, there is no awareness or conviction of the existence of a Creator of any form who rewards and punishes the good and ill deeds of the creatures of his creation. A Buddhist takes refuge in the Buddha (*Buddhaṁ saraṇaṁ gacchāmi*) but not in the hope that he will be saved by the Master. There is no such guarantee. The Buddha is only a teacher who points out the way and guides the followers to their individual deliverance.

A sign-board at the parting of roads, for instance, indicates directions, and it is left to the wayfarer to tread along the way watching his steps. The board certainly will not take him to his desired destination.

A doctor diagnoses the ailment and prescribes; it is left to the patient to test the prescription. The attitude of the Buddha towards

1. *M.* 7.
2. *The Shorter Oxford English Dictionary*, 1956.

his followers is like that of an understanding and compassionate teacher or a physician.

The highest worship is that paid to the best of men, those great and daring spirits who have, with their wide and penetrating grasp of reality, wiped out ignorance, and rooted out defilements. The men who saw Truth are true helpers, but Buddhists do not pray to them. They only reverence the revealers of Truth for having pointed out the path to true happiness and deliverance. Happiness is what one must achieve for oneself; nobody else can make one better or worse. 'Purity and impurity depend on oneself. One can neither purify nor defile another.'[1]

While lying on his death-bed between the two Sāla trees at Kusinārā the eighty-year-old Buddha seeing the flowers offered to him, addressed the Venerable Ānanda thus: 'They who, Ānanda, are correct in life, living according to the *Dhamma*—it is they who rightly honour, reverence and venerate the Tathāgata (the Perfect One) with the worthiest homage. Therefore, Ānanda, be ye correct in life, living according to the *Dhamma*. Thus, should you train yourselves.'[2] This encouragement of the Buddha on living according to the *Dhamma* shows clearly that what is of highest importance is training in mental, verbal and bodily conduct, and not the mere offering of flowers to the Enlightened Ones. The emphasis is on living the right life.

Now when a Buddhist offers flowers, or lights a lamp before the Buddha image or some sacred object, and ponders over the supreme qualities of the Buddha, he is not praying to anyone; these are not rites, rituals or acts of worship. The flowers that soon fade, and the flames that die down speak to him, and tell him of the impermanency (*anicca*) of all conditioned things. The image serves him as an object for concentration, for meditation; he gains inspiration and endeavours to emulate the qualities of the Master. Those who do not understand the significance of this simple offering, hastily conclude: 'This is idol worship.' Nothing could be more untrue.

Jawaharlal Nehru in his autobiography writes:

'At Anurādhapura,[3] I liked greatly an old seated statue of the Buddha. A year later, when I was in Dehra Dun Gaol, a friend in Ceylon sent me a picture of this statue. and I kept it on my little table in my cell. It became a precious companion for me, and the

1. *Dhp.* 165. 2. *D.* 16. 3. In Ceylon.

strong, calm features of the Buddha's statue soothed and gave me strength and helped me to overcome many a period of depression.'[1]

P. D. Ouspensky, seeing a Buddha image in a monastery near Mount Lavinia in Ceylon, wrote:

'The face of the Buddha was quite alive; he was not looking straight at me, and yet he saw me. At first I felt nothing but wonder. I had not expected and could not have expected anything like it. But very soon wonder and all other feelings and thoughts disappeared in new and strange sensations. The Buddha *saw* me, saw in me that which I could not see myself, all that was hidden in the most secret recesses of my soul. And under his gaze, which, as it were, passed me by, I began to see all this myself. Everything that was small, superfluous, uneasy and troubled came to the surface and displayed itself under this glance. The face of the Buddha was quite calm, but not expressionless, and full of deep thought and feeling. He was lying here deep in thought and I had come, opened the doors and stood before him, and now he was involuntarily judging me. But there was no blame or reproach in his glance. His look was extraordinarily serious, calm and full of understanding. But when I attempted to ask myself what the face of the Buddha expressed, I realized that there could be no answer. His face was neither cold nor indifferent. On the other hand it would be quite wrong to say that it expressed warmth, sympathy or compassion. All this would be too small to ascribe to him. At the same time it would also be wrong to say that the face of the Buddha expressed unearthly grandeur or divine wisdom. No, it was a human face, yet at the same time a face which men do not happen to have. I felt that the words that I could command would be wrong if applied to the expression of this face. I can only say that here was *understanding*.

'Simultaneously I began to feel the strange effect which the Buddha's face produced on me. All the gloom that rose from the depths of my soul seemed to clear up. It was as if the Buddha's face communicated its calm to me. Everything that up to now had troubled me and appeared so serious and important, now became so small, insignificant and unworthy of notice, that I only wondered how it could ever have affected me. And I felt that no matter how agitated, troubled, irritated and torn with contradictory thoughts

1. Jawaharlal Nehru, *An Autobiography* (John Lane, The Bodley Head, London), p. 271.

and feelings a man might be when he came here, he would go away calm, quiet, enlightened, *understanding*. . . .'[1]

As to whether Buddhism is a philosophy, that depends upon the definition of the word; and whether it is possible to give a definition that will cover all existing systems of philosophical thought is doubtful. Etymologically philosophy means to love (Gr. *philein*) wisdom (*sophia*). 'Philosophy has been both the seeking of wisdom and the wisdom sought.' In Indian thought philosophy is termed *darśana*, vision of truth. In brief, the aim of philosophy should be to find out the ultimate truth.

Buddhism also advocates the search for truth. But it is no mere speculative reasoning, a theoretical structure, a mere acquiring and storing of knowledge. The Buddha emphasises the practical aspect of his teaching, the application of knowledge to life—looking into life and not merely at it.

For the Buddha, the entire teaching is just the understanding of the unsatisfactory nature of all phenomenal existence and the cultivation of the path leading away from this unsatisfactoriness. This is his 'philosophy'.

In Buddhism wisdom is of the highest importance; for purification comes through wisdom, through understanding.[2] But the Buddha never praised mere intellect. According to him, knowledge should go hand in hand with purity of heart, with moral excellence (*vijjā-caraṇasampanna*). Wisdom gained by understanding and development of the qualities of mind and heart is wisdom par excellence (*bhāvanāmaya paññā*). It is saving knowledge, and not mere speculation, logic or specious reasoning. Thus it is clear that Buddhism is neither mere love of, nor inducing the search after wisdom, nor devotion (though they have their significance and bearing on mankind), but an encouragement of a practical application of the teaching that leads the follower to dispassion, enlightenment and final deliverance.

Though we call the teaching of the Buddha 'Buddhism', thus including it among the '*isms*' and '*ologies*', it does not really matter what we label it. Call it religion, philosophy, Buddhism or by any other name you like. These labels are of little significance to one who goes in search of truth and deliverance.

When Upatissa and Kolita (who were later to become Sāriputta

1. P. D. Ouspensky, *A New Model of the Universe*, third edition (Kegan Paul, London, 1938), pp. 360–72.

2. *S.* i. 214.

and Mahā Moggallāna, the two chief disciples of the Buddha) were wandering in search of the doctrine of deliverance, Upatissa saw the Venerable Assaji (one of the first five disciples of the Master) who was on his alms-round. Upatissa was greatly struck by the dignified deportment of the Elder. Thinking it not the right time to inquire and question, Upatissa followed the Elder Assaji to his resting place, and then approached and greeted him and asked about his master's teaching.[1] The Venerable Assaji, rather reluctant to speak much, humbly said: 'I cannot expound the doctrine and discipline at length, but I can tell you the meaning briefly.' Upatissa's reply is interesting: 'Well, friend, tell little or much; what I want is just the meaning. Why speak many words?' Then the Venerable Assaji repeated a single verse which embraces the Buddha's entire doctrine of causality:

'Whatever from a cause proceeds, thereof
The Tathāgata has explained the cause,
Its cessation too he has explained.
This is the teaching of the Supreme Sage.'[2]

Upatissa instantly grasped the meaning and attained the first stage of realization, comprehending 'whatever is of the nature of arising, all that is of the nature of ceasing' (*yaṁkiñci samudaya-dhammaṁ sabbaṁ taṁ nirodhadhammaṁ*).[3]

No amount of talk and discussion not directed towards right understanding will lead us to deliverance. What is needed is right instruction and right understanding. We may even derive right instructions from nature, from trees and flowers, from stones and rivers. There are many instances where people gained enlightenment and release from taints by merely watching a leaf fall, the flow of water, a forest fire, the blowing out of a lamp. This struck a chord in them, and realizing the impermanent nature of things, they gained deliverance. Yes, the lotus awaits the sunlight, and no sooner does the sun shine than the lotus opens and brings delight to all.

Here in this teaching no attempt is made to probe into the ultimate origin of man and things—to inquire into the question: 'Is the universe eternal or not? Is it finite or infinite?'

1. Compare this with the story of Kassapa, p. 55, n.2.
2. *Ye dhammā hetuppabhavā—tesaṁ hetuṁ tathāgato āha*
   Tesaṁ ca yo nirodho—evaṁ vādi Mahā Samaṇo'.
3. *Vinaya Mahāvagga.*

The Buddha was not concerned with such metaphysical problems which only confuse man and upset his mental equilibrium. Their solution surely will not free mankind from misery and ill. That was why the Buddha hesitated to answer such questions, and at times refrained from explaining those which were often wrongly formulated. The Buddha was a practical teacher. His sole aim was to explain in all its detail the problem of *dukkha*, suffering, the universal fact of life, to make people feel its full force, and to convince them of it. He has definitely told us what he explains and what he does not explain.[1]

Some scholars, however, do not appreciate this attitude of the Master, they even doubt his enlightenment and label him an agnostic. Scholars will ever argue and speculate. These are not questions of today or yesterday, they were raised in the time of the Buddha. Even Sakuludāyi the Wanderer, for instance, asked about the past and the future and the Buddha's reply was categorical:

'Let be the past, let be the future, I will teach you the *Dhamma*:

> "When this is, that comes to be,
> With the arising of this, that arises,
> When this is not, that does not come to be,
> With the cessation of this, that ceases." '[2]

This in a nutshell is the Buddhist doctrine of conditionality or Dependent Arising (*paṭicca samuppāda*).[3] And this forms the foundation of the Four Noble Truths, the central conception of Buddhism.

1. See p. 39.
2. *Imasmiṁ sati idaṁ hoti,*
imassuppādā idaṁ uppajjati,
imasmiṁ asati idaṁ na hoti,
imassa nirodhā idaṁ nirujjhati.
M. ii. 32. See also the dialogue between the Buddha and Māluṅkyaputta in *M.* 63.
3. For the whole formula consisting of the twelve factors, see p. 56.

3

THE CENTRAL CONCEPTION OF BUDDHISM

(*The Four Noble Truths*)

THE FIRST NOBLE TRUTH

Dukkha: Suffering

THE Four Noble Truths realized by the Buddha while seated in contemplation under the Bodhi tree at Gayā were made known by him to his erstwhile companions, the five ascetics, when he gave his first sermon at the deer park at Isipatana (modern Sarnath) near Benares. These Four Noble Truths form the central conception of Buddhism.

They are:

1. *Dukkha*, suffering,
2. *Samudaya*, the arising of suffering,
3. *Nirodha*, the cessation of suffering,
4. *Magga*, the path leading to the cessation of suffering.

The word *dukkha* (or Sanskrit *duḥkha*) is one of those Pāli[1] terms that cannot be translated adequately into English, by one word, for no English word covers the same ground as *dukkha* in Pāli. Suffering, ill, anguish, unsatisfactoriness are some favourite renderings; the words pain, misery, sorrow, and so forth, are also used. The word *dukkha*, however, includes all that, and more than that. Though one likes to leave the term untranslated, for convenience sake both the words suffering and *dukkha* will be used wherever possible. After a perusal of this chapter the reader may be able to understand what *dukkha* means in the Buddha's teaching.

1. Pāli is the language or dialect in which the Buddhist texts, or the Buddhist Canon (*tipiṭaka*), and the commentaries are written. They were committed to writing (inscribed on palm leaves) for the first time during the reign of King Vaṭṭhagāmani Abhaya (101–77 B.C.) at *Aḷu-vihāra*, Mātale near Kandy in Ceylon.

In Buddhism awakening from ignorance to full knowledge always implies the comprehension of the Four Noble Truths. The Enlightened One is called the Buddha simply because he understood the Truths in all their fullness. The whole of his first sermon is devoted to the formulation of these Truths; for they are the essence of the Buddha's teaching. 'As the footprint of every creature that walks the earth can be contained in an elephant's footprint, which is pre-eminent for size, so does the doctrine of the four Noble Truths embrace all skilful *Dhamma*[1] (the entire teaching of the Buddha).'

In the original Pāli texts, specifically in the discourses (*suttas*), these Four Truths are made clear in detail and in diverse ways. Without a clear idea of the Truths, one cannot know what the Buddha taught for forty-five years. To the Buddha the entire teaching is just the understanding of *dukkha*, the unsatisfactory nature of all phenomenal existence, and the understanding of the way out of this unsatisfactoriness.

Even when the recluses and brahmins of his time misrepresented him by saying:

'The recluse Gotama is a nihilist (*venayiko*) who makes known the destruction and disappearance of being', the Buddha, without any feeling of indignation, or dissatisfaction, emphatically said: 'formerly (as early as the first proclamation of the *Dhamma* to the five ascetics) as well as now, monks, I make known only suffering and the cessation of suffering (*dukkhaṁceva paññapemi dukkhassa ca nirodhaṁ*)'.[2]

To understand this unequivocal saying is to understand Buddhism; for the entire teaching of the Buddha is nothing else than the application of this one principle. It seems to me that what can be called the discovery of a Buddha, is just these Four Truths, and the rest are logical developments and more detailed explanations of the Four Noble Truths. This is the typical teaching of the Buddhas of all ages, peculiar to them and none else (*Buddhānaṁ sāmukkaṁsikā dhammadesanā*).[3] The supremacy of the Four Truths in the teaching of the Buddha is abundantly clear from the message of the siṁsapa grove as from the message of the deer park:

Once the Buddha was living at Kosambi (near Allahabad) in the siṁsapa grove. Then gathering a few leaves in his hand, the Buddha addressed the monks:

1. *M.* 28. 2. *M.* 22. 3. *Vinaya Mahāvagga.*

– What do you think, monks, which is greater in quantity, the handful of siṁsapa leaves gathered by me, or what is in the forest overhead?

– Not many, trifling, Venerable Sir, are the leaves in the handful gathered by the Blessed One, many are the leaves in the forest overhead.

– Even so, monks, many are the things I have fully realized, but not declared unto you; few are the things I have declared unto you. And why, monks, have I not declared them? They, monks, are, indeed, not useful, are not essential to the life of purity, they do not lead to disgust, to dispassion, to cessation, to tranquillity, to full understanding, to enlightenment, to Nibbāna. That is why, monks, they are not declared by me.

And what is it, monks, that I have declared?

This is suffering—this have I declared.

This is the arising of suffering—this have I declared.

This is the cessation of suffering—this have I declared.

This is the path leading to the cessation of suffering—this have I declared.

And why, monks, have I declared these truths? They are, indeed useful, are essential to the life of purity, they lead to disgust, to dispassion, to cessation, to tranquillity, to full understanding, to enlightenment, to Nibbāna. That is why, monks, they are declared by me.'[1] Thus spoke the Buddha.

The Buddha is known as the peerless physician (*bhisakko*), the supreme surgeon (*sallakatto anuttaro*). He indeed is an unrivalled healer. The Buddha's method of exposition of the Four Truths is comparable to that of a physician. As a physician, he first diagnosed the illness, next he discovered the cause or the arising of the illness, then considered its removal and lastly applied the remedy.

Suffering (*dukkha*) is the illness; craving (*taṇhā*) is the arising or the root cause of the illness (*samudaya*); through the removal of craving the illness is removed and that is the cure (*nirodha = nibbāna*). The Eightfold Path (*magga*) is the remedy.

A sick man should become aware of his ailment, he should take notice of it lest it becomes acute, he should then think of a way of removing its cause; with this end in view he goes to a physician who diagnoses and prescribes a remedy. Through the efficacy of the remedy the patient gets rid of the ailment and that is the cure.

1. *S.* v. 437.

Thus suffering is not to be ignored, but to be known (*abhiññeyya*); for it is the dire disease. Craving, the cause, is to be removed, to be abandoned (*pahātabba*); the Eightfold Path is to be practised, to be cultivated (*bhāvetabba*); for it is the remedy. With the knowledge of suffering, with the removal of craving through the practice of the path, Nibbāna's realization (*saccikātabba*) is ensured. It is the cure, the complete detachment, the release from craving.

The Buddha's reply to Sela, the brahmin, who doubted the Master's enlightenment is interesting:

'I know what should be known, what should
Be cultivated I have cultivated,
What should be abandoned that have I let go,
Hence, O brahmin, I am Buddha—the Awakened One.'[1]

The reply clearly indicates that it was for no other reason than a perfect comprehension of the Four Truths that the Master is called a Buddha. The Buddha himself says: 'Monks, by the fact of understanding as they really are, these Four Noble Truths, a Tathāgata is called an Arahat, a Fully Enlightened One.'[2]

The First Noble Truth: *Dukkha*: Suffering.

In the early Buddhist scriptures the word *dukkha* is used in more than one sense. It is used in the psychological, physical and philosophical sense according to the context.

To those who try to see things as they really are, the concept of *dukkha* (suffering) is no insignificant thing. It is the key-stone in Buddhist thought. To ignore this essential concept implies ignoring the remaining three truths. The importance of knowing *dukkha* is seen in these words of the Buddha:

'He who sees suffering, sees also the arising of suffering, the cessation of suffering, and the path leading to the cessation of suffering.'[3]

As these truths are interconnected and interdependent, seeing one or more of the four truths implies seeing the others as well.[4] To one who denies suffering, a path, treading along which one gains deliverance from suffering, is meaningless. In brief, denying

1. *M.* 92: *Sn.* 558: *Thag.* 828; *Vinaya* i. 245.
2. *S.* v. 433.
3. *S.* v. 437.
4. *S.* v. 437.

one single truth amounts to denying the other three as well, and that is to deny the entire teaching of the Buddha.

To the staunch materialist who says: 'I do not want to swallow all this nonsense,' this teaching may appear rather jejune, puzzling and out of place, but to those who strive to cultivate a realistic view of life, this is no myth, no imaginary tale told to fools.

To those who view the sentient world from the correct angle, that is with dispassionate discernment, one thing becomes abundantly clear; there is only one problem in the world, that of suffering (*dukkha*). All other problems known and unknown are included in this one which is universal. As the Buddha says: The world is established on suffering, is founded on suffering (*dukkhe loko patiṭṭhito*).[1] If anything becomes a problem there is bound to be suffering, unsatisfactoriness, or if we like, conflict—conflict between our desires and the facts of life. And naturally, man's every endeavour is to solve the problem, in other words, to remove unsatisfactoriness, to control conflict, which is pain, a wretched state of mind.

To this single problem we give different names: economic, social, political, psychological and even religious problems. Do not they all emanate from that one single problem, *dukkha*, namely, unsatisfactoriness? If there is not unsatisfactoriness, why need we strive to solve them? Does not solving a problem imply reducing the unsatisfactoriness? All problems bring about unsatisfactoriness, and the endeavour is to put an end to them, but they beget each other. The cause is often not external, but in the problem itself, it is subjective. We often think that we have solved problems to the satisfaction of all concerned, but they often crop up in other forms, in diverse ways. It seems as if we are constantly confronted with fresh ones, and we put forth fresh efforts to solve them, thus they and the solving of them go on incessantly. Such is the nature of suffering, the universal characteristic of sentient existence. Sufferings appear and pass away only to reappear in other forms. They are both physical and psychological, and some people are capable of enduring the one more than the other and vice versa.

Life according to Buddhism is suffering; suffering dominates all life. It is the fundamental problem of life. The world is suffering and afflicted, no being is free from this bond of misery and this is a universal truth that no sensible man who sees things in their proper perspective can deny. The recognition of this universal fact, however,

1. *S.* i. 40.

is not a total denial of pleasure or happiness. The Buddha, the Lord over suffering, never denied happiness in life when he spoke of the universality of suffering. In the *Aṅguttara Nikāya*, one of the five original Collections of Pāli, there is a long enumeration of the happinesses that beings are capable of enjoying.[1]

In answering a question of Mahāli Licchavi, the Buddha says:

'Mahāli, if visible forms, sound, smell, taste and tactile objects (these, as you know, are sense objects which man experiences through his sense faculties), are entirely subject to suffering, beset with suffering, and entirely bereft of pleasure and happiness, beings will not take delight in these sense objects; but, Mahāli, because there is pleasure and happiness in these sense objects, beings take delight in them and cling to them; because of this clinging they defile themselves.'[2]

Through sense faculties man is attracted to sense objects, delights in them and derives enjoyment (*assāda*). It is a fact that cannot be denied, for you experience it. Neither the delightful objects nor the enjoyments, however, are lasting. They suffer change. Now when a man cannot retain or is deprived of the pleasures that delight him, he often becomes sad and cheerless. He dislikes monotony, for lack of variety makes him unhappy, and looks for fresh delights, like cattle that seek fresh pasture, but these fresh delights, too, are fleeting and a passing show. Thus all pleasures, whether we like it or not, are preludes to pain and disgust. All mundane pleasures are fleeting, like sugar-coated pills of poison they deceive and harm us.

A disagreeable dish, an unpleasant drink, an unlovely demeanour, and a hundred other trifles, bring pain and dissatisfaction to us—Buddhist or non-Buddhist, rich or poor, high or low, literate or illiterate. Shakespeare merely gives voice to the words of the Buddha when he writes in *Hamlet:* 'When sorrows come they come not single spies, but in battalions.'

Now when man fails to see this aspect of life, this unsteadiness of pleasures, he becomes disappointed and frustrated, may even behave foolishly, without sense or judgement and even lose balance of mind. This is the danger, the evil consequence (*ādīnava*). Mankind is frequently confronted with these two pictures of life (*assāda* and *ādīnava*). Yet the man who endeavours to get rid of his deep fondness for things, animate and inanimate, and views life with a

1. *A.* i. 80. 2. *S.* iii. 69.

detached outlook, who sees things in their proper perspective, whose cultural training urges him to be calm under all life's vicissitudes, who can smile when things go wrong, and maintain balance of mind putting away all likes and dislikes—he is never worried but liberated (*nissaraṇa*). These three, *assāda*, *ādīnava* and *nissaraṇa*, or enjoyment, its evil consequences and liberation are facts of experience—a true picture of what we call life.

In answering the question of Mahāli the Buddha continues: 'Mahāli, if visible forms, sound, smell, taste and tactile objects are entirely subject to pleasure, beset with pleasures and not bereft of pain, beings will not be disgusted with sense objects, but, Mahāli, because there is pain and no lasting pleasure in these sense objects, they feel disgusted, being disgusted they do not delight in and cling to them; not clinging, they purify themselves.'[1]

Now there are these three aspects of suffering: (1) suffering in its most obvious ordinary form (*dukkha-dukkhatā*); (2) suffering or the unsatisfactoriness of conditioned states (*saṁkhārā-dukkhatā*); (3) suffering caused by change (*viparināma dukkhatā*).[2]

All mental and bodily sufferings such as birth, ageing, disease, death, association with the unloved, dissociation from the loved, not getting what one wants[3] are the ordinary sufferings of daily life and are called *dukkha-dukkhatā*. Not much science is needed to understand this fact of life.

Saṁkhārā-dukkhatā, unsatisfactoriness of conditioned states, is of philosophical significance. Though the word *saṁkhārā* implies all things subject to cause and effect, here in the context of *dukkha* the five groups or aggregates (pañcakkhandha) are meant. They are the aggregates of matter (in this case the visible, tangible body of form), of sensations, of perceptions, of mental formations and of consciousness.[4] They are known briefly as *nāma-rūpa*, the psycho-physical entity. *Rūpa* includes the physical aggregate and *nāma* the remaining four aggregates. The combination of the five constitutes a sentient being.

A being and the empirical world are both constantly changing. They come into being and pass away. All is in a whirl, nothing escapes this inexorable unceasing change, and because of this transitory nature nothing is really pleasant. There is happiness, but very

1. *S.* iii. 69.
2. *D.* 33; *Saṁyutta*, *Jambukhādaka-sutta*; *Vism.* 499 (*The Path of Purification*, p. 568).
3. *S.* v. 421; *Vin.* i. 10.
4. The five aggregates are discussed in full on p. 45.

momentary, it vanishes like a flake of snow, and brings about unsatisfactoriness. This is why the Buddha in his formulation of the Noble Truth of *dukkha* concluded with the words: 'In brief the five aggregates of grasping are *dukkha* (suffering or unsatisfactory). This is what is called the unsatisfactoriness of conditioned states (*saṁkhāra dukkha*).

Viparināma dukkha comes under the category of unsatisfactoriness due to impermanence. All the pleasant and happy feelings that man can experience fade away and disappear. As the Buddha says, even the feelings that a yogi or meditator experiences by attaining the four meditative absorptions (*jhāna*), come under the category of *viparināma dukkha*, because they are transient (*anicca*), *dukkha*, and subject to change (*viparināmadhamma*).[1] But the *dukkha* mentioned here is certainly not the pain and suffering that people in general endure. What the Buddha points out is that all things impermanent are unsatisfactory.

They suffer change every moment and this change brings about unsatisfactoriness; for whatever is impermanent is unsatisfactory (*yadaniccaṁ taṁ dukkhaṁ*). That is, there is no lasting bliss.

In his formulation of the Noble Truth of Suffering, the Buddha says: In short, the five aggregates of clinging are suffering.[2] According to this teaching suffering cannot be separated from the five aggregates. It cannot exist independently of them. The five aggregates of grasping and suffering are the same and not two different things. 'Monks, what is suffering? It should be said that it is the five aggregates of grasping.'[3]

The Buddha says elsewhere: 'In this very body, a fathom long, with its consciousness and perception I declare are the world, its arising, its cessation and the path that leads to the cessation of the world.'[4] Here the word '*world*' denotes suffering, *dukkha*.

From the above it becomes clear that to understand properly the first noble truth, as well as the other three, it is essential to have a clear idea of the five aggregates (*pañcakkhandha*).

Let us therefore try to understand the significance of the aggregates. Buddhism speaks of two truths, the apparent or conventional truth (*sammuti sacca*) and the ultimate or highest truth (*paramattha sacca*).[5] In ordinary parlance we speak of a 'being', but in the ultimate sense there is no such 'being'; there is only a manifestation of ever-changing psycho-physical forces or energies. These forces

1. *M.* i. *Mahādukkhakkhandha-sutta,* no. 13, p. 90.
2. *S.* v. 421.
3. *S.* iii. 158.
4. *A.* ii. 48.
5. *DA. Com.* to discourse 9, *Poṭṭhapāda-sutta.*

or energies form the five aggregates, and what we call a 'being' is nothing but a combination of these everchanging five aggregates.

Now what are the five Aggregates?

1. The first is the Aggregate of Matter (*rūpakkhandha*). Matter contains and comprises the Four Great Primaries (*cattāri mahābhūtāni*) which are traditionally known as, solidity, fluidity, heat or temperature and motion or vibration (*paṭhavi, āpo, tejo, vāyo*).[1] In this context, they are not simply earth, water, fire and wind, though conventionally they may be so called. In Buddhist thought, especially in the *Abhidhamma*, the Higher Doctrine, they are more than that.

Paṭhavi or solidity is the element of expansion. It is due to this element of expansion that objects occupy space. When we see an object we only see something extended in space and we give a name to it. The element of expansion is present not only in solids, but in liquids, too; for when we see the sea stretched before us even then we see *paṭhavi*. The hardness of rock and the softness of paste, the quality of heaviness and lightness in things are also qualities of *paṭhavi*, or are particular states of it.

Āpo or fluidity is the element of cohesion. It is this element that heaps particles of matter together without allowing them to scatter. The cohesive force in liquids is very strong, for unlike solids, they coalesce even after their separation. Once a solid is broken up or separated the particles do not recoalesce. In order to join them it becomes necessary to convert the solid into a liquid by raising the temperature, as in the welding of metals. When we see an object we only see an expansion with limits, this expansion or 'shape' is possible because of the cohesive force.

Tejo is the element of heat or temperature. It is this element which matures, intensifies or imparts heat to the other three primaries. The vitality of all beings and plants is preserved by this element. From every expansion and shape we get a sensation of heat. This is relative; for when we say that an object is cold, we only mean that the heat of that particular object is less than our body heat, in other words, the temperature of the object is lower than the temperature of our body. Thus it is clear that the so-called 'coldness', too, is an element of heat or temperature, of course in a lower degree.

Vāyo is the element of motion. It is displacement. This, too, is relative. To know whether a thing is moving or not we need a point which we regard as being fixed, by which to measure that

1. *M.* 28.

motion, but there is no absolutely motionless object in the universe. So the so-called stability, too, is an element of motion. Motion depends on heat. In the complete absence of heat atoms cease to vibrate. Complete absence of heat is only theoretical, we cannot feel it, because then we would not exist, as we, too, are made of atoms.

Every material object is made up of the Four Great Primaries though one or other seems to preponderate; if, for instance, the element of solidity (*paṭhavi*) preponderates, the material object is called solid, and so on.

From these Great Primaries which always co-exist are derived twenty-four other material phenomena and qualities; among these Derivatives (*upadāyarūpa*) are included the five sense faculties, namely, the faculties of eye, ear, nose, tongue and body, and their corresponding sense objects, namely, visible form, sound, smell, taste and tangible things. The aggregate of matter includes the whole realm of physical substance, both in one's body and in the external world.

2. The second is the Aggregate of Feeling or Sensation (*vedanākkhandha*). All our feelings are included in this group. Feelings are threefold: pleasant, unpleasant and neutral. They arise dependant on contact. Seeing a form, hearing a sound, smelling an odour, tasting a flavour, touching some tangible thing, cognizing a mental object, (an idea or thought) man experiences feeling.[1] When, for instance, eye, form and eye-consciousness (*cakkhu-viññāṇa*) come together, it is their coincidence that is called contact. Contact means the combination of the organ of sense, the object of sense, and sense consciousness. When these are all present together there is no power or force that can prevent the arising of feeling.

Such is the intrinsic nature of contact and feeling. It cannot, however, be said that all beings experience the same feeling from the same object. One person may derive a pleasant feeling from a particular object while another has an unpleasant feeling and still another a neutral feeling from the same object. This depends on how the mind and its factors function. Further, a sense object which once evoked a pleasant feeling in a man, may produce an unpleasant or a neutral feeling in him under different circumstances, and so on. Again, what is pleasant to one sense faculty may be unpleasant to another faculty; for instance, a luscious fruit un-

1. These six kinds of feelings are experienced through the eye, ear, nose, tongue, body and the mind, respectively. Mind is regarded as the sixth faculty in Buddhist thought.

pleasant to the sight may prove very pleasant to the tongue and so on. Thus we learn how feeling is conditioned by contact in diverse ways.

3. The third is the Aggregate of Perception (*saññākkhandha*). The function of perception is recognition (*saṁjānana*) of objects both physical and mental. Perception, like feeling, also is sixfold: perception of forms, sounds, smells, tastes, bodily contacts and mental objects. Perception in Buddhism is not used in the sense that some Western philosophers like Bacon, Descartes, Spinoza and Liebnitz used the term, but as a mere sense perception.

There is a certain affinity between awareness (*vijānana*, which is the function of consciousness) and recognition (*saṁjānana*, the function of perception). While consciousness becomes aware of an object, simultaneously the mental factor of perception takes the distinctive mark of the object and thus distinguishes it from other objects. This distinctive mark is instrumental in cognizing the object a second and a third time, and in fact, every time we become aware of the object. Thus, it is perception that brings about memory.

It is important to note that perceptions often deceive us. Then they become known as illusion or perversity of perceptions (*saññā-vipallāsa*, see below p. 96).

A simile will illustrate the point. A farmer after sowing a field, will set up a scare-crow to protect the seed and for a time the birds will mistake it for a man and will not settle. That is an illusion of perception. Similarly sense and mental objects deceive our mind by producing a false impression. The Buddha, therefore, compares perception to a mirage.[1]

When a particular perception, perverted or not, occurs frequently, it grows stronger and grips our mind. Then it becomes difficult to get rid of that perception, and the result is well explained in this verse of the *Suttanipāta*.[2]

'Who is free from sense perceptions
In him no more bonds exist;
Who by Insight freedom gains
All delusions cease in him;
But who clings to sense perceptions
And to view-points wrong and false
He lives wrangling in this world.'

1. *Marīci*. See p. 94.
2. *Sn*. 847.

4. The fourth is the Aggregate of Mental (Volitional) Formations (*saṁkhārakkhandha*).[1] In this group are included all mental factors except feeling (*vedanā*) and perception (*saññā*) mentioned above. The *Abhidhamma* speaks of fifty-two mental concomitants or factors (*cetasika*). Feeling and perception are two of them, but they are not volitional activities. The remaining fifty are collectively known as *saṁkhārā*, Mental or Volitional Formations. Volition (*cetanā*) plays a very important role in the mental realm. In Buddhism no action is considered as *karma* (*kamma*) if that action is void of volition. And like feeling and perception, it is of six kinds: Volition directed to forms, sounds, smells, tastes, bodily contacts and mental objects.

5. The fifth is the Aggregate of Consciousness (*viññāṇakkhandha*)[2] which is the most important of the aggregates; for it is the receptacle, so to speak, for all the fifty-two mental concomitants or factors, since without consciousness no mental factors are available. Consciousness and the factors are interrelated, inter-dependent and co-existent.

Now what is the function of consciousness? Like feeling, perception and volitional formations, consciousness also has six types and its function is varied. It has its basis and objects. As explained above all our feelings are experienced through the contact of sense faculties with the external world.

The faculty of mind (*manindriya*) which cognizes mental objects, we know, is not something tangible and perceptible like the other five faculties, which cognize the external world. The eye cognizes the world of colours (*vaṇṇa*) or visible objects, the ear audible sounds, and so forth. The mind, however, cognizes the world of ideas and thoughts. *Indriya* (faculty) literally means 'chief' or 'lord'. Forms can only be seen by the faculty of the eye and not by the ear, hearing by the faculty of the ear, and so on. When it comes to the world of thoughts and ideas the faculty of the mind is lord over the mental realm. The eye cannot think thoughts, and collect ideas, but it is instrumental in seeing visible forms, the world of colours.

It is very important here to understand the function of consciousness. Although there is this functional relationship between the faculties and their objects, for instance, eye with forms, ear with

1. 'Mental formations' is the popular term for the word *saṁkhāra* in the list of the five aggregates. In other contexts *saṁkhāra* may signify anything conditioned and compounded. In this sense all the five aggregates are *saṁkhāra*.

2. Loosely the three words *viññāna*, *citta* (thought) and *mano* (mind) are synonymous (*S.* ii. 94–5). Technically, however, they go in different ways.

sounds and so on, awareness comes through consciousness. In other words, sense objects cannot be experienced with the particular sensitivity without the appropriate kind of consciousness. Now when eye and form are both present, visual consciousness arises dependent on them. Similarly with ear and sound, and so on, down to mind and mental objects.[1] Again when the three things, eye, form and eye-consciousness, come together, it is their coincidence that is called 'contact'. From contact comes feeling and so on (as explained in Dependent Arising or *Paṭicca Samuppāda*).[2]

Thus consciousness originates through a stimulus arising in the five sense doors and the mind door, the sixth. As consciousness arises through the interaction of the sense faculties and the sense objects, it also is conditioned and not independent. It is not a spirit or soul opposed to matter. Thoughts and ideas which are food for the sixth faculty called mind are also dependent and conditioned. They depend on the external world which the other five sense faculties experience.

The five faculties contact objects, only in the present, that is when objects come in direct contact with the particular faculty. The mind faculty, however, can experience the sense object, whether it is form, sound, smell, taste or touch, already cognized by the sense organs. For instance, a visible object, with which the eye came in contact in the past, can be visualized by the mind faculty just at this moment although the object is not before the eye. Similarly with the other sense objects. This is subjective, and it is difficult to experience some of these sensations. This sort of activity of the mind is subtle and sometimes beyond ordinary comprehension.

Thus the whole cosmos becomes a mere mass of sensation. When we see colour patches and something solid or expanded we make an entity out of them but in reality it is not so. The mind is merely giving a certain interpretation to phenomena which exist in the external world, but which are not necessarily the same as they appear through the channels of the senses.

As this mind or consciousness lies outside the realm of the physical world it cannot be submitted to a chemical test; it has neither size, shape dimension nor bulk. It is invisible, intangible and as such cannot be discerned by the five senses. It is not under the control of other factors, but is master of them. And it must clearly be understood that mind is not an everlasting spirit in the form of a

1. *M.* 148.
2. See below p. 56.

'Self' or a 'Soul' or an Ego-entity. It is neither a spirit opposed to matter nor a projection, an offspring of matter.

There were many during the time of the Buddha who thought, and there are many who continue to think that consciousness in the form of a permanent enduring self or soul exists in man, and that it continues through life and at death transmigrates from one life to another and binds lives together.

We see a glaring instance of this in the thirty-eighth discourse of the *Majjhima Nikāya*. One of the Buddha's own disciples, Sāti by name, held the following view: 'In so far as I understand the *Dhamma* taught by the Buddha, it is the same consciousness that transmigrates and wanders about (in rebirth)'. When Sāti intimated his point of view to the Master, the Buddha questioned him: 'What is this consciousness, Sāti?' 'It is that which expresses, which feels (*vado vedeyyo*) and experiences the result of good and evil deeds now here now there.'

'But to whom, foolish man, have you heard me teaching the *Dhamma* in this wise? Have I not in many ways explained consciousness as arising out of conditions, that apart from conditions there is no arising of consciousness?' The Buddha then explained the different types of consciousness and made clear, by means of examples, how consciousness arises depending on conditions.

These are the five aggregates explained briefly. None of these aggregates are permanent. They are ever subject to change. Leaving aside philosophy, and looking at the matter from a purely scientific standpoint, nothing conditioned and compounded is permanent. Whatever is impermanent is pain-laden, is sorrow-fraught.

It is not at all astonishing if the reader concludes that this Buddhist concept of suffering is very uninviting. As the Buddha has pointed out, all beings crave for the pleasant and the pleasurable. They loathe the unpleasant and the non-pleasurable. The grieving ones seek pleasures while those already happy seek more and more.

It is, however, wrong to imagine that the Buddhist outlook on life and the world is a gloomy one, and that the Buddhist is in low spirits. Far from it, he smiles as he walks through life. He who understands the true nature of life is the happiest individual, for he is not upset by the evanescent nature of things. He tries to see things as they are, and not as they seem to be. Conflicts arise in man when he is confronted with the facts of life such as ageing, illness, death and so forth, but frustration and disappointment do not vex him when he is ready to face them with a brave heart. This view of life is neither pessimistic nor optimistic, but the realistic view. The man who ignores the principle of unrest in things, the intrinsic nature of suffering, is upset when confronted with the vicissitudes of life, because he has not trained his mind to see things as they really are. Man's recognition of pleasures as lasting, leads to much vexation, when things occur quite contrary to his expectations. It is therefore necessary to cultivate a detached outlook towards life and things pertaining to life. Detachment cannot bring about frustration, disappointment and mental torment, because there is no clinging to one thing and another, but letting go. This indeed is not easy, but it is the sure remedy for controlling, if not eradicating, unsatisfactoriness.

The Buddha sees suffering as suffering, and happiness as happiness, and explains that all cosmic pleasure, like all other conditioned things, is evanescent, is a passing show. He warns man against attaching too much importance to fleeting pleasures, for they sooner or later beget discontent. Equanimity is the best antidote for both pessimism and optimism. Equanimity is evenness of mind and not sullen indifference. It is the result of a calm, concentrated mind. It is hard, indeed, to be undisturbed when touched by the vicissitudes of life, but the man who cultivates equanimity is not upset.

A mother was asked why she did not lament over the death of her beloved son. Her answer was philosophical: 'Uninvited he came, uninvited he passed away, as he came so he went, what use is there in lamenting, weeping and wailing?'[1] Thus people bear their misfortune with equanimity. Such is the advantage of a tranquil mind. It is unshaken by loss and gain, blame and praise, and undisturbed by adversity. This frame of mind is brought about by viewing the sentient world in its proper perspective. Thus calm or evenness of mind leads man to enlightenment and deliverance from suffering.

Absolute happiness cannot be derived from things conditioned and compounded. What we hug in great glee this moment, turns into a source of dissatisfaction the next moment. Pleasures are short-lived, and never lasting. The mere gratification of the sense faculties we call pleasure and enjoyment, but in the absolute sense of the word such gratification is not happy. Joy too is *dukkha*, unsatisfactory (*nandipidukkhā*); for it is transient. If we with our inner eye try to see things in their proper perspective, in their true light, we will be able to realize that the world is but an illusion (*māyā*)

1. *Uraga Jātaka*, no. 354.

that leads astray the beings who cling to it. All the so-called mundane pleasures are fleeting, and only an introduction to pain. They give very temporary relief from life's miserable ulcers. This is what is known as suffering (*dukkha*) produced by change. Thus we see that *dukkha* never ceases work, it functions in some form or other and is always at work—as *dukkha-dukkhatā*, *saṁkhāra dukkhatā* and *viparināma dukkhatā*, as explained above.

All kinds of suffering man can conceive of come into being, reach a peak, and cease in the five Aggregates of Grasping. Apart from the five Aggregates of Grasping, which are constantly changing, no suffering, gross or subtle, can exist.

Wittingly or not, all beings exert themselves to avoid disharmony and unsatisfactoriness, and to gain pleasure, joy and happiness. The exertion goes on continuously, but no lasting happiness is ever experienced. Pleasure seems to be an interval between two pains. This is a clear indication that wherever there are the five Aggregates of Grasping there is *dukkha*, suffering, unsatisfactoriness. It may be noted that like happiness, suffering is not lasting, because it too is conditioned and subject to change.

Sir Edwin Arnold paints this picture of pain in *The Light of Asia*:

> 'Ache of birth, ache of helpless days,
> Ache of hot youth and ache of manhood's prime,
> Ache of chill grey years and choking death
> These fill your piteous time.'

As the Buddha says:

> 'A burden, indeed, are the five aggregates,
> Happy it is to lay down that burden.'[1]

This is *Nibbāna*, the absolute happiness (*nibbānaṁ paramaṁ sukhaṁ*).[2]

The Buddha, the Lord over suffering, did not have a funereal expression on his face when he explained to his followers the import of *dukkha*, suffering; far from it, his face was always happy, serene and smiling for it showed his contented mind:

1. *S.* iii. 26.
2. *Dhp.* 204; *M.* 75.

'Happy, indeed, we live,
We who have no burdens.
On joy we ever feed
Like radiant deities.'[1]

He encouraged his disciples not to be morbid, but to cultivate the all important quality of joy (*pīti*) which is a factor of enlightenment. The result of this admonition of the Buddha is seen in 'Psalms of the Early Buddhists'[2] in which are recorded the joyful songs (*udāna*) of the disciples, male and female. A dispassionate study of Buddhism will tell us that it is a message radiating joy and hope and not a defeatist philosophy of pessimism.

1. *Dhp.* 200.
2. *Thera-gāthā:* Psalms of the Brethren.
Theri-gāthā: Psalms of the Sisters.

4

THE SECOND NOBLE TRUTH

Samudaya: The Arising of Suffering

BEFORE treating a sick man it is essential to discover the cause of his ailment. The efficacy of the treatment depends on the removal of the cause. The Buddha discourses on suffering but goes a step further and points out the arising of suffering thus administering an efficacious cure. The hasty critic, therefore, is not justified in labelling the Buddha a pessimist. The optimist will be pleased to hear that in the exposition of the Four Noble Truths there is a way out of the 'pessimism'. What then, according to the teaching of the Buddha, is the Noble Truth of the arising of suffering?

As there is no arbitrary creator who controls the destinies of man in Buddhist thought, Buddhism does not attribute suffering or the arising of suffering to an external agency, to 'supernatural' power, but seeks it in the innermost recesses of man himself. In the first sermon of the Buddha and in many another discourse in the early scriptures, the second Noble Truth is formulated in the following words:

It is this craving ('thirst', *taṇhā*[1]) which causes re-becoming, rebirth, accompanied by passionate pleasure, and finding fresh delight now here, now there, namely, craving for sense pleasures (*kāma-taṇhā*), craving for continued existence, for becoming (*bhava-taṇhā*), and craving for non-existence, for self-annihilation (*vibhava-taṇhā*).

Thus it is clear that suffering is the effect of craving which is the cause. Here we see seed and fruit, action and reaction, cause and effect, a reign of natural law, and this is no great mystery. Now this most powerful force, this mental factor, craving or 'thirst', keeps existence going. It makes and remakes the world. Life depends on the desires of life. It is the motive force behind not only the present existence, but past and future existence, too. The present

1. In Sanskrit '*trishṇā*' which is etymologically the same as 'thirst'.

is the result of the past, and the future will be the result of the present. This is a process of conditionality. This force is compared to a river (*taṇhā-nadī*); for like a river that when in flood submerges villages, suburbs, towns and countries, craving flows on continuously through re-existence and re-becoming. Like fuel that keeps the fire burning, the fuel of craving keeps the fire of existence alive.

The Buddha says: 'Monks, I do not see any other single fetter bound by which beings for a long, long time wander and hurry through the round of existence, like this fetter of craving (*taṇhā saṁyojanaṁ*). Truly, monks, bound by this fetter of craving, beings do wander and hurry through the round of existence.'[1]

It is important to understand that craving here is not regarded as the First Cause with a capital '*F*' and a capital '*C*'; for according to Buddhism there is no 'First Cause', but beginningless causes and effects and naught else ruling the universe. Things are neither due to one single cause nor are they causeless, but as explained in the formula of Dependent Arising things are multiple-caused. Craving, like all other things, physical or mental, is also conditioned, interdependent and relative. It is neither a beginning nor an end in itself. Though craving is cited as the proximate cause of suffering, it is not independent, but interdependent. Dependent on feeling or sensation arises craving, feeling arises dependent on contact and so forth.[2] The following dialogue explains the standpoint of the Buddha regarding the arising of suffering:

Once a certain ascetic named Kassapa questioned the Buddha thus:[3]

1. *Iti*, I, ii, v.

2. Also compare *M*. i. 51 *Sammādiṭṭhi sutta*. From the arising of feeling is the arising of craving, from the cessation of feeling is the cessation of craving; the way leading to the cessation of craving is this Noble Eightfold Path itself.

3. It is interesting, or rather strange, to note how Kassapa approached the Blessed One to put his question: The Blessed One was staying at Rājagaha, and one forenoon went out for his almsround. Kassapa, seeing the Blessed One from a distance, approached, greeted him and said: 'We would ask the Venerable Gotama concerning a certain point, if the Venerable Gotama gives us the opportunity of hearing his reply to our question.'

'It is not the right time just now for questions, Kassapa, we have entered the village (for alms),' said the Buddha. Kassapa, however, repeated his question up to the third time, and received the same reply. Then said Kassapa: 'We do not intend asking many questions from the Venerable Gotama.'

'Ask, Kassapa, what you will,' said the Blessed One.

Compare this with the story of Upatissa, p. 34.

– Now then, Venerable Gotama, is suffering self-wrought?
– Not so, verily, Kassapa.
– What then, Venerable Gotama, is suffering wrought by another?
– Not so, verily, Kassapa.
– What then, Venerable Gotama, is suffering wrought both by one's self and by another?
– Not so, verily, Kassapa.
– What then, Venerable Gotama, is suffering wrought neither by one's self nor by another, arisen without cause (due to purely fortuitous circumstances, *adhicca samuppanna*)?
– Not so, verily, Kassapa.
– Well then, Venerable Gotama, is suffering non-existent (is there no suffering)?
– Surely, Kassapa, suffering is not non-existent. Suffering is.
– Then the Venerable Gotama neither knows nor sees suffering.
– Nay, Kassapa, I am not one who neither knows nor sees suffering; I am one who knows suffering and sees suffering.
– How now, Venerable Gotama, you have answered all my questions, as 'not so, verily, Kassapa'. You affirm that suffering is, and that you know and see suffering. May the Venerable Gotama teach me what suffering is?
– The statement, Kassapa, that one and the same person produces and experiences suffering amounts to the Eternalist Theory (*sassatavāda*). To say that, 'one produces and another experiences suffering', this, Kassapa, which to one afflicted with feeling occurs as suffering wrought by another, amounts to the Annihilationist Theory (*uccheda vāda*). The Tathāgata, Kassapa, avoiding these two extremes teaches the *Dhamma* by the Median Path:

'Dependent on ignorance (of the true nature of existence), arise volitional or *karma* formations.
Dependent on volitional-formations, arises (rebirth) consciousness.
Dependent on consciousness, arises mentality-materiality (mental and physical combination).
Dependent on mentality-materiality, arises the sixfold base (the five physical sense organs with consciousness as the sixth).
Dependent on the sixfold base, arises contact.
Dependent on contact, arises feeling.
Dependent on feeling, arises craving.
Dependent on craving, arises clinging.
Dependent on clinging, arises the process of becoming.

Dependent on the process of becoming, arise ageing and death,[1] sorrow, lamentation, pain, grief and despair. Thus does this whole mass of suffering arise. (This is called the Noble Truth of the Arising of Suffering or *dukkha*.)

'Through the entire cessation of ignorance cease volitional formations; through the cessation of volitional formations, consciousness . . . (and so on). Thus does this whole mass of suffering cease. (This is called the Noble Truth of the Cessation of Suffering.')

Kassapa, being convinced by this exposition of the doctrine, took refuge in the Buddha, Dhamma, and Sangha, entered the Order, and later became one of the Arahats.[2]

Thus this doctrine of Dependent Arising, in its direct order, makes plain how suffering arises due to causes and conditions, and how suffering ceases with the removal of its causes and conditions.

How Buddha himself expressed this appears in the *Aṅguttara Nikāya*.

'And what, monks, is the Noble Truth of the Arising of Suffering? Dependent on ignorance arise volitional formations; dependent on volitional formations, consciousness . . . (and so on). . . . Thus does this whole mass of suffering arise. This, monks, is called the Noble Truth of the Arising of Suffering.

'And what, monks, is the Noble Truth of the Cessation of Suffering? Through the complete cessation of ignorance cease volitional formations; through the cessation of volitional formations, consciousness . . . (and so on), the whole mass of suffering. This, monks, is called "the Cessation of Suffering".'[3]

It is now quite clear that Dependent Arising is an essential corollary to the second and third of the Four Noble Truths, and is not, as some are inclined to think, a later addition to the teachings of the Buddha.

1. The Pāli equivalents of the factors of the formula are: *avijjā, saṁkhārā, viññāṇa, nāma-rūpa, saḷāyatana, phassa, vedanā, taṇhā, upādāna, bhava, jāti, jarā-maraṇa.* For a detailed study see *Dependent Origination* by Piyadassi Thera (Buddhist Publication Society, Kandy, Ceylon).

2. *S.* ii. 19.

3. *A.* i. 177.

This Dependent Arising, this doctrine of conditionality, is often explained in severely practical terms, but it is not a mere pragmatical teaching, though it may appear to be so, owing to the shortness of the explanations. Those conversant with the Buddhist Canon (*Tipiṭaka*) know that in the doctrine of Dependent Arising is found that which brings out the basic principles of knowledge (*ñāṇa*) and wisdom (*paññā*) in the *Dhamma*. In this teaching of the conditionality of everything in the world, that is the five aggregates, can be realized the essence of the Buddha's outlook on life. So if the Buddha's explanation of the world is to be rightly understood, it has to be through a full grasp of the central teaching summed up in the dictum: '*Ye dhammā hetuppabhavā* . . .' (Whatsoever things proceed from a cause. . . .) referred to above.[1]

When the cause and condition of a thing is removed, so does the effect cease. Following the Buddha's doctrine of conditionality, this idea is pithily expressed by Sister Selā, well known for her deep knowledge of the *Dhamma*, in this verse:

'Not-self-wrought is this puppet-form,
Nor other-wrought this mass of woe;
Condition-based it comes to be,
Condition-ceased it endeth, lo.'[2]

As we saw above, 'Not so, verily, Kassapa, not so, verily, Kassapa' was the Buddha's answer to Kassapa's question: 'Is suffering self-wrought or wrought by another?' The answer clearly shows that the Buddha disapproves of both the self-agency (that suffering is caused solely by self) and the external agency (that suffering is caused solely by other than the self).

To say that suffering is solely due to the individual's own agency (*sayaṁkāra*) is meaningless; for he is in the environment of the sentient world of beings and surely that environment influences him in diverse ways. To say that man's action, his behaviour, is solely determined by external agency (*para-kāra*) is also equally meaningless; for then man's moral responsibility and 'freedom of will' is denied. The Buddha's doctrine of the middle path, Dependent Arising, which avoids the two extremes, explains that all

1. See p. 35.
2. '*Nayidaṁ attakataṁ bimbaṁ*
Nayidaṁ parakataṁ aghaṁ;
Hetuṁ paṭicca sambhūtaṁ,
Hetu bhaṅgā nirujjhati. *S*. i. 134.

dhammas, things or phenomena, are causally dependent on one another and interrelated.

This conditionality goes on uninterrupted and uncontrolled by self-agency or external agency of any sort. The doctrine of conditionality (*idhappaccayatā*) cannot be labelled as determinism, because in this teaching both the physical environment and the moral causation (psychological causation) of the individual function together. The physical world influences man's mind, and mind, on the other hand, influences the physical world, obviously in a higher degree, for as the Buddha says: 'the world is led by the mind' (*cittena nīyati loko*).[1]

If we fail to understand the real significance and application to life of the Dependent Arising, we mistake it for a mechanical law of causality or even a simple simultaneous arising, a first beginning of all things, animate and inanimate. As there is no origination out of nothing in Buddhist thought, Dependent Arising shows the impossibility of a first cause. The first beginning of existence, of the life stream of living beings is inconceivable and as the Buddha says: 'Notions and speculations concerning the world (*loka-cintā*) may lead to mental derangement.'[2] 'O monks, this wheel of existence, this cycle of continuity (*saṁsāra*) is without a visible end, and the first beginning of beings wandering and hurrying round, wrapt in ignorance (*avijjā*) and fettered by craving (*taṇhā*) is not to be perceived.[3]

It is, in fact, impossible to conceive of a first beginning. None can trace the ultimate origin of anything, not even of a grain of sand, let alone of human beings. It is useless and meaningless to seek a beginning in a beginningless past. Life is not an identity, it is a becoming. It is a flux of physiological and psychological changes.

If one posits a first cause one is justified in asking for the cause of that 'First Cause'; for nothing can escape the law of condition and cause which is patent in the world to all but those who will not see. A theist, however, who attributes beings and events to an omnipotent Creator-God would emphatically say: 'It is God's will: it is sacrilege to question the Authority.' Does not this God-idea stifle the human liberty to investigate, to analyse, to scrutinize, to see what is beyond this naked eye, and so retards insight?

Let us grant that 'X' is the 'first cause'. Now does this assumption bring us one bit nearer to our deliverance? Does it not close the

1. *S.* i. 39. 2. *A.* ii. 80. 3. *S.* iii. 149, 151: *S.* ii. 179.

door to it? We see a natural law—beginningless causes and effects—and naught else ruling the universe.

As explained in the Dependent Arising the proximate cause of craving is feeling or sensation. Craving has its source, its rise in feeling.

All forms of appetite are included in *taṇhā* (craving). Greed, thirst, desire, lust, burning, yearning, longing, inclination, affection, household love are some of the many terms that denote *taṇhā* which in the word of the Buddha leads to becoming (*bhava-netti*). Becoming, which manifests itself as *dukkha*, as suffering, frustration, painful excitement, unsatisfactoriness, is our own experience.

The enemy of the whole world is lust, craving, or thirst through which all evils come to living beings. It is not only greed for or attachment to pleasures caused by the senses, wealth and property and by the wish to defeat others and conquer countries, but also attachment to ideals and ideas, to views, opinions and beliefs (*dhamma-taṇhā*) which often lead to calamity and destruction and bring untold suffering to whole nations, in fact to the whole world.

Now where does this craving arise and take root? Where there is delight and pleasure, there craving arises and takes root. What are delightful and pleasurable? The eye, ear, nose, tongue, body and mind (because it is through these avenues, these fivefold bases, that man cognizes the sense objects, the external world, and through the mind door, as the sixth, he entertains ideas and thoughts). There craving arises and takes root. Forms, sounds, smells, tastes, bodily contacts and ideas are delightful and pleasurable and there craving arises and takes root.[1]

Man is always attracted by the pleasant and the delightful, and in his search for pleasure, he runs after the five kinds of sense objects; cognizes ideas and clings to them. He little realizes that no amount of forms, sounds, smells, tastes, tangibles and mental objects or ideas will ever satisfy the eye, ear, nose, tongue, body and mind. Beings in their intense thirst for either possession or the satisfaction of desires, become bound to the wheel of existence, are twisted and torn between the spokes of agony, and securely close the door to final deliverance. The Buddha was most emphatic against this mad rush, and warned:

> 'Pleasure is a bond, a joy that's brief,
> Of little taste, leading to drawn-out pain.
> The wise know that the hook is baited.'[2]

1. *D.* 22. 2. *Sn.* 61.

The poet only echoes the Buddha's words when he writes:

> 'Pleasures are like poppies spread,
> You seize the flower, its bloom is shed;
> Or, like the snow fall on the river,
> A moment white, then melts for ever.'[1]

Whenever craving for these objects is connected with sense pleasure it is called 'Sensuous Craving' (*kāma-taṇhā*). When it is associated with the belief in eternal personal existence, then it is called 'Craving for Existence and Becoming' (*bhava-taṇhā*). This is what is known as the View of Eternalism (*sassata diṭṭhi*), attachment to becoming, the desire for continuing to exist for ever. When craving is associated with the belief in 'self-annihilation' it is called craving for non-existence (*vibhava-taṇhā*). This is what is known as the View of Annihilationism (*uccheda-diṭṭhi*).

It may be remembered that craving is conditioned not only by pleasurable and agreeable feelings, but also by unhappy and unpleasant feelings. A man in distress craves to be rid of it, and longs for happiness and release. To put it another way, the poor and the needy, the sick and the disabled, in brief, all 'sufferers' crave for happiness, pleasure and solace. On the other hand, the rich and the healthy who are already experiencing pleasure, also crave, but for more and more acute pleasure. Thus this thirst, this craving, is insatiable, and people pursue fleeting pleasures, constantly seeking fuel for this life-flame. Their greed is inordinate.

It is only when suffering comes, as its consequence, and not before, that one realizes the viciousness of this poisonous creeper of craving which winds itself round all who are not Arahats or perfectly pure ones who have uprooted its tap-root, ignorance. The more we crave, the more we suffer; sorrow is the tribute we have to pay for having craved.

> 'From craving grief arises,
> From craving arises fear,
> For him who is from craving free
> There is no grief, then whence comes fear?'[2]

Wherefore, know this craving as your foe here, that guides you

1. Robert Burns, *Tam O'Shanter*. 2. *Dhp.* 216.

to continued and repeated sentient existence, to rebirth, and thus builds the 'House of Being!'

The Buddha said: 'Dig up the root of craving.' (*Taṇhāya mūlaṁ khaṇatha*).[1]

> 'As a tree with firm, uninjured
> Roots, though cut down, grows up again,
> So when latent craving is not rooted out
> Suffering again and again arises.'[2]

No sensible man will deny the existence of suffering or unsatisfactoriness in this sentient world, nevertheless it is difficult for him to comprehend how this craving or thirst brings about re-existence. To do this one must understand two principal teachings of Buddhism: *karma* and rebirth.

If our present birth here is the beginning, and our death is the end of this life, we need not worry and try to understand the problem of suffering. A moral order in the universe, the reality of right and wrong, may not be of any significance to us. To enjoy and avoid suffering at any cost, may seem to be the sensible thing to do, during this brief span of life. This view, however, does not explain the inequality of mankind, and in general, man is conscious of a moral causation. Hence the need to seek the cause of this ill. The Pāli word *kamma* (Skt. *karma*, from the root *kr* to do) means literally 'action' or 'doing'. Not all actions, however, are considered as *karma*. The growing of hair and nails and the digesting of food, for instance, are actions of a sort, but not *karma*. Reflex actions also are not karma, but activities without moral significance.

'Volition, O monks, I declare, is *kamma*' (*cetanāhaṁ bhikkhave kammaṁ vadāmi*)[3] is the Buddha's definition. Volition is a factor of the mind, a psychological impulse which comes under the group of formations (*saṁkhāra*). So volition is part and parcel of the five groups of grasping that constitute the 'individual'. *Karma* is the action or seed. The effect or fruit is known as *karma-vipāka*. 'Having willed, man acts by deed, word or thought[4] and these volitions may be good or ill, so actions may be wholesome, unwholesome or neutral according to their results. This endless play of action and reaction, cause and effect, seed and fruit, continues in perpetual motion, and this is becoming, a continually changing process of psycho-physical phenomena of existence (*saṁsāra*).

1. Ibid. 337. 2. Ibid. 338. 3. *A*. iii. 415. See below, p. 93.
4. *A*. iii. 415.

It is clear that *karma* is volition which is a will, a force, and this force is classified into three types of craving: Craving for sense pleasures, for existence and for non-existence.[1] Having willed, man acts, through body, speech and mind, and actions bring about reactions. Craving gives rise to deed, deed produces results, results in turn bring about new desires, new craving. This process of cause and effect, action and reaction, is a natural law. It is a law in itself, with no need for a law-giver. An external agency, power, or God that punishes the ill and rewards the good deeds, has no place in Buddhist thought. Man is always changing either for good or for evil. This changing is unavoidable and depends entirely on his own will, his own action, and on nothing else. 'This is merely the universal natural law of the conservation of energy extended to the moral domain.'

Not much science is needed to understand how actions produce reactions, how effects follow causes and seed brings forth fruit, but how this karmic force, these acts of will, bring fruit in another birth after the dissolution of this body, is hard to grasp. According to Buddhism there is no life after death or before birth which is independent of *karma* or acts of will. *Karma* and rebirth go arm in arm, *karma* being the corollary of rebirth and vice versa. Here, however, we must understand that the Buddhist doctrine of *karma* is not fatalism, is not a philosophical doctrine that human action is not free but determined by motives which are regarded as external forces acting upon the will, or predetermined by God. The Buddha neither subscribed to the theory that all things are unalterably fixed, that they happen by inevitable necessity—that is Strict Determinism (*niyati-vāda*): nor did he uphold the theory of Complete Indeterminism (*adhicca-samuppanna*).

There is no eternal survival in heaven or hell in Buddhist thought. Birth precedes death, and death also precedes birth, so that the pair follow each other in bewildering succession. Still there is no soul, self, or fixed entity that passes from birth to birth. Though man comprises a psycho-physical unit of mind and matter, the 'psyche' or mind is not a soul or self, in the sense of an enduring entity, something ready-made and permanent. It is a force, a dynamic continuum capable of storing up memories not only of this life, but also of past lives. To the scientist matter is energy in a state of stress, change without real substance. To the psychologist the 'psyche' is no more a fixed entity. When the Buddha stressed that the so-

1. See above, p. 54.

called 'being' or 'individual' is nothing but a combination of physical and mental forces, or energies, a change with continuity, did he not antedate modern science and modern psychology by twenty-five centuries?

This psycho-physical organism undergoes incessant change, creates new psycho-physical processes every instant and thus preserves the potentiality for future organic processes, and leaves no gap between one moment and the next. We live and die every moment of our lives. It is merely a coming into being and passing away, a rise and fall (*udaya-vaya*), like the waves of the sea.

This change of continuity, this psycho-physical process, which is patent to us in this life does not cease at death but continues incessantly. It is the dynamic mind-flux that is known as will, thirst, desire or craving which constitutes karmic energy. This mighty force, this will to live, keeps life going. According to Buddhism it is not only human life, but the entire sentient world that is drawn by this tremendous force—this mind with its mental factors, good or ill.

The present birth is brought about by the craving and clinging karma-volitions (*taṇhā-upādāna*) of past births, and the craving and clinging acts of will of the present birth bring about future rebirth. According to Buddhism it is this karma-volition that divides beings into high and low.[1]

'Beings are heirs of their deeds; bearers of their deeds, and their deeds are the womb out of which they spring,'[2] and through their deeds alone they must change for the better, remake themselves, and win liberation from ill. It should, however, be remembered that according to Buddhism, not everything that occurs is due to past actions. During the time of the Buddha, sectarians like the Nigaṇṭha Nātaputta held the view that whatever the individual experiences, be it pleasant or unpleasant or neither—all come from former actions or past *kamma*.[3] The Buddha, however, rejected this theory of an exclusive determination by the past (*pubbekatahetu*) as unreasonable. Many a thing is the result of our own deeds done in this present life, and of external causes.

One with an inquiring mind may ask, if there is no transmigrating permanent Soul or Self to reincarnate, what is it that is reborn? The answer is that there is no permanent substance of the nature of Self or Soul (*Ātman*) that reincarnates or transmigrates. It is impossible to conceive of anything that continues without change.

1. *M.* 135. 2. *M.* 135.
3. *M.* iii. 214, *Devadaha-sutta*. This view is examined at *A.* i. 173.

All is in a state of flux. What we call life here is the functioning of the five Aggregates of Grasping which we have discussed earlier,[1] or the functioning of mind and body which are only energies or forces. They are never the same for two consecutive moments, and in the conflux of mind and body we do not see anything permanent. The grown-up man is neither the child nor quite a different person; there is only a relationship of continuity. The conflux of mind and body or mental and physical energy is not lost at death, for no force or energy is ever lost. It undergoes change. It resets, re-forms in new conditions. This is called rebirth, re-existence or re-becoming (*punabbhava*).

Karmic process (*kammabhava*) is the energy that out of a present life conditions a future life in unending sequence. In this process there is nothing that passes or transmigrates from one life to another. It is only a movement that continues unbroken. The 'being' who passes away here and takes birth elsewhere is neither the same person nor a totallv different one (*na ca so na ca añño*).[2]

There is the last moment of consciousness (*cuti citta* or *viññāṇa*) belonging to the immediately previous life; immediately next, upon the cessation of that consciousness, but conditioned by it, there arises the first moment of consciousness of the present birth which is called a relinking or rebirth-consciousness (*paṭisandhi viññāṇa*).[3] Similarly the last thought-moment in this life conditions the first thought-moment in the next. In this way consciousness comes into being and passes away yielding place to new consciousness. Thus this perpetual stream of consciousness goes on until existence ceases. Existence in a way is consciousness—the will to live, to continue.

According to modern biology, 'a new human life begins in that miraculous instant when a sperm cell from the father merges with an egg cell or ovum within the mother'. This is the moment of birth. Science speaks of only these two physical common factors. Buddhism, however, speaks of a third factor which is purely psychic.

According to the *Mahātaṇhāsaṁkhaya-sutta*,[4] 'by the conjunction of three factors does conception take place. If mother and father come together, but it is not the mother's proper season, and the being to be reborn (*gandhabba*) does not present itself, a germ of life is not planted. If the parents come together, and it is the mother's proper season, but the *gandhabba* is not present, then

1. See chapter 3 above. 2. *Milindapañha*.
3. The third proposition in the formula of 'Dependent Arising'. See above, p. 56.
4. *M.* 38 .

there is no conception. If the mother and father come together, and it is the mother's proper season and the *gandhabba* is also present, then a germ of life is planted there.'

The third factor is simply a term for the *paṭisandhi-viññāṇa*, rebirth-consciousness. It should be clearly understood that this rebirth-consciousness is not a Self or a Soul or an Ego-entity that experiences the fruits of good and evil deeds.[1] Consciousness is also generated by conditions. Apart from condition there is no arising of consciousness.

We give names, such as birth, death, thought-processes and so on, to a stream of consciousness. There are only thought-moments. As explained above, the last thought-moment we call death, and the first thought-moment we call birth; thus births and deaths occur in this stream of consciousness, which is only a series of ever continuing thought-moments.

So long as man is attached to existence through his ignorance, craving and clinging, to him death is not the final end. He will continue his career of whirling round the 'Wheel of Existence'. This is the endless play of action and reaction kept in perpetual motion by *karma* concealed by ignorance propelled by craving or thirst. As *karma*, or action, is of our own making, we have the power to break this endless chain. It is through the eradication of ignorance (*avijjā*) and of this driving force, craving, this thirst for existence, this will to live (*taṇhā*), that the Cycle of Existence (*saṁsāra*) ceases. The Buddha explains thus: 'How is there not re-becoming in the future? By the cessation of ignorance, by the arising of knowledge (*vijjā*), by the cessation of craving there is thus no re-becoming in the future.'[2]

The Buddha on attaining Enlightenment spoke these joyful words:

> 'Repeated births are each a torment.
> Seeking but not finding the "House Builder",
> I wandered through many a Saṁsāric birth.
> O "House Builder", thou art seen,
> Thou wilt not rebuild the house.
> All thy rafters have been shattered,
> Demolished has thy ridge pole been.
> My mind has won the Unconditioned (*Nibbāna*),
> The extinction of craving is achieved (arahatship).'[3]

1. This view is discussed at *M.* 38. See above, p. 50.
2. *M.* 43.
3. *Dhp.* 153, 154.

5

THE THIRD NOBLE TRUTH

Nirodha: The Cessation of Suffering

In chapters 3 and 4 we discussed suffering and its arising. Let us now try to understand the meaning of the Cessation of Suffering (*dukkha-nirodha*) which is known as *Nibbāna* (Sanskrit *Nirvāṇa*). The etymological meaning of the latter is given as *ni* + *vāna*, freedom from craving, a departure from craving, or *nir* + *vā*, to cease blowing or to be extinguished.

Though the Pāli and Sanskrit etymological meanings may help us to understand the term, they do not help us to realize the bliss of *Nirvāṇa*. Realization, as we shall see in the next chapter, comes through Virtue (*sīla*), Concentration (*samādhi*) and Wisdom (*paññā*). *Nirvāṇa* is a *dhamma*, an experience that cannot be explained because of its subtlety. It is known as the Supramundane (*lokuttara*), the Absolute, the Unconditioned (*asaṁkhata*). *Nirvāṇa* is to be realized by the wise, each one individually.

Let alone *Nirvāṇa*, a simple thing like the taste of sugar cannot be made known to one who has no previous experience of it by advising him to read a book on the chemistry of sugar. But if he puts a small lump on his tongue, he will experience the sweet taste and no more theorizing on sugar is needed.

'What is *Nirvāṇa*?' is a question that a Buddhist or a non-Buddhist may prefer to ask at the outset. This is not a question of today or yesterday. Clever answers may be given and *Nirvāṇa* explained in glowing terms, but no amount of theorizing will bring us one whit nearer to it, for it is beyond words, logic and reasoning (*atakkāvacara*). It is easier and safer to speak of what *Nirvāṇa* is not, for it is impossible to express it in words. *Nirvāṇa* is ineffable and incommunicable. In our attempt to explain it we use words which have limited meanings, words connected with the cosmos, whereas *Nirvāṇa*, the Absolute Reality, which is realized through the highest mental training and wisdom, is beyond any cosmic experience, beyond the reach of speech. Then why write about it? It is to prevent misconceptions about the Buddhist concept of *Nirvāṇa*.

The Buddha says:

'It occurred to me, monks, that this *Dhamma* I have realized is deep, hard to see, hard to understand, peaceful and sublime, beyond mere reasoning, subtle and intelligible to the wise. But this generation delights, revels and rejoices in sensual pleasures. For a generation delighting, revelling and rejoicing in sensual pleasures, it is hard to see this conditionality, this dependent arising. Hard, too, is it to see this calming of all conditioned things, the giving up of all substance of becoming, the extinction of craving, dispassion, cessation, *Nibbāna*. And if I were to teach the *Dhamma* and others were not to understand me, that would be a weariness, a vexation for me.'[1]

This is a clear indication from the Buddha himself that the extirpation of craving (*Nirvāṇa*) is hard to see, hard to understand.

In his explanation of the Third Noble Truth, in his first sermon, the Buddha says: 'This, monks, is the Noble Truth of the Cessation of Suffering: the complete cessation (*nirodho*), giving up (*cāgo*), abandoning (*paṭinissaggo*), release (*mutti*) and detachment (*anālayo*) from that very craving.'[2]

Though in this definition the word *Nibbāna* is not mentioned, 'complete cessation of craving' implies *Nibbāna*. Elsewhere this is made clear by the Buddha. 'Verily, Radha, the extinction of craving (*taṇhakkhayo*) is *Nibbāna*.'[3] Replying to a deity he says: 'The abandoning of craving (*taṇhāya vippahānena*) is *Nibbāna*.[4] Then in the words of the Venerable Sāriputta: 'The subduing and abandoning of passionate desire (*chandarāga*) for these Five Aggregates of Grasping: that is the cessation of suffering.'[5]

It is clear from the above that *nirodha* or *Nibbāna* is the cessation, the extinction of craving (*taṇhā*). As we have seen in the preceding chapter craving is the arising of suffering which ceases only when its origin, craving, ceases. With the giving up of craving one also gives up suffering and all that pertains to suffering. *Nibbāna*, therefore, is explained as the extinction of suffering.

It may be noted that though negative terms are often used to define *Nibbāna*, they do not imply that *Nibbāna* is mere negation or annihilation of a self. After all negation does not mean an

1. *M.* 26: *S.* i. 136. 2. *S.* v. 421. 3. *S.* iii. 190
4. *S.* i. 39. 5. *M.* 28.

absolute void, a vacuum, but simply the absence of something. An Arahat who has realized *Nibbāna* is free from craving. Craving no more exists in him, and this is not mere nothingness, or annihilation of self, because there is no self to be annihilated.

It is also evident from the texts that positive terms like *Khemaṁ* (Security), *Suddhi* (Purity), *Paṇītaṁ* (Sublime), *Santi* (Peace), *Vimutti* (Release), are used to denote the Unconditioned *Nirvāṇa*. Nevertheless, the real significance of these terms is restricted to the known experiences of the sentient world. All positive definitions are from our experience of the phenomenal world. A worldling's conception of things is *saṁsāric*, that is, belonging to existence or becoming. So all his conceptions concerning *Nirvāṇa* also are in terms of becoming, and therefore, he cannot have a true picture of *Nirvāṇa*. All his thoughts, concepts and words are limited, conditioned, and cannot be applied to the Unproduced, Unconditioned, Uncompounded *Nirvāṇa*.

Conventionally we speak of positive and negative terms; they are like everything else, relative; but *Nirvāṇa* is beyond both positive and negative and is not related to anything conditioned. The Buddha has used the terms of the world, knowing their limitations. Regarding the question, what is *Nirvāṇa*? let us hear the words of the Buddha:

'There are, monks, two *Nibbāna* elements (*Nibbāna dhātuyo*). What two? The *Nibbāna* element with a basis remaining (*saupādisesa*)[1] and the *Nibbāna* element without a basis remaining (*anupādisesa*). Which, monks, is the *Nibbāna* element with a basis remaining? Here, monks, a monk is an Arahat, one whose taints (*āsava*) are destroyed, who has lived the life, done what was to be done, laid down the burden, attained Arahatship by stages, destroyed completely the bond of becoming, one who is free through knowing rightly. As his faculties have not been demolished he experiences what is agreeable and disagreeable, he experiences pleasure and pain. The five aggregates remain. It is his extinction of lust, hate and delusion, monks, that is called the *Nibbāna* element with a basis remaining (*saupādisesa nibbānadhātu*).

'And which, monks, is the *Nibbāna* element without a basis remaining (*anupādisesa nibbānadhātu*)?

'Here, monks, a monk is an Arahat, one whose taints are destroyed, who has lived the life, done what was to be done, laid down the

1. *Upādi* here means the five aggregates.

burden, attained Arahatship by stages, destroyed completely the bond of becoming, one who is free through knowing rightly. All his feelings not being welcomed, not being delighted in (*anabhinanditāni*), will here and now become cool: it is this, monks, that is called the *Nibbāna* element without a basis remaining.

'These, monks, are the two *Nibbāna* elements.'

This fact the Blessed One declared:

'Thus this is said:

These two *Nibbāna* elements are explained
By the Seeing One, steadfast and unattached:
When one element with basis belonging to this life
Remains, destroyed is that which to becoming leads;[1]
When one without that basis manifests
In the hereafter, all becomings cease.

The minds of those who know this unconditioned state
Are delivered by destroying that to which becoming leads:
They realize the *Dhamma*'s essence[2] and in stillness
Delighting, steadfast they abandon all becoming.'[3]

A being consists of the five aggregates or mind and matter. They change incessantly and are therefore impermanent. They come into being and pass away, for, 'whatever is of the nature of arising, all that is of the nature of ceasing'.[4]

Lust, hate and delusion in man bring about repeated existence, for it is said: without abandoning lust, hate and delusion, one is not free from birth. . . .[5]

One attains arahatship, that is deliverance even while alive, by rooting out lust, hate and delusion. As stated above this is known as the *Nibbāna* element with a basis remaining (*saupādisesa nibbānadhātu*). The Arahat's five aggregates or the remaining bases are conditioned by the lust, hate and delusion of his infinite past. As he still lives his aggregates function: he, therefore, experiences the pleasant as well as painful feelings that his sense faculties entertain

1. *Bhavanetti*, a synonym for *taṇhā*, craving or thirst.
2. *Dhamma-sāra* here means arahatship.
3. *Iti.* pp. 38, 39.
4. *M.* iii. 280: *S.* v. 423: *S.* iv. 47, 107: *Vinaya Mhvg.*
5. *A.* ii. i. 6.

through contact with sense objects. But since he is freed from attachment, discrimination and the idea of selfhood, he is not moved by these feelings.[1]

Now when an Arahat passes away his aggregates, his remaining bases, cease to function; they break up at death; his feelings are no more, and because of his eradication of lust, hate and delusion, he is not reborn, and naturally there is then no more entertaining of feelings; and therefore is it said: 'his feeling will become cool (*sītibhavissanti*)'.

This idea is expressed in the *Udāna* thus:

> 'The body broke up, perception ceased,
> All feelings cooled, all formations stilled,
> Consciousness disappeared.'[2]

This is known as the *Nibbāna* element without a basis remaining (*anupādisesa nibbānadhātu*).

From the foregoing the position of the Arahat, the Consummate One, is clear. When a person totally eradicates the trio that leads to becoming—lust, hate and delusion—he is liberated from the shackles of *saṁsāra*, from repeated existence. He is free in the full sense of the word. He no longer has any quality which will cause him to be reborn as a living being, because he has realized *Nibbāna*, the entire cessation of continuity and becoming (*bhava-nirodha*); he has transcended common or worldly activities and has raised himself to a state above the world while yet living in the world: his actions are issueless, are karmically ineffective, for they are not motivated by the trio, by the mental defilements (*kilesa*). He is immune to all evil, to all defilements of the heart. In him there are no latent or underlying tendencies (*anusaya*); he is beyond good and evil, he has given up both good and bad:[3] he is not worried by the past, the future, nor even the present. He clings to nothing in the world and so is not troubled. He is not perturbed by the vicissitudes of life. His mind is unshaken by contact with worldly contingencies; he is sorrowless, taintless and secure (*asokaṁ, virajaṁ, khemaṁ*).[4] Thus *Nibbāna* is a 'state' realizable in this very life (*diṭṭhadhamma-nibbāna*). The thinker, the inquiring mind, will not find it difficult to understand this state, which can be postulated only of the Arahat and

1. Cf. Arahat Sona's statement: 'sights, tastes, sounds, smells, touches . . . do not cause the steadfast one (*tādino*) to tremble. His mind stands firm and fully free. *A.* iii. 377.

2. *Ud.* viii. 9.

3. *Dhp.* 39.

4. *Sn. Maṅgala-sutta* 11.

not of any other being, either in this world or in the realms of heavenly enjoyment.

Though the sentient being experiences the unsatisfactory nature of life, and knows at first hand what suffering is, what defilements are, and what it is to crave, he does not know what the total extirpation of defilements is, because he has never experienced it. Should he do so, he will know, through self-realization, what it is to be without defilements, what *Nirvāṇa* or reality is, what true happiness is. The Arahat speaks of *Nirvāṇa* with experience, and not by hearsay, but the Arahat can never, by his realization, make others understand *Nirvāṇa*. One who has slaked his thirst knows the release he has gained, but he cannot explain this release to another. However much he may talk of it, others will not experience it; for it is self-experience, self-realization. Realization is personal to each individual. Each must eat and sleep for himself, and treat himself for his ailments; these are but daily requirements, how much more when it is concerned with man's inner development, his deliverance of the mind.

What is difficult to grasp is the *Nibbāna* element without a basis remaining (*anupādisesa-nibbāna*), in other words, the *parinibbāna* or final passing away of the Arahat.

An oft-quoted passage from the Udāna runs:

'Monks, there is the unborn, unoriginated, unmade and unconditioned. Were there not the unborn, unoriginated, unmade and unconditioned, there would be no escape for the born, originated, made and conditioned. Since there is the unborn, unoriginated, unmade and unconditioned, so there is escape for the born, originated, made and conditioned.[1]

'Here there is neither the element of solidity (expansion), fluidity (cohesion), heat and motion, nor the sphere of infinite space, nor the sphere of infinite consciousness, nor the sphere of nothingness, nor the sphere of neither perception nor non-perception, neither this world nor the other, nor sun and moon. Here there is none coming, none going, none existing, neither death nor birth. Without support, non-existing, without sense objects is this. This indeed is the end of suffering (*dukkha*).[2]

It is clear from the above that this *parinibbāna* (the ultimate *Nibbāna*) is a state where the five aggregates: form, feeling,

1. *Ud.* viii. 3.
2. *Ud.* viii. 1. Also Cf. *Sarasutta, Devatā Saṁyutta.*

perception, mental formations and consciousness, and all that pertains to the aggregates have ceased. This, therefore, is a state where relativity has no place. It is beyond and outside everything that is relative. It is neither the effect of a cause, nor does it as cause give rise to an effect. It is neither the path (*magga*) nor the fruit (*phala*). It is the Absolute, the Unconditioned, the Uncompounded.

Suffering and its arising (cause) which is craving is mundane (*lokiya*), but *Nirvāṇa* not being in the world, stands outside conditioned things and, therefore, beyond cause and effect. All things mundane are relative, but *Nirvāṇa* being that which has no relativities is Absolute.

In a very important discourse (*Dvayatānupassanā-sutta*)[1] wherein the Dependent Arising and the Four Noble Truths are enumerated, the Buddha addressing the monks says:

'What the world at large considers Truth (*idaṁ saccaṁti upanijjhāyitaṁ*) has been viewed as falsehood by the Noble (*Ariya*) through their consummate comprehension, whilst the Noble hail as Truth what the world deems falsehood', and further says:

> '*Nibbāna* is no lie (no state unreal)
> For it is known as truth by the Noble Ones.
> But since they realize that truth
> Desireless they pass away.'[2]

This is not the only instance where the Buddha used Truth as a substitute for *Nibbāna*, for we find the following:

> 'Reality, monk, is a name for *Nibbāna*.'[3]

> 'In reality they are released
> Destroying craving for becoming.'[4]

As stated in an equally important discourse (*Dhātuvibhaṅga-sutta*)[5] the Arahat who is absolutely calm within (the threefold fire of lust, hate and delusion fully extinguished, blown out within,

1. *Sn.* 2. *Sn.* 758.
3. *S.* iv. 195: *'yathābhūtaṁ vacanaṁ ti kho bhikkhu nibbānassetaṁ adhivacanaṁ.'*
4. *Iti.* ii. 12: *'yathābhūte vimuccanti-bhavataṇhāparikkhayā'*. Reality, *yathābhūta* = *nibbāna*, see Commentary.
5. *M.* 140.

'*paccattaṁ yeva parinibbāyati*') when experiencing a pleasant, unpleasant or neutral feeling, knows that it is impermanent, that it is not clung to with the idea of my and mine; that it is not experienced with feelings of enjoyment (with passion).

'Whatever feeling he experiences, be it pleasant, unpleasant or neutral, he experiences it without being attached to it, without being bound to it (*visaṁ-yutto*). He knows that with the dissolution of the body (after the life principle has come to an end) all feelings, all experiences will become cool, will be tranquillized (*sītibhavissanti*) just as an oil lamp burns dependent upon oil and wick and through the coming to an end of its oil and wick it goes out for lack of fuel. Even so when a monk experiences a feeling that the body has come to an end, he knows, "I experience a feeling that the body has come to an end", and when he experiences a feeling that life has come to an end he knows, "I experience a feeling that life has come to an end", and he knows, "with the breaking up of the body and the coming to an end of life, all feeling, not being delighted in here and now, will become cool". Therefore, monk, a person thus endowed is endowed with this supreme wisdom, because the knowledge of the destruction of all suffering (*dukkha*) is the supreme noble wisdom.

'This deliverance of his, founded on Truth, is unshakable. False is that which is unreality; that which is reality (not false), *Nibbāna*, is Truth (*taṁ saccaṁ*). Therefore, monk, a person thus endowed is endowed with this supreme Truth, because the Supreme Noble Truth (*paramaṁ ariya saccaṁ*) is *Nibbāna*, which is reality (not false).'

In the *Ratana-sutta*[1] it is said:

> 'Their past is dead, the new[2] no more arises,
> Mind to future becoming is unattached,
> The germ has died[3], they have no more desire for growth,
> Those wise (and steadfast ones) go out as did this lamp.'[4]

This is the position of the Arahat who has passed away (*parinib-*

1. The Jewel Discourse, *Sn.* 14.
2. The past and the new *kamma* are meant here.
3. Here germ means the rebirth consciousness.
4. It is said that as the Buddha spoke these words he saw the flame of a lamp go out.

buto). His path, like that of birds in the sky,[1] cannot be traced. It is therefore wrong to say that the Arahat or the Buddha entered *Nibbāna*, because it is not a place or a state or a 'heaven' where beings continue to live eternally. *Nibbāna* has no location. The final passing away of the Buddha or the Arahat is expressed in the texts as *parinibbuto*, *parinibbāyi*, meaning fully passed away, fully extinct, which is a clear indication that it is the cessation of becoming (*bhavanirodha*)—the journey's end. Now what that is—what happens to the Buddha or the Arahat after his passing away—cannot be theorized, cannot be defined. There is no measure, no dimension. It is an 'unanswered', 'undetermined' question (*avyākata*). The highest (ultimate) Truth is inexpressible and undeclared (*anakkhāta*).

When Upasīva questioned whether one who passed away ceased to exist, or lasted for ever in bliss, the Buddha's answer was categorical:

> 'Of one who's passed away there is no measure,
> Of him there's naught whereby one may say aught;
> When once all things have wholly been removed,
> All ways of saying, too, have been removed.'[2]

In the absence of an *Atta* (*Ātman*), Soul or Self, what attains *Nibbāna*, or who realizes *Nibbāna* is a baffling question. Let us first try to understand who or what this so-called being is. A being is a conflux of mind and matter. It is a process that undergoes change not remaining the same for two consecutive moments, and herein, there is no permanent something: the complete cessation of this process—this flux of physical and psychological categories—is known as *Parinibbāna* (fully blown out or passed away). No 'I' Self or Soul enters *Nibbāna*, is eternalized or annihilated in *Nibbāna*.

The question of what attains or who realizes *Nibbāna* arises because of the strong notion of 'I', ME and MINE (*ahaṁkāra*, *mamiṁkāra*) in man, and all the questions are round this 'I'; but there is no 'I' or Self behind our actions, mental, verbal and physical. There is no doer of a deed. There is no thinker of a thought. *Nibbāna* is, but not the man (being) who realizes it. Phenomena alone flow on. In conventional language we speak of man, woman, I, me and so forth, but in the ultimate sense no such individual

1. *Dhp.* 92, 93.
2. *Sn.* 1076. Compare this with the Buddha's reply to Vaccha: 'To say that he (an Arahat) is reborn does not fit the case; to say that he is not reborn, does not fit the case.' *M.* i. 486. Discourse 72.

exists. Only a process comes into being and a process ceases. 'Whatever is of the nature of arising, all that is of the nature of ceasing.'[1]

The five aggregates of grasping form the 'being'. Craving which is the arising (cause) of suffering arises in the five aggregates of grasping. The cessation of craving is also within these aggregates. Thus a process comes into being, and a process ceases, and there is no permanent Self or 'I' that produces the aggregates and finally extirpates them, much less an external agency. Here there is a becoming and a cessation of becoming. This is the right view.

The Buddhist *Nibbāna* is called the Supreme Happiness (*paramaṁ sukhaṁ*) and as we have seen above, this happiness is brought about by the complete calming, the utter ceasing of all sensations. Now this saying, indeed, baffles us completely, we who have experienced so many pleasant feelings with our sense faculties.

The Venerable Udāyi, a disciple of the Buddha, was confronted with this very problem. The Venerable Sāriputta addressing the monks said: 'It is *Nibbāna*, friends, that is happiness; it is *Nibbāna*, friends, that is happiness.' Then the Venerable Udāyi asked: 'But what, friend Sāriputta, is happiness, since herein there is no feeling?' 'Just this, friend, is happiness, that herein there is no feeling.'[2] This saying of the Venerable Sāriputta is fully supported by the following one of the Buddha: 'Whatever is experienced, sensed, felt, all that is suffering' (*yaṁkiñci vedayitaṁ taṁ dukkhasmiṁ ti*[3]).

The essential steps of the path to the removal of suffering—to *Nibbāna*—are pointed out by the Buddha. It is the way of careful cultivation of the mind so as to produce unalloyed happiness and supreme rest from the turmoil of life. The path is indeed very difficult, but if we, with constant heedfulness, and complete awareness, walk it watching our steps, we will one day reach our destination. A child learns to stand and walk gradually and with difficulty. So too have all great ones, in the march to perfection, moved from stage to stage through repeated failure to final success.

'Mindful of the yogis of the past
And remembering their ways of life,
Even though today be but the after-time[4]
One may yet attain the Peace perennial.[5]'

1. *M.* iii. 280; *S.* iv. 47, 107. 2. *A.* iv. 414. 3. *S.* ii. 53.
4. i.e. after the passing away of the Buddha.
5. '*Saritvā pubbake yogi—tesaṁ vattaṁ anussaraṁ*
Kiñcāpi pacchimo kālo—phuseyya amataṁ padaṁ.' *Thag.* 947.

6

THE THREEFOLD DIVISION OF THE NOBLE EIGHTFOLD PATH

WHILE lying on his death-bed, addressing the disciples the Buddha said: 'The Doctrine and the Discipline (*dhamma-vinaya*) which I have set forth and laid down for you, let them, after I am gone, be your teacher.'[1]

From this it is quite clear that the Buddha's way of life, his religious system, comprises the doctrine and the discipline. Discipline implies moral excellence, the taming of the tongue and the bodily actions, the code of conduct taught in Buddhism. This is generally known as *sīla*, virtue or moral training. The doctrine deals with man's mental training, taming of the mind. It is meditation or the development of Mental Concentration, *samādhi*, and Wisdom, *paññā*. These three, Virtue, Concentration and Wisdom, are the cardinal teachings which when carefully and fully cultivated raise man from lower to higher levels of mental life; lead him from darkness to light, from passion to dispassion, from turmoil to tranquillity.

These three are not isolated reactions, but integral parts of the Path. This idea is crystallized in the clear admonition of the Enlightened Ones of all ages—'Cease from all evil; cultivate the good; cleanse your own mind.'[2]

These oft-quoted but ever fresh words convey briefly the Message of the Master indicating the path to purification and deliverance. The Path, however, is generally referred to as the Noble Eightfold Path (*ariyo aṭṭhaṁgiko maggo*). Though some prefer to call this the Āriyan Eightfold Path, it may be noted that the term '*Āriyan*' does not here stand for any race, caste, class or clan. It simply means noble or excellent.

1. *Mahā Parinibbāna-sutta*, D. 16.
2. '*Sabba pāpassa akaraṇaṁ—kusalassa upasampadā, Sacittapariyodapanaṁ—etaṁ buddhānasāsanaṁ.*' *Dhp.* 183.

The Eightfold Path is arranged in three groups: Virtue, Concentration and Wisdom (*sīla, samādhi* and *paññā*).[1] This Path is unique to Buddhism and distinguishes it from every other religion and philosophy.

The eight factors of the Path are:[2]

1. Right Understanding (*sammā-diṭṭhi*) 2. Right Thought (*sammā-saṁkappa*)	Wisdom Group (*paññā*)
3. Right Speech (*sammā-vācā*) 4. Right Action (*sammā-kammanta*) 5. Right Livelihood (*sammā-ājīva*)	Virtue Group (*sīla*)
6. Right Effort (*sammā-vāyāma*) 7. Right Mindfulness (*sammā-sati*) 8. Right Concentration (*sammā-samādhi*)	Concentration Group (*samādhi*)

Referring to this Path, in his First Discourse,[3] the Buddha called it the Middle Path (*majjhimā paṭipadā*), because it avoids two extremes: Indulgence in sensual pleasures which is low, worldly and leads to harm is one extreme; self-torture in the form of severe asceticism which is painful, low and leads to harm is the other.

Living in the palace amidst song and dance, luxury and pleasure, the Bodhisatta[4] knew by experience that sense pleasures do not lead mankind to true happiness and deliverance. Six years of rigorous mortification, which he, as an ascetic, so zealously practised in search of purification and final deliverance, brought him no reward. It was a vain and useless effort. Avoiding these two extremes he followed a path of moral and mental training and through self-experience discovered the Middle Path consisting of the three groups.

In this chapter a brief account of the three groups and how they aim at promoting and perfecting a path that consists of eight factors will be discussed. The factors will be dealt with in their entirety in the chapters that follow.

It must always be borne in mind that the term 'path' is only a figurative expression. Though conventionally we talk of treading a path, in the ultimate sense the eight steps signify eight mental factors. They are interdependent and interrelated, and at the

1. *M.* 44. 2. *M.* 44.
3. Known as 'Setting in Motion the Wheel of Truth' (*Dhamma-cakkappavattana*), *S.* v. 420; *Vin.* i. 10. See above, p. 18.
4. See above, p. 14, n.2.

highest level they function simultaneously; they are not followed and practised one after the other in numerical order. Even on the lower level each and every factor should be tinged with some degree of right understanding; for it is the key-note of Buddhism.

Let us first hear these words of the Buddha:

'O monks, it is through not understanding, not penetrating four things (*dhammā*) that we have run so long, wandered on so long in this round of existence both you and I. And what four? Virtue, Concentration, Wisdom and Deliverance. But when these four things, O monks, are understood and penetrated, rooted out is the craving for existence, destroyed is that which leads to renewed becoming, and there is no more coming to be.'[1]

Further says the Master:

'Concentration (meditation), O monks, supported by virtue brings much fruit, brings much advantage. The mind supported by wisdom is wholly and entirely freed from the intoxication of sense desires, from becoming, wrong views and ignorance.'[2]

These sayings of the Buddha explain the function and the purpose of cultivating Virtue, Meditation and Wisdom. Deliverance means living experience of the cessation of the three root causes of evil, Greed, Hatred and Delusion or Ignorance (*lobha*, *dosa* and *moha*), that assail the human mind. These root causes are eliminated through training in Virtue, Meditation and Wisdom.

Thus it is clear that the Buddha's teaching aims at the highest purification, perfect mental health, free from all tainted impulses.

Now this deliverance from mental taints, this freedom from ill, lies absolutely and entirely in a man's own hands, in those of no one else, human or divine. Not even a Supreme Buddha can redeem a man from the fetters of existence except by showing him the path.

The path is: Virtue, Concentration and Wisdom, which are referred to in the discourses as the threefold training (*tividhā-sikkhā*) and none of them is an end in itself; each is a means to an end. One cannot function independently of the others. As in the case of a tripod which falls to the ground if a single leg gives way, so here one cannot function without the support of the others.

1. *D.* 16.	2. *D.* 16.

These three go together supporting each other. Virtue or regulated behaviour strengthens meditation and meditation in turn promotes Wisdom. Wisdom helps one to get rid of the clouded view of things—to see life as it really is—that is to see life and all things pertaining to life as arising and passing away.

It is now quite clear that in the interplay of doctrine and discipline (*dhamma-vinaya*) or knowledge and conduct (*vijjā-caraṇa*) the two constitute a single process of growth. 'As hand washes hand, and foot washes foot, so does conduct purify wisdom and wisdom conduct.'[1] This fact may be borne in mind by students of Buddhism, as there is a tendency, especially in academic circles, to regard the teachings of the Buddha as mere speculation, as a mere doctrine of metaphysics without practical value or importance.

The Buddhist way of life, however, is an intense process of cleansing one's speech, action and thought. It is self-development and self-purification. The emphasis is on practical results and not mere philosophical speculation, logical abstraction or even mere cogitation.

In strong language did the Buddha warn his followers against mere book learning thus:

'Though he recites the sacred texts a lot, but acts not accordingly that heedless man is like a cowherd counting others' cattle (not obtaining the products of the cow). He shares not the fruits of the tranquil man.

'Though he recites only a little of the sacred texts, but acts in accordance with the teaching, abandoning lust, hate and delusion, possessed of right understanding, his mind entirely released and clinging to nothing here or hereafter, he shares the fruits of the tranquil man.'[2]

These are clear indications that the Buddhist way of life, the Buddhist method of grasping the highest truth, awakening from ignorance to full knowledge, does not depend on mere academic intellectual development, but on a practical teaching that leads the follower to enlightenment and final deliverance.

The Buddha was more concerned with beings than with inanimate nature. His sole object was to unravel the mystery of existence, to solve the problems of becoming. This he did by comprehending in all their fullness the Four Noble Truths, the eternal verities of life.

1. *D.* 4. 2. *Dhp.* 19, 20.

This knowledge of the truths he tried to impart to those who sought it, and never forced it upon others. He never compelled or persuaded people to follow him, for compulsion and coercion were foreign to his method of teaching. He did not encourage his disciples to believe him blindly, but wished them to investigate his teaching which invited the seeker to 'come and see' (*ehipassika*). It is seeing and understanding, and not blind believing, that the Master approves.

To understand the world within, one must develop the inner faculties, one's mind. The Buddha says: 'Mind your mind'.[1] 'The wise tame themselves.'[2]

Today there is ceaseless work going on in all directions to improve the world. Scientists are pursuing their methods and experiments with undiminished vigour and determination. Modern discoveries and methods of communication and contact have produced startling results. All these improvements, though they have their advantages and rewards, are entirely material and external.

Within this conflux of mind and body of man, however, there are unexplored marvels to occupy men of science for many many years.

Really, the world, which the scientists are trying to improve, is, according to the ideas of Buddhism, subject to so much change at all points on its circumference and radii, that it is not capable of being made sorrowfree.

Our life is so dark with ageing, so smothered with death, so bound with change, and these qualities are so inherent in it—even as greenness is to grass, and bitterness to quinine—that not all the magic and witchery of science can ever transform it. The immortal splendour of an eternal sunlight awaits only those who can use the light of understanding and the culture of conduct to illuminate and guard their path through life's tunnel of darkness and dismay.

The people of the world today mark the changing nature of life. Although they see it, they do not keep it in mind and act with dispassionate discernment. Though change again and again speaks to them and makes them unhappy, they pursue their mad career of whirling round the wheel of existence and are twisted and torn between the spokes of agony.

After all, a scientist or a plain man, if he has not understood the importance of conduct, the urgency for wholesome endeavour, the necessity to apply knowledge to life, is, so far as the doctrine of the Buddha is concerned, an immature person, who has yet to negotiate

1. *D.* 16. 2. *Dhp.* 80.

many more hurdles before he wins the race of life and the immortal prize of *Nibbāna*.

For an understanding of the world within, science may not be of much help to us. Ultimate truth cannot be found in science. To the scientist, knowledge is something that ties him more and more to this sentient existence. That knowledge, therefore, is not saving knowledge. To one who views the world and all it holds in its proper perspective, the primary concern of life is not mere speculation or vain voyaging into the imaginary regions of high fantasy, but the gaining of true happiness and freedom from ill or unsatisfactoriness (*dukkha*). To him true knowledge depends on the central question: Is this learning according to actuality? Can it be of use to us in the conquest of mental peace and tranquillity, of real happiness?

To understand the world within we need the guidance, the instruction of a competent and genuine seer whose clarity of vision and depth of insight penetrate into the deepest recesses of life and cognize the true nature that underlies all appearance. He, indeed, is the true philosopher, the true scientist who has grasped the meaning of change in the fullest sense and has transmuted this understanding into a realization of the deepest truths fathomable by man—the truths of the three signs or characteristics (*ti-lakkhaṇa*): Impermanence, Unsatisfactoriness, Non-self (*anicca, dukkha, anatta*).[1] No more can he be confused by the terrible or swept off his feet by the glamour of things ephemeral. No more is it possible for him to have a clouded view of phenomena; for he has transcended all capacity for error through the perfect immunity which insight (*vipassanā ñāṇa*) alone can give.

The Buddha is such a seer, and his path to deliverance is open to all who have eyes to see and minds to understand. It is different from other paths to 'salvation'; for the Buddha teaches that each individual, whether layman or monk, is solely responsible for his own liberation.

Mankind is caught in a tangle, inner as well as outer, and the Buddha's infallible remedy, in brief, is this: 'The prudent man full of effort, established well in Virtue, develops Concentration and Wisdom and succeeds in solving the tangle.[2]

The Buddha's foremost admonition to his sixty immediate Arahat disciples was that the *Dhamma* should be promulgated for the welfare and happiness of many; out of compassion for the world.[3]

1. For a detailed explanation of the Three Signs see below, p. 95.
2. *S*. i. 13.
3. *Vinaya Mahāvagga*.

The whole dispensation of the Master is permeated with that salient quality of universal loving compassion.

Sīla or Virtue, the initial stage of the Path, is based on this loving compassion. Why should one refrain from harming and robbing other people? Is it not because of love for self and others? Why should one succour the poor, the needy and those in distress? Is it not out of compassion for those others?

To abstain from evil and do good is the function of *sīla*,[1] the code of conduct taught in Buddhism. This function is never void of loving compassion. *Sīla* embraces within it qualities of the heart, such as love, modesty, tolerance, pity, charity and happiness at the success of others, and so forth. *Samādhi* and *Paññā*, or Concentration and Wisdom, are concerned with the discipline of the mind.

As stated above, three factors of the Eightfold Path (Nos: 3, 4 and 5) form the Buddhist code of conduct (*sīla*). They are: Right Speech, Right Action and Right Livelihood.

Right Speech is to abstain (a) from falsehood and always speak the truth; (b) from tale-bearing which brings about discord and disharmony, and to speak words that are conducive to concord and harmony; (c) from harsh and abusive speech, and instead to speak kind and refined words; and (d) from idle chatter, vain talk or gossip and instead to speak words which are meaningful and blameless.

Right Action is abstention from (a) killing, (b) stealing, and (c) illicit sexual indulgence, and cultivating compassion, taking only things that are given, and living pure and chaste.

Right Livelihood is abandoning wrong ways of living which bring harm and suffering to others: Trafficking (a) in arms and lethal weapons, (b) in animals for slaughter, (c) in human beings (i.e. dealing in slaves which was prevalent during the time of the Buddha), (d) in intoxicating drinks and (e) poisons, and living by a profession which is blameless and free from harm to oneself and others. (These factors will be discussed in detail in the chapters that follow.)

From this outline of Buddhist ethics, it is clear that the code of conduct set forth by the Buddha is no mere negative prohibition but an affirmation of doing good—a career paved with good intentions for the welfare and happiness of all mankind. These moral principles aim at making society secure by promoting unity, harmony and right relations among people.

1. *Vism: sīlaniddesa.*

This code of conduct (*sīla*) is the first stepping stone of the Buddhist Way of Life. It is the basis for mental development. One who is intent on meditation or concentration of mind must develop a love of virtue; for it is virtue that nourishes mental life and makes it steady and calm.

The next stage in the Path to Deliverance is Mental Culture, Concentration (*samādhi*), which includes three other factors of the Eightfold Path: they are, Right Effort, Right Mindfulness and Right Concentration (Nos. 6, 7 and 8).

Right Effort is the persevering endeavour (a) to prevent the arising of evil and unwholesome thoughts that have not yet arisen in a man's mind, (b) to discard such evil thoughts already arisen, (c) to produce and develop wholesome thoughts not yet arisen and (d) to promote and maintain the good thoughts already present.

The function of this sixth factor, therefore, is to be vigilant and check all unhealthy thoughts, and to cultivate, promote and maintain wholesome and pure thoughts arising in a man's mind.

The prudent man who masters his speech and his physical actions through *sīla* (virtue) now makes every endeavour to scrutinize his thoughts, his mental factors, and to avoid distracting thoughts.

Right Mindfulness is the application or arousing of attention in regard to the (a) activities of the body (*kāyānupassanā*), (b) feelings or sensations (*vedanānupassanā*), (c) the activities of the mind (*cittānupassanā*) and (d) mental objects (*dhammānupassanā*).

As these factors of the Path are interdependent and co-operating, Right Mindfulness aids Right Effort and together they can check the arising of unwholesome thoughts and develop the good and wholesome thoughts already entertained. The man vigilant in regard to his actions, verbal, physical and mental, avoids all that is detrimental to his mental (spiritual) progress. Such a one cannot be mentally indolent and supine. The well-known discourse on the Foundations of Mindfulness (*Satipaṭṭhāna-sutta*) deals comprehensively with this fourfold Mindfulness.[1]

Right Concentration is the intensified steadiness of the mind comparable to the unflickering flame of a lamp in a windless place. It is concentration that fixes the mind right and causes it to be unmoved and undisturbed. The correct practice of *Samādhi* (concentration or mental discipline) maintains the mind and the mental properties in a state of balance. Many are the mental impediments

1. See chapter 13 on Right Mindfulness.

that confront a yogi, a meditator, but with the support of Right Effort and Right Mindfulness the fully concentrated mind is capable of dispelling the impediments, the passions that disturb man. The perfectly concentrated mind is not distracted by sense objects, for it sees things as they really are, in their proper perspective.[1]

Thus mastering the mind, and not allowing the mind to master him, the yogi cultivates true Wisdom (*paññā*) which consists of the first two factors and the final stage of the Path, namely, Right Understanding and Right Thought.

Thought includes thoughts of renunciation (*nekkhamma-saṁkappa*), good will (*avyāpāda-saṁkappa*) and of compassion or non-harm (*avihiṁsā-saṁkappa*). These thoughts are to be cultivated and extended towards all living beings irrespective of race, caste, clan or creed. As they embrace all that breathes there are no compromising limitations. The radiation of such ennobling thoughts is not possible for one who is egocentric and selfish.

A man may be intelligent, erudite and learned, but if he lacks right thoughts, he is, according to the teachings of the Buddha, a fool (*bāla*) not a man of understanding and insight. If we view things with dispassionate discernment, we will understand that selfish desire, hatred and violence cannot go together with true Wisdom. Right Understanding or true Wisdom is always permeated with right thoughts and never bereft of them.

Right Understanding, in the ultimate sense, is to understand life as it really is. For this, one needs a clear comprehension of the four Noble Truths, namely: The Truth of (a) *Dukkha*, Suffering or Unsatisfactoriness, (b) the Arising of *Dukkha*, (c) the Cessation of Dukkha and (d) the Path leading to the Cessation of *Dukkha*.

Right Understanding or penetrative Wisdom is the result of continued and steady practice of meditation or careful cultivation of the mind. To one endowed with Right Understanding it is impossible to have a clouded view of phenomena, for he is immune from all impurities and has attained the unshakable deliverance of the mind (*akuppā ceto vimutti*).

The careful reader will now be able to understand how the three groups, Virtue, Concentration and Wisdom, function together for one common end: Deliverance of the Mind (*ceto vimutti*), and how through genuine cultivation of man's mind, and through control of actions, both physical and verbal, purity is attained. It is through self-exertion and self-development that the aspirant secures free-

1. See chapter 14 on Right Concentration.

dom, and not through praying to and petitioning an external agency. This indeed is the *Dhamma* discovered by the Buddha, made use of by him for full enlightenment and revealed to the others:

> 'Virtue, and concentration, wisdom, supreme freedom,
> These things the Illustrious Gotama realized.
> Thus fully understanding them the Buddha,
> Ender of Ill, the Teacher, the Seeing One
> Utterly calmed, taught the *Dhamma* to the monks.'[1]

In spite of the scientific knowledge that is steadily growing the people of the world are restless and racked with fear and discontent. They are intoxicated with the desire to gain fame, wealth, power and to gratify the senses. To this troubled world still seething with hate, distrust, selfish desire and violence, most timely is the Buddha's Message of love and understanding, the Noble Eightfold Path, referring to which the Buddha says:

> 'This is the path itself,
> For none other leads
> To purity of vision:
> If you follow it and so confuse
> King Māra, all suffering will end.
> Since I have learned how to remove
> The thorns,[2] I have revealed the path.
> You yourselves should (always) strive,
> Tathāgatas only teach.
> Those who walk in meditation[3]
> Free themselves from Māra's bondage.'[4]

1. *A.* ii. 2; *A.* iv. 106; *D.* ii. 123. In the *Path of Freedom, Vimuttimagga*, Colombo, 1961, p. 1, only the first two lines forming the introductory stanza are found. This is a recent, and only translation in English by the Ven. N. R. M. Ehara, Soma Thera and Kheminda Thera.
2. Thorns of passionate desire and so forth.
3. Both concentrative calm (*samatha*) and insight (*vipassanā*).
4. *Dhp.* 274, 275.

7

THE FOURTH NOBLE TRUTH

Magga: The Path

RIGHT UNDERSTANDING

(*Sammā-diṭṭhi*)

'AS THIS great ocean has but one taste, that of salt, so has this *Dhamma* but one taste, that of freedom.'[1]

Freedom, supreme security from bondage,[2] is the clarion call of the Buddha's teaching. It is for this end—freedom—that the Master points out a path.

At the parting of roads a pedestrian gets bewildered, not knowing the right path to take. He looks round for help, and to his delight, sees a signboard with directions. Now if he is really intent on reaching his destination, he will not hesitate—but will proceed with zest watching his steps. So do people in this cycle of existence (*saṁsāra*), get bewildered as long as they do not know the path to freedom. The Buddha, like the signboard, indicates the sublime path of understanding and freedom, but people still cling to the by-paths that lead deeper into the morass of *dukkha* (suffering). That is because they have woven previous habits into the texture of their being while wandering through the jungles of saṁsāric life.

It is very difficult, indeed, for people to turn away from accustomed modes of conduct, thought and action.[3] However, if one wants to conquer the burdensome cares of worldly life, and gain true happiness and freedom one has gradually to turn away from things seemingly dear and congenial, and enter the path trodden by the Supremely Enlightened Ones of all ages and pointed out by them—the ANCIENT PATH.[4]

1. *Udāna*, p. 56. 2. *M.* 26. 3. *S.* ii. Discourse 61.
4. *S.* ii. 106, *purāṇamaggaṁ, purāṇaṁjasaṁ, pubbakehi sammā-sambuddhehi anuyātaṁ.*

It is by advancing step by step along the Ancient Path that one reaches the goal—freedom. One cannot attain freedom all at once. As the sea deepens gradually, so in the doctrine and discipline of the Buddha there is gradual training, gradual doing, and gradual practice.[1] All the practical guidance and instructions given by the Buddha to remove mental conflicts due to the unsatisfactoriness of life and gain final peace and happiness, are to be found on the Eightfold Path.

To one who views the modern world with dispassionate discernment, right understanding seems to be a very essential, nay an indispensable, factor of human life. With the advance of modern science, people, both in the East and West, seem to have become more and more materially minded and have almost ignored the mental realm, the world within, so that they seem to be lop-sided and even ill-disposed. Slogans and political propaganda seem to mould man's mind, and life to be mechanical; man has become like a puppet controlled by others.

Modern man seems to be enmeshed in all sorts of ideas, views, opinions and ideologies both wise and foolish. He is film-fed, television-minded, and radio-trained. Today what is presented by the newspapers, radio, television, some novels and pictures, by certain literature on sex psychology, and by sex-ridden films tends to confuse man, and turn him from the path of rectitude and understanding.

Wrangling, animosity, petty quarrels and even wars are the outcome of wrong ways of thinking and false views propagated by craving and hate. Today more than at any other time right understanding is needed to guide mankind through the turmoil of life, to 'straighten the restless mind as a fletcher straightens his shaft',[2] and to conform to justice and rectitude.

From the early Buddhist writings it becomes quite clear that the Buddha was not a teacher who leaned to the right or left, for his path was straight. He avoided all extremes, whether of Self Indulgence and Self Mortification; of Eternity or Annihilation; of Complete Indeterminism (*adhiccasamuppanna*) or Accidentalism and Strict Determinism (*Niyati-vāda*) or Fatalism; or of any other 'ism' that tends towards extremes. His Way of Life, as he explained in his first sermon, is the Middle Path. It is a teaching that has direct bearing on the lives of mankind, a practical application, without bias, prejudice or emotion—the active and practical aspect of the

1. *A.* iv. 200; *Udāna*, p. 54. 2. *Dhp.* 33.

entire teaching of the Master. It is not mere speculation, philosophizing and rationalizing, for it entails engaging oneself in the real task of applying each and every factor of the path[1] to life; in coming to grips with the true meaning of life, for the sole purpose of freedom from the taints that haunt the human heart.

The first factor of the path is known as right understanding which means to understand things as they really are and not as they appear to be. It is important to realize that right understanding in Buddhism has a special meaning which differs from that popularly attributed to it. In Buddhism right understanding is the application of Insight to the five aggregates of clinging, and understanding their true nature, that is understanding oneself. It is self-examination and self-observation. This point we shall discuss presently.

Right understanding is of the highest importance, for the remaining seven factors of the path are guided by it.[2] It ensures that right thoughts are held and it co-ordinates ideas; when as a result thoughts and ideas become clear and wholesome, man's speech and action are also brought into proper relation. Again it is through right understanding that one gives up harmful or profitless effort and cultivates right effort which aids the development of right mindfulness. Right effort and right mindfulness guided by right understanding bring about right concentration. Thus right understanding, which is the main spring in Buddhism, causes the other limbs of the co-ordinate system to move in proper relation.[3]

Now there are two conditions that are conducive to right understanding: Hearing from others, that is hearing the *Saddhamma*, the Good Law, from others (*paratoghosa*),[4] and systematic (wise) attention (*yoniso-manasikāra*).[5] The first condition is external, that is, what we get from outside, while the second is internal, what we cultivate (*manasikāra* literally means doing-in-the-mind).

What we hear[6] gives us food for thought and guides us in forming our own views. It is, therefore, necessary to listen, but only to that which is conducive to right understanding and to avoid all the harmful and unwholesome utterances of others which prevent straight thinking.

The second condition, systematic attention, is more difficult to

1. For the factors, see p. 78. 2. See *M.* 117. 3. See *M.* 117.
4. As in the case of Upatissa hearing from Arahat Assaji, see above, p. 35.
5. *M.* 43.
6. In the past people learnt by hearing and became 'learned', *bahussuta*; nowadays people learn mainly by reading and become known as well read.

cultivate, because it entails constant awareness of the things that one meets with in everyday life. The word *yoniso-manasikāra* which is often used in the discourses is most important, for it enables one to see things deeply (*yoniso*, lit. by-way-of womb) instead of only on the surface. Metaphorically, therefore, it is 'radical' or 'reasoned attention'. *Ayoniso-manasikāra*, unwise or unsystematic attention, is always deplored by the Buddha for it never helps one to consider conditionality, or to analyse the aggregates. Hence the importance of developing systematic and avoiding unsystematic attention. These two conditions, learning and systematic attention, together help to develop right understanding.

One who seeks truth is not satisfied with surface knowledge, with the mere external appearance of things, but wants to delve deep and see what is beyond the reach of the naked eye. That is the sort of search encouraged in Buddhism, for it leads to right understanding. The man of analysis states a thing after resolving it into its various qualities, which he puts in proper order, making everything plain. He does not state things unitarily, looking at them as a whole, but divides them up according to their outstanding features so that the conventional and the highest truth can be understood unmixed.

The Buddha was discriminative and analytical to the highest degree (*vibhajjavādi*). As a scientist resolves a limb into tissues and the tissues into cells, he analysed all component and conditioned things into their fundamental elements, right down to their ultimates, and condemned shallow thinking, unsystematic attention, which tends to make man muddle-headed and hinders the investigation of the true nature of things. It is through right understanding that one sees cause and effect, the arising and ceasing of all conditioned things. The truth of the *Dhamma* can be only grasped in that way, and not through blind belief, wrong view, speculation or even by abstract philosophy.

The Buddha says: 'This *Dhamma* is for the wise and not for the unwise,'[1] and explains the ways and means of attaining wisdom by stages, and avoiding false views. Right understanding permeates the entire teaching, pervades every part and aspect of the *Dhamma* and functions as the key-note of Buddhism.

What then is right understanding? It is the understanding of *dukkha* or suffering—its arising, its cessation and the path leading to its cessation.[2]

1. *A.* iv. 232. 2. *D.* 22; M. 141.

Thus ignorance of the real nature of life is primarily ignorance of the Four Noble Truths.[1] It is because of their ignorance of these truths that beings are tethered to becoming and are born again and again. Hear these words of the Buddha:

'Monks, it is through not understanding, not penetrating the Four Noble Truths that we have run so long, wandered so long in *saṁsāra*, in this cycle of continuity, both you and I. . . . But when these Four Noble Truths are understood and penetrated, rooted out is the craving for existence, destroyed is that which leads to renewed becoming, and there is no more coming to be.'[2]

In his first proclamation of the *Dhamma*, addressing the five ascetics, the Buddha says:

'So long as my knowledge and vision of reality regarding these Four Noble Truths, in three phases and twelve aspects was not fully clear to me, I did not claim to have attained incomparable supreme enlightenment in the world. But when my knowledge and vision of reality regarding these Four Noble Truths was clear to me, then I claimed to have won incomparable supreme enlightenment in this world.'[3]

These words clearly indicate that right understanding in the highest sense is comprehension of the Four Noble Truths. To grasp these truths is to understand the intricacies of nature. 'A person who fully understands these truths is truly called "Intuitively Wise".'[4]

Now right understanding is of two kinds, mundane and supramundane. An ordinary worldling's[5] knowledge of the efficacy of moral causation or of actions and their results (*kamma*, and *kamma-vipāka*) and the knowledge that accords with the Four Noble Truths (*saccānulomikañāṇa*) is called mundane (*lokiya*) right understanding. It is mundane because the understanding is not yet free from taints. This may be called 'knowing accordingly' (*anubodha*). But right understanding experienced at the moment of attaining

1. Discussed above in chapters 3 and 4.
2. *S.* v. 431; D. 16; *Vin.* i. 231. Also see above, p. 79.
3. *Mhvg.* v. 423.
4. *M.* 43.
5. A worldling (*puthujjana*) is one who has not yet attained to any of the four stages of realization. See p. 92, n. 1.

one or the other of the four stages of realization[1] is called Supramundane (*lokuttara*), right understanding. This is what is known as 'penetration' (*paṭivedha*).

Thus there is right understanding cultivated by the worldling (*puthujjana*) and by the Noble Ones (*Ariyas*). It is at the higher level that right understanding, in conjunction with the remaining seven factors, reaches consummation.

Due to lack of right understanding, the ordinary man is blind to the true nature of life and fails to see the universal fact of life, *dukkha*, unsatisfactoriness. He does not even try to grasp these facts but hastily considers the doctrine as pessimism. It is natural perhaps, for beings engrossed in mundane pleasures, beings who crave more and more for gratification of the senses and loathe pain, to resent the very idea of suffering and turn their backs on it. They do not, however, realize that even as they condemn the idea of *dukkha* and adhere to their own convenient and optimistic view of things, they are still being oppressed by the ever recurring unsatisfactory nature of life.

It is a psychological fact that people often do not want to reveal their true natures, to unfold what is in the deepest recesses of their minds, while they apparently wish others to believe that they are hale and hearty and free from worries and tribulations. It is for this same psychological reason that many people, wittingly or not, do not want to speak or hear of the universal malady of *dukkha*, unsatisfactoriness. They love pleasure, imagine that they are in a state of security and live in a mind-made paradise.

Although people see and accept change as the salient feature of existence they cannot rid themselves of the fascination and thrill which change has for men in general. They cherish the belief that it is possible to discover a way of happiness in this very change, to find a centre of security in this circle of impermanence. They imagine that although the world is uncertain they can make it certain and give it a solid basis, and so the unrelenting struggle for worldly improvement goes on with persevering effort and futile enthusiasm.

This effort to improve themselves and the world in every possible way, to secure better conditions in every sphere of human living and ensure against risks, reveals, without a shadow of a doubt, that there is no real happiness, no real rest in the world. This un-

1. The first stage of realization is technically known as *sotāpatti* 'Stream Entry'; the second stage is *sakadāgāmi* 'Once-Return'; the third is *anāgāmi* 'Non-Return'; the fourth and the last stage is *Arahatta*, Arahatship, the stage at which all fetters are severed and taints rooted out.

satisfactory nature of the world, this picture of pain, is clear to all who have eyes to see and minds to understand. It is right understanding that brings this clear picture of what we call life before our mind's eye, and this is the realistic view (*yathābhūtadassana*) in which there is no question of optimism and pessimism, of looking at things from the most favourable or unfavourable point of view.

When we turn to *Sammādiṭṭhi-sutta*, the ninth discourse of the *Majjhima Nikāya*, one of the five original collections, we find that the method of gaining right understanding is explained in sixteen different ways, which can be reduced to the following four: (a) Explanation by way of Moral Causation, (b) by way of the Four Truths, (c) by way of Nourishment, and (d) by way of Dependent Arising. The second and the fourth ways of explanation are almost identical; for both explain the same characteristic feature, namely, the process of arising and that of ceasing (*samudaya*, *nirodha*), in other words, becoming (*bhava*) and the cessation of becoming (*bhava-nirodha*).

Nourishment (*āhāra*) is of four kinds: (a) ordinary material food (*kabaliṅkārāhāra*), (b) contact (of sense organs with sense objects, *phassāhāra*), (c) consciousness (*viññāṇāhāra*) and (d) mental volition (*manosañcetanāhāra*).[1] It is not necessary here to explain all the methods mentioned in the discourse.[2]

In its lower stage right understanding urges a man to understand moral causation (*kammassakata ñāṇa*), which implies the understanding of the ten 'karmically wholesome actions' (*kusala-kamma*) and the ten 'karmically unwholesome actions (*akusala-kamma*).[3] Wholesome actions bring good results, they are meritorious and lead to happiness here and hereafter. The ten wholesome actions, therefore, are called 'Good Courses of Action' (*kusala-kammapatha*). Unwholesome actions give rise to evil consequences, they are demeritorious and lead to suffering, to painful happenings here and hereafter. The ten unwholesome actions, therefore, are called 'Evil Courses of Action' (*akusala-kammapatha*).

The Buddha, in more than one place, has emphatically stressed the psychological importance of action (*kamma*); 'O monks, it is volition that I call kamma. Having willed one acts through body, speech and mind.'[4] It is the understanding of moral causation that

1. *M.* i. 48.
2. For a detailed explanation read *Right Understanding* by Soma Thera (Buddhist Literature Society, Colombo, 1946).
3. For details see chapters on Right Speech and Right Action.
4. *A.* iii. 415. See also above, p. 62.

urges a thinking man to refrain from evil and to do good. He who acknowledges moral causation well knows that it is his own actions that make his life miserable or otherwise. He knows that the direct cause of the differences and inequalities of birth in this life, are the good and evil actions of each individual in past lives and in this life. His character is predetermined by his own choice. The thought, the act which he chooses, that by habit he becomes. Thus he understands his position in this mysterious universe and behaves in such a way as to promote moral and spiritual progress. This type of right understanding on the mundane level paves the way towards the realization of conditionality and the Four Truths.

Now let us discuss the method of gaining right understanding by way of the Four Truths. We have seen earlier[1] that the Four Truths are not separated from the five aggregates, outside of which they are not to be sought. The understanding of the true nature of the aggregates implies the realization of the Four Truths. It is, therefore, very necessary to have a clear idea of the five aggregates which have been explained in detail in chapter 3 (pp. 45–9).

The Buddha's analysis of the so-called being into five ever changing aggregates, makes it clear that there is nothing abiding, nothing eternally conserved, in this conflux of aggregates (*khandha-santati*).

Change or impermanence is the essential characteristic of phenomenal existence. We cannot say of anything, animate or inanimate, 'this is lasting'; for even while we say it, it is undergoing change. The aggregates are compounded and conditioned and therefore ever subject to cause and effect. Unceasingly does consciousness or mind and its factors change, and just as unceasingly, though at a slower rate, the physical body also alters from moment to moment. He who sees clearly that the impermanent aggregates are impermanent, has right understanding.[2]

The Buddha gives five very striking similes to illustrate the changing nature of the five aggregates. He compares material form or body to a lump of foam, feeling to a bubble, perception to a mirage, mental formations to a plantain-trunk and consciousness to an illusion, and asks: 'What essence, monks, could there be in a lump of foam, in a bubble, in a mirage, in a plantain-trunk, in an illusion?' Continuing the Buddha says:

'Whatever material form there be whether past, future or present; internal or external; gross or subtle; low or lofty; far or near; that

1. See above, p. 44. 2. *S.* iii. 51.

material form the monk sees, meditates upon, examines with systematic attention, he thus seeing, meditating upon, and examining with systematic attention, would find it empty, he would find it unsubstantial and without essence. What essence, monks, could there be in material form?' The Buddha speaks in the same manner of the remaining aggregates and asks: 'What essence, monks, could there be in feeling, in perception, in mental formation and in consciousness?'[1]

Thus we see that a more advanced range of thought comes with the analysis of the five aggregates. It is at this stage that right understanding known as Insight (*vipassanā*) begins to work. It is through this Insight that the true nature of the aggregates is grasped and seen in the light of the three signs or characteristics (*ti-lakkhaṇa*), namely: Impermanence, Unsatisfactoriness and No-Self.

The Master explains it thus:

'The five aggregates, monks, are impermanent; whatever is impermanent, that is *dukkha*, unsatisfactory; whatever is *dukkha*, that is without Self. What is without Self, that is not mine, that I am not, that is not my Self. Thus should it be seen by perfect wisdom (*sammappaññāya*) as it really is. Who sees by perfect wisdom as it really is, his mind not grasping is detached from taints, he is liberated.[2] Nāgarjuna only echoes these words when he says: "When the notion of an Ātman, Self or Soul ceases, the notion of 'mine' also ceases and one becomes free from the idea of I and mine."'[3]

It is not only the five aggregates that are impermanent, unsatisfactory and without a Self, but the causes and conditions that produce the aggregates are also impermanent, unsatisfactory and without a Self. This point the Buddha makes very clear:

'Material form, feeling, perception, mental formations and consciousness, monks, are impermanent; whatever causes and conditions there are for the arising of these aggregates, they too are impermanent. How, monks, could aggregates arising from what is impermanent, be permanent?

1. *S.* iii. 140 2. *S.* iii. 44.
3. *ātmanyasati cātmiyaṁ kuta eva bhaviṣyati nirmamo nirahaṁkāraḥ śamādātmātmanīnayoḥ* (*Mādhyamika-kārikā*, xviii. 2).

'Material form . . . and consciousness, monks, are unsatisfactory; whatever causes and conditions there are for the arising of these aggregates, they too are unsatisfactory. How, monks, could aggregates arising from what is unsatisfactory be pleasant and pleasurable?

'Material form . . . and consciousness, monks, are without a Self (*anatta*); whatever causes and conditions there are for the arising of these aggregates, they too are without a Self. How, monks, could aggregates arising from what is without a Self be Self (*atta*)?

'The instructed noble disciple (*sutavā ariyasāvako*), monks, seeing thus becomes dispassionate towards material form, feeling, perception, mental formations and consciousness. Through dispassion he is detached, through detachment he is liberated; in liberation the knowledge comes to be that he is liberated, and he understands: "Destroyed is birth, lived is the life of purity (lit. noble life), done is what was to be done, there is no more of this to come (meaning that there is no more continuity of the aggregates, that is no more becoming or rebirth)." '[1]

By the ceasing of ignorance, by the arising of knowledge, by the cessation of craving, there is thus no more becoming, no more rebirth.[2]

It is always when we fail to see the true nature of things that our views become clouded; because of our preconceived notions, our greed and aversion, our likes and dislikes, we fail to see the sense organs and sense objects in their respective and objective natures, and go after mirages and deceptions. The sense organs delude and mislead us and then we fail to see things in their true light, so that our way of seeing things becomes perverted (*viparīta dassana*).

The Buddha speaks of three kinds of illusion (*vipallāsa*, Skt. *viparyāsa*) that grip man's mind, namely: the illusions of perception, thought and view.[3] Now when a man is caught up in these illusions, he perceives, thinks and views incorrectly:

(a) He perceives permanence in the impermanent; (b) satisfactoriness in the unsatisfactory (ease and happiness in suffering); (c) Self in what is not Self (a Soul in the Soulless); (d) beauty in the repulsive.

He thinks and views in the same erroneous manner. Thus each illusion works in four ways,[4] and leads man astray, clouds his

1. *S.* iii. 23. Discourses 7, 8, 9 abridged.
2. *M.* 43.
3. *Saññā vipallāsa, citta-v, diṭṭhi-v.*
4. *A.* ii. 52.

vision, and confuses him. This is due to unwise reflections, to unsystematic attention (*ayoniso-manasikāra*). Right understanding alone removes these illusions and helps man to cognize the real nature that underlies all appearance. It is only when man comes out of this cloud of illusions and perversions that he shines with true wisdom like the full moon that emerges brilliant from behind a black cloud.

The Buddha gave full freedom to sceptics and inquirers to doubt and question what is doubtful and questionable; for there was no secrecy in his teaching. 'Monks, the doctrine and discipline set forth and laid down by the Tathāgata, shines when brought to light, and not when hidden.'[1] As a result the disciples were not reluctant to question the Buddha on doctrinal points—to question him point blank.

The Venerable Kaccāyana, for instance, approached the Buddha and asked him:

'Venerable sir, "right understanding", "right understanding", it is said. How far is there "right understanding"?'

'This world (i.e. being) for the most part, Kaccāyana, is concerned with these two (views): existence and non-existence (eternalism and annihilationism). Now he who with perfect wisdom sees the arising of the world (of aggregates) as it really is, does not hold with the view of existence.

'This world for the most part, Kaccāyana, hankers after thoughts of grasping and habitually clings to objects of sense desire. The *ariya*, the noble one, does not harbour thoughts of grasping, and does not cling habitually to objects of sense desire, thinking: "this is my Self (Soul)".

'That which arises is just suffering (*dukkha*, that is the five aggregates of clinging);[2] that which ceases is suffering (the five aggregates of clinging). The noble disciple who thus thinks, doubts not, he is not perplexed. He realizes it on his own, unaided by others. Thus far, Kaccāyana, is right understanding.

'Everything exists, this is one extreme. Nothing exists, this is the other extreme. Avoiding these two extremes, Kaccāyana, the Tathāgata teaches the *Dhamma* by the median path: dependent on ignorance arise volitional formations, dependent on volitional formations arises consciousness . . . (and so on). . . . Thus does this

1. *A.* i. 283.
2. 'Monks, what is suffering? It should be said that it is the five aggregates of clinging.' *S.* ii. 158. See above, p. 44.

whole mass of suffering arise.[1] Through the complete cessation of ignorance cease volitional formations . . . (and so on). . . . Thus does this whole mass of suffering cease.'[2]

It should now be clear that this being whom for all practical purposes we call a man, woman or individual, is not something static, but kinetic, being in a state of constant and continuous change. Now when a person sees life and all that pertains to life in this light, and understands analytically his so-called being as a mere succession of mental and bodily aggregates, he sees things as they really are. He does not hold the wrong view of 'Personality Belief', belief in a Soul or Self (*sakkāya-diṭṭhi*), because he knows through right understanding that all phenomenal existence is causally dependent (*paṭicca-samuppanna*), that each is conditioned by something else, and that its existence is relative to that condition. He knows that as a result there is no 'I', no persisting psychic entity, no ego principle; no Self or anything pertaining to a Self in this life process. He is therefore free from the notion of a microcosmic soul (*Jīvātma*), or a Macrocosmic Soul (*Paramātma*).

Thus the realization of the Four Noble Truths dawns through a complete comprehension, a full penetration, of the five aggregates, that is through seeing the aggregates as impermanent, unsatisfactory and without a Self. Hence the Buddha's repeated request to his disciples to understand analytically the so-called being built up by the aggregates. Many examples of how the disciples gained deliverance of mind by seeing the true nature of the aggregates are recorded in the *Psalms of the Early Buddhists*. Mittā Kālī, for instance, tersely states her experience in this verse:

'Contemplating as they really are
The rise and fall of aggregates
I rose up with mind free (of taints).
Completed is the Buddha-word.'[3]

These aggregates of mind and body being ever subject to cause and effect, as we saw above, pass through the inconceivably rapid moments of arising, existing and ceasing (*uppāda, ṭhiti, bhaṅga*) just as the unending waves of the sea or as a river in flood sweeps to

1. For the whole formula of twelve factors see above, p. 56.
2. *S.* ii. 17.
3. *Theri-gāthā*. Verse 96.

a climax and subsides. Indeed human life is compared to a mountain stream that flows and rushes on, changing incessantly.[1]

Thus the sum total of the doctrine of change taught in Buddhism is that all component things that have conditioned existence are a process and not a group of abiding entities, but the changes occur in such rapid succession that people regard mind and body as static entities. They do not see their arising and their breaking up, but regard them unitarily, see them as a lump (*ghana saññā*) or whole.

'Those ascetics and brahmins, O monks, who conceive a Self in diverse ways conceive it as either the five aggregates of clinging, or as any one of them. What five?

'Herein the untaught worldling . . . considers body as the Self, Self as possessed of body, body as included in the Self, Self as included in the body . . . similarly as to feeling, perception, volitional formations, and consciousness. . . .[2] Thus this is the (wrong) view. The "I am" notion is not abandoned. . . .'[3]

It is very hard indeed for people who are accustomed continually to think of their own mind and body and the external world with mental projections as wholes, as inseparable units, to get rid of the false appearance of 'wholeness'. So long as man fails to see things as processes, as movements, he will never understand the *Anatta* (no-Soul) doctrine of the Buddha. That is why people impertinently and impatiently put the question: If there is no persisting entity,

1. *A.* iv. 137. Compare '*nadī soto viya*', like a flowing stream.

A few years after the passing away of the Buddha, Heraclitus taught the '*Panta Rhei*' doctrine, the flux theory, at Athens, and one wonders if that teaching was transmitted to him from India. 'There is no static being', says Heraclitus, 'no unchanging substratum.' 'Change, movement, is Lord of the Universe. Everything is in a state of becoming, of continual flux (*Panta Rhei*)'. He continues: 'You cannot step twice into the same river; for fresh waters are ever flowing in upon you.' (A. K. Rogers. *A Student's History of Philosophy* (London, 1920), p. 15). But one who understands the root of the *Dhamma* would go a step further and say: 'The same man cannot step twice into the same river; for the so-called man who is only a conflux of mind and body, never remains the same for two consecutive moments.' ('*Philosophy of Change*', Piyadassi Thera, *Dharmodaya Sabhā* (Kathmandu, Nepal, 1956), p. 7).

2. The idea of a Self is applied to each aggregate in four ways. Thus when applied to all the five aggregates it become twentyfold. This is what is known as *viṁsatiākāra sakkāyadiṭṭhi*, or the twenty kinds of self-illusion. (See *M.* i. 8; iii. 17; *Vbh.* 364.) When this self-illusion is removed, the sixty-two (wrong) views also are removed. (For the sixty-two views see *D.* i. *Brahmajāla sutta.*)

3. *S.* iii. 46 *sutta* 47.

no unchanging principle, like Self or Soul (*Ātman*), what is it that experiences the results of deeds here and hereafter?

Two different discourses[1] deal with this burning question. The Buddha was explaining in detail to his disciples the evanescent nature of the five aggregates, how they are devoid of Self, and how the latent conceit 'I am' and 'mine' ceases to exist, and then there arose a thought in the mind of a certain monk thus: 'Material body is not self, feeling is not self, perception is not self, mental formations are not self, consciousness is not self. Then what self do selfless deeds affect?'

The Buddha, reading the thoughts of that monk's mind, said: 'the question was beside the point' and made the monks understand the impermanent, unsatisfactory and not-self nature of the five aggregates.

'It is wrong to say that the doer of the deed is the same as the one who experiences its results. It is equally wrong to say that the doer of the deed and the one who experiences its results are two different persons';[2] for the simple reason that what we call life, as we saw earlier, is a flow of physical and psychic processes or energies arising and ceasing constantly, and it is not possible to say that the doer himself experiences the results because he is changing now, every moment of his life; but at the same time we must not forget the fact that the continuity of life, that is the continuance of experience, the procession of events, is not lost; it continues without a gap. The child is not the same as the adolescent, the adolescent is not the same as the adult, they are neither the same nor totally different persons (*na ca so, na ca añño*).[3] There is only a flow of bodily and mental processes. Therefore said the ancients:

> 'No doer of the deed is there,
> No one who experiences its result;
> Bare phenomena flow on.
> This alone is the right view.'[4]

What does this mean? The answer is that there is no permanent 'I' or 'mine' in the form of a Self or Soul in this psycho-physical process. There is a seeing, a feeling, an experiencing, etc., but not an unchanging never-ending Self or Soul behind the scene. That is all.[5]

1. *M.* iii. 19, Discourse No. 109; *S.* iii. 103. Discourse No. 82.
2. *A.* ii. 70. 3. *Miḷinda Pañha.* 4. *Vism.* xix.
5. For a very comprehensive and brilliant exposition of 'The Doctrine of No-Soul: *Anatta*', see *What the Buddha Taught* by Walpola Rahula (Gordon Fraser, London, 1959), chapter VI.

Before concluding this chapter a challenging question raised by some against the doctrine of *anatta* should be answered. Those who consider the word *anatta* in Buddhism as something diametrically opposed to the so-called *atta*, ask: 'How can one speak of *anatta*, no Self, if there is no *atta*, Self?' They treat them as relative terms. But we must understand what the Buddha meant by *anatta*. He never meant anything in contradistinction to *atta*. He did not place the two terms in juxtaposition and say: 'this is my *anatta* in opposition to *atta*.' The term *anatta*, since the prefix '*an*' indicates non-existence, *abhāva*, and not opposition, *viruddha*, means literally *no atta*, that is the mere denial of an *atta*, the non-existence of *atta*.

The believers in an *atta* tried to keep their *atta*. The Buddha simply denied it, by adding the prefix '*an*'. As this concept of an *atta*, Self or Soul, was deep rooted in many whom the Buddha met, he had to discourse at length on this pivotal question of Self to learned men, dialecticians and hair-splitting disputants. The *Sutta Piṭaka*, wherein are recorded thousands of discourses of the Buddha, became so voluminious mainly because of this question of Self. The careful reader of the discourses will note how the Buddha's answers and elucidations concerning this vexed question of Self developed into lengthy sermons.

From the foregoing exposition of the Buddha it will now be clear that right understanding, at the highest level, is merely the avoidance of all wrong views, illusions and perversions which according to Buddhism are mainly due to the notion of a Self or to belief in a Personality (*sakkāya diṭṭhi*): it is the understanding of the arising and ceasing of the aggregates. Through understanding of the aggregates, that is through an intellectual grasp of the nature of the so-called being, dawns the knowledge of the Four Noble Truths.

The Buddha's doctrine of *anicca* and *dukkha* (impermanence and suffering) was not new to the people of India. In the early *Upanishads* like *Chāndogya* we come across such expressions as '*tarati śokaṁ ātmavit*', 'knowledge of the Self ferries a person across (the world of) sorrow'. But what baffled Indian thinkers was the Buddhist doctrine of *anatta* (No Self). They were so steeped in the belief of a Self that when the Buddha denied a Self and discoursed against it, it was a real shock to them, and they were up in arms to safeguard the long-standing and central conception of their religion and philosophy—Self, *Ātman*.

As they failed to understand the meaning of *anatta* they did not hesitate to label the Buddha a nihilist (*venayika*).[1] It was the recognition that this Self or Soul is an illusion that made the Buddha's doctrine so revolutionary. The doctrine of *anatta* is unique in the world history of religion and philosophy.

'The distinguishing characteristic of Buddhism was that it started in a new line, that it looked at the deepest questions men have to solve from an entirely different standpoint. It swept away from the field of its vision the whole of the great soul-theory which had hitherto so completely filled and dominated the minds of the superstitious and of the thoughtful alike. For the first time in the history of the world, it proclaimed a salvation which each man could gain for himself, and by himself, in this world during this life, without any the least reference to God, or to gods, either great or small.

'Like the Upanishads, it placed the first importance on knowledge; but it was no longer a knowledge of God, it was a clear perception of the real nature, as they supposed it to be, of men and things. And it added to the necessity of knowledge, the necessity of purity, of courtesy, of uprightness, of peace, and of a universal love, "far-reaching, grown great, and beyond measure." '[2]

1. *M.* Discourse 22. See above, p. 38.
2. The *Hibbert Lectures*, 1881, Professor T. W. Rhys Davids, p. 28.

8

RIGHT THOUGHT

(*Sammā-saṁkappa*)

RIGHT thought, which is the second factor of the Path, is the outcome of right understanding. These two comprise the Wisdom spoken of in the context of the Noble Eightfold Path. Right thought is the result of seeing things as they are. Thoughts are all important; for a man's words and acts have thoughts as their source. It is thoughts that are translated into speech and deed. The good or ill results of our words and actions depend solely on our thoughts, on the way we think. Hence the importance of learning to think straight instead of crooked. The oft-quoted but ever-fresh opening verses of the *Dhammapada*, speak to us of the great importance and significance of thought:

'Mental states have mind as their fore-runner,
As their chief; and of mind are they made.
If one speaks or acts with a polluted mind
Suffering follows one as the wheel the oxen's feet.

'All mental states have mind as their fore-runner,
As their chief; and of mind are they made.
If one speaks or acts with a pure mind
Happiness follows one as the shadow that ne'er departs.'

From these words of the Buddha it becomes clear that the beauty or the ugliness of our words and deeds depend on our own thoughts, which are real. Thoughts travel swifter than anything we can conceive of and they roam whither-so-ever they list. Their influence on us and the external world is tremendous. Each and every ugly, vicious and morally repulsive thought pollutes the human heart and may cause untold harm. Wrong words and deeds are expressions of a wrong condition of mind. But if man concentrates on right thoughts with right understanding the good results that mind can produce are immense.

What then is right thought?

It is thoughts of renunciation, of good-will and of not harming or compassion.[1]

Their opposites are: thoughts of sense desire, of ill-will and of harm.[2]

In the discourse on the Twofold Thought,[3] the Buddha has explained in detail how before enlightenment he experienced the Twofold Thought.

Thoughts of sense desire, ill-will and harm he put in one category, those of renunciation, good-will and compassion into the other. When thoughts of sense desire, ill-will and harm arose in him, he knew that they led to harming oneself and others, obstructed intuitive wisdom, caused pain and did not lead to *Nibbāna*. Thus reflecting he kept on getting rid of such thoughts, driving them away and making an end of them.

When thoughts of renunciation, good-will and compassion arose in him, he knew that they led neither to harming oneself nor others; they developed intuitive wisdom, did not cause pain, and led to *Nibbāna*.

Continuing the Buddha explains, how, through reflection, he made his mind firm, how he calmed it and made it unified and concentrated within his subject of meditation. He then tells how, aloof from unwholesome states of mind, he attained to and abided in the first *jhāna* (meditative absorption), the second *jhāna*, the third *jhāna* and the fourth *jhāna*,[4] and how he finally comprehended, as they really are, the Four Noble Truths.

It is important here to observe how the removal of the three root causes of all evil, namely lust, hate and delusion, depends upon right understanding and right thought.

Delusion which is another term for ignorance, as we saw earlier, is rooted out by right understanding. Sense desire and ill-will are wiped out by right thought. Right understanding and right thought are both supported by the remaining factors of the Path.

Let us now try to understand the importance of removing evil

1. *Nekkhamma-saṁkappa, abyāpāda-saṁkappa, avihiṁsā-saṁkappa, M.* 17, 117 and passim.

2. *kāma-saṁkappa, byāpāda-saṁkappa, vihiṁsā-saṁkappa, M.* 78, 117 and passim.

3. *Dvedhāvitakka sutta, M.* 19.

4. For a description of the *jhānas* see p. 208, n. 2.

thoughts and the method of so doing, which is by the correct practice of renunciation, good-will and compassion. When a man's mind is obsessed by lust or hate it is quite impossible for him to see things clearly. But the removal of these impediments does not mean struggling with the baneful thoughts that grip the mind. One must learn to see such thoughts face to face—how they appear, reappear and overpower the mind; one must study their nature. Now if a man allows his mind continually to entertain thoughts of lust and hate and does not try to control them those thoughts are strengthened and hold sway over his mind. But if a man is really bent on removing evil thoughts, he will try gradually to cultivate good thoughts that will counteract the harmful ones and clear his mind. For instance, when a man is disturbed by sensuality through seeing, hearing and so on, thoughts of renunciation will bring him peace of mind. Similarly, good-will and compassion will soothe a mind that cherishes ill-will, anger, cruelty and revenge. However, we must admit that this is no easy task. It needs much determination and effort.

Some consider that since lust or sense desire is a natural impulse it should therefore not be balked. Others think that it should be put down by force. From the highest standpoint lust or hate is just a thought, a mentation (*vitakka*). Before one allows one's lust to go its own way, or suppresses it, one must try to look at the thought of lust itself without any prejudice. Then only will one see the origin, the cause, of that thought. Whether one allows it to grow strong, weakens it or removes it altogether depends on oneself. Again, when a sense organ comes in contact with some sense object, or the mind with a mental object, which is disagreeable, then there arises conflict, which causes anger, revulsion, ill-will or hate.

Thus we see that through a stimulant arising at the sense doors, lust, hate and other unwholesome thoughts, due to delusion, come into being. When a person is deluded by an external object feeling arises in him; he either becomes attached to the sense object or resents it (*anurodhavirodhaṁ samāpanno*).[1] There is attraction or repulsion, as in the case of the atom. If we look round we notice that human society is often obsessed by these two strong impulses—attachment and resentment. So long as man is influenced by these taints, the vicissitudes of life will continue to oppress him; but when these taints are controlled, if not eliminated, he will not be too affected by the changes. One cannot altogether avoid the vicissitudes

1. *M.* 38.

of life so long as one lives in the world; nevertheless one can develop one's mind and self-mastery to such a pitch that one can remain undisturbed by the upsets which these changes have brought about.

The Buddha's exposition of the *Dhamma* was methodical. He would not talk of the Four Noble Truths, the essence of his teaching, to everyone he met. When he knew that a person was not mature enough to grasp the deeper doctrine, he would instruct him only on the simpler side of the *Dhamma* in a progressive manner: he would speak to him on charitable giving (*dāna*), on virtue or moral habits (*sīla*), on the heavens (these are the simpler aspects),[1] on the disadvantage, emptiness and impurity of the pleasures of the senses and on the advantage of renunciation.

When the Master knew that a person's mind was ready, pliable, void of hindrances, uplifted, pleased, only then did he explain to him the *Dhamma* which the Enlightened Ones themselves have discovered, the *Dhamma* peculiar to them: *dukkha* (suffering), its arising, its ceasing, and the path.[2]

From the foregoing it is obvious that a man's mind can only grasp the highest Truth if he is ready to give up thoughts of sense desire. When his mind is released from such thoughts, he realizes the Truths and gains right understanding. Thus we see how right thoughts aid right understanding. They are interdependent and bring about true Wisdom (*sammā-paññā*).

The Buddha speaks of renunciation by personal experience and not through hearsay. He himself relates the story of his own renunciation:

'I too, monks, before enlightenment, while I was still a Bodhisatta being liable to birth, ageing, disease, dying, sorrow and defilements, sought what was liable to birth, ageing, disease, dying, sorrow and defilements. Then it occurred to me, monks, why do I, liable to birth . . . and defilements seek what is likewise liable to birth . . . and defilements. What if I, being liable to birth . . . and defilements, were to seek the unborn, the supreme security from bondage, *Nibbāna*?

'Then I, monks, after a time . . . in the prime of life, in radiant

1. The practice of *dāna* and *sīla* according to Buddhism is instrumental in causing a good rebirth, i.e. a rebirth in a good state of existence, but it does not bring about release from suffering, cessation from becoming—*Nirvāṇa*.

2. *Vinaya Mhvg*. The pliability and so on of the mind is brought about by the release from sense pleasures.

youth, cut off my hair and beard, donned a dyed robe and went forth from home into homelessness (I renounced).'[1]

This is the Noble Quest (*ariya-pariyesana*).

Again, this idea is conveyed in the very inspiring discourse[2] on the 'Going Forth' of Gotama, the Bodhisatta, who gave up his crown and went into solitude. As the discourse says, one day he entered the city of Rājagaha for his alms round. King Bimbisāra looking down from his palace saw the Bodhisatta walking the streets bowl in hand, with measured steps and down-cast eyes. Struck by his mien the King sent men to find out where he would go and stay. On receiving their report, he hurried to Mount Paṇḍava, met the Bodhisatta and said:

'You are young, in the prime of life, handsome, and you appear to be a kṣatriya.'[3]

'O Mahārāja, by lineage I am a "Kinsman of the Sun", a Sākyan. Such is the stock I left behind me. I do not long for sense pleasures, knowing their peril and seeing renunciation's peace I go my way striving (for *Nibbāna* the Highest Renunciation). My mind takes delight in the striving (not in sense pleasures).'

From the above, we understand that 'going forth' (*pabbajjā*) and separation from the pleasures of sense (*nekkhamma*) are identical. The purpose of going forth is to turn away from thoughts of sensuality (*kilesa-kāma*) and from the objects of sense (*vatthu-kāma*). 'Going forth' is really self-sacrifice and the urge to do so should be genuine if it is to bear pleasant fruit.

This is not a course that all can follow, for to leave behind the world's attractive and sensuous life is no easy task. It may not be possible for all to cut themselves off from the world and all it holds. And the Buddha does not expect all his followers to become ascetics.

'Hard it is to go forth
From home to homelessness;
To take delight in it is hard.'[4]

1. *M.* 26, 36. 2. *Pabbajjā sutta, Sn.*

3. In India there were four principal castes: *Kṣatriyas* (rulers), *Brāhmaṇas* (priests), *Vaiśyas* (householders), *Śūdras* (lowest castes, outcasts). The first three are described as higher, or superior castes.

4. *Dhp.* 302.

In the Buddha's Dispensation full liberty is granted to the disciples to leave the Order if they find it difficult to live the monk's life any more. There is no coercion and compulsion whatsoever and the person reverting to a lay life is not stigmatized.

The Buddha says: 'Monks, there are two kinds of happiness, that of a lay life (*gihisukhaṁ*) and that of "going forth" (*pabbajjā sukhaṁ*): that of sensual indulgence (*kāma sukhaṁ*) and that of renunciation (*nekkhamma sukhaṁ*). Of these, monks, the happiness of "going forth" and of renunciation are superior.'[1]

This does not imply that the Buddha belittled lay life, he was only giving expression to his own experience. He had, as a matter of fact, enjoyed both these happinesses. One thing, however, should be remembered: whether monk or layman, one has to follow the same path, namely the Ancient Path, the way of Virtue, Concentration and Wisdom.

Genuine renunciation, it may be borne in mind, is not escapism. Those who do not understand the real significance of renunciation, and those who judge it by bogus 'recluses' who lead an indolent, worthless and parasitical life, hastily conclude that 'going forth' or turning from the world is a sort of escapism, a selfish way of life. The ideal recluse, the bhikkhu, however, is an altruist of the highest type who takes least from, and gives much to, society. The *Dhammapada* says: 'As a bee, without harming the flower, its colour or fragrance, takes the honey (pollen) even so should the sage move in the village.'[2]

It is true that, with the passage of time, many changes have taken place, yet the true Buddhist monk who has given up worldly pleasures, endeavours to lead a life of voluntary poverty and complete celibacy with the high aim of serving others selflessly within the bounds of a bhikkhu's life, and of attaining deliverance of mind. There are two ways of leading the life of a bhikkhu: one entails continuous meditation (*vipassanā-dhura*) and the other part-time meditation, and studying and teaching the *Dhamma* (*gantha-dhura*). It is obligatory on every bhikkhu to take up one or other of these ways according to his temperament, age and environment.

When discussing the question of 'going forth', that is becoming a monk, hermit or recluse, it should not be thought that the practice of Buddhism is only for monks and not for the laity. The Buddha's teaching, the Noble Eightfold Path, is for all—man or woman, householder or one who has renounced. Can we restrict the *Dhamma*

1. *A.* i. 80. 2. *Dhp.* 49.

only to a few recluses? It is certainly true that the monk's life is more conducive to the practice of meditation, to the giving up of harmful thoughts, than the householder's life which is filled with toil and need. It is not easy to live the 'noble life' while a householder. The life of an ideal hermit who is free from household worries and other worldly cares, is more congenial to the development of mental peace. This one cannot deny, but that does not mean that the laity are quite incapable of gaining mental purification. Far from it, if a person can tame his fickle mind while living a lay life, if he can refrain from overindulging in pleasures of the body, from nourishing sexual desires and stimulants, he too is destined to reach the mental heights which a hermit enjoys. Of course, it goes without saying that complete purification and deliverance comes through complete detachment and renunciation. All these achievements depend on how his mind works, whether he is layman or monk.

A man may live in the forest away from the tumult of the town, but if his mind is not concentrated, if it is in a tumult, and evil thoughts play havoc with it, he should leave that forest because the purpose for which he had entered it is not achieved. He should delight in that forest only if his mind is calm and the taints tend to disappear. And, on the other hand, if a person can calm his mind even while living in a village where people's voices are heard, he is far superior to a forest-dweller whose mind is impure.[1]

In this connection the story of the Venerable Meghiya is interesting. In the thirteenth year of the Buddha's enlightenment, the Elder Meghiya was his personal attendant, and they were staying on a hill called *Cālika*. What follows is a condensed account of the story.

The Venerable Meghiya being attracted by a beautiful mango grove near a river thought of going there to meditate if the Buddha gave him leave. So he went to the Master and told him of his wish. 'Wait a little, Meghiya, till some other monk arrives, for we are alone,' said the Master. In spite of the Buddha's warning, a second and a third time, the Elder repeated his request. Then the Blessed One replied: 'Well, what can I say, Meghiya, when you talk of striving for concentration? Do now as you think fit.'

Accordingly the Venerable Meghiya went to that mango grove to meditate. And while he was there three evil unwholesome thoughts came to him, namely: thoughts of sense pleasure, ill-will and harm. And the Elder wondered thus: 'It is strange, it is amazing!

1. For detailed explanations see *M.* Discourses 5 and 17.

I who in faith left home for the homeless state am yet assailed by these unwholesome thoughts.'

So the elder returned to the Blessed One and told him what had happened. Then the Master said:

'Meghiya, for the deliverance of the mind of the immature, five things are conducive to their maturing: (a) a good friend; (b) virtuous behaviour, guided by the essential precepts for training; (c) good counsel tending to dispassion, calm, cessation, enlightenment and *Nibbāna*; (d) the effort to abandon evil thoughts and acquire wholesome thoughts; and (e) the acquisition of wisdom that discerns the rise and fall of things.'[1]

Going beyond the pleasures of sense is characteristic of renunciation. Renunciation is the very opposite of all that is carnal and sensual (*kāma*). It focusses the whole mind naturally on the object of *Nirvāṇa*.

In many a discourse the Buddha has explained the characteristics of sensuality, its danger and disadvantages. In his very first sermon he defined sensual indulgence as a low, common, ignoble and worldly thing. Impressing on his disciples the need for giving up sense pleasures, the Buddha compares them to a skeleton, a (bare) bone, a piece of flesh, a torch of dry grass, a pit of red hot coals, a dream, borrowed goods, a fruit-tree, a slaughter house, a sword and a chopping block, a stake, and a snake's head. They bring much pain, much disappointment. The danger in them is great.[2]

Further says the Buddha: 'Impermanent, monks, are pleasures of the senses, empty, false, unreal;[3] this prattle of fools is made of illusion. . . . Here these evil unwholesome thoughts lead to covetousness, ill-will and quarrels.[4]

To the pleasure-seeker, to the strong materialist, however, this may appear rather a dull sermon on morals, but to those who try

1. The whole of this discourse is at *A*. iv. 354; *Ud*. p. 34 and in brief at *Dhp. com*. i. 287. The Elder's verse (66) is in *Thg*. It is said that the Venerable Meghiya was of a Sākyan rājā's family. The *Dhp*. verses (33, 34) are as follows:

'The unsteady fickle mind, hard to guard and hard to control, the wise man straightens even as a fletcher, an arrow.

'Like a fish jerked out of its watery abode and cast on land, this mind quakes. (Therefore) the realm of *Māra* (passions) should be abandoned.'

2. *M*. Discourse 22. Cf. this with *Potaliya-sutta, M*. 54.

3. *aniccā, tucchā, musā, mosadhammā*.

4. *M*. Discourse 106.

to face facts and see things in their true light, with dispassionate discernment, this is no lie. Modern psychologists and moralists are only trying to rediscover what the Buddha said twenty-five centuries ago, when they probe into the question of sex psychology.

In the threefold classification of Right Thought, thoughts of good-will and of doing no harm follow. They correspond with *mettā* and *karuṇā*, lovingkindness and compassion which are among the four sublime states or *brahma-vihāra*.[1] *Mettā* and *karuṇā* are two excellent states of mind conducive to noble living. They banish selfishness and disharmony and promote altruism, unity and brotherhood. They are thoughts to be cultivated towards all beings irrespective of race, caste, colour, community, creed, East or West, and therefore they are known as boundless states (*appamaññāyo*), for they are not limited, are not confined to watertight compartments. They enfold all beings without any partiality or grading according to rank, quality, position, power, learning, value and so on which keep men apart. They give security to all living beings.

As the books point out this pair of virtues can be cultivated not only as a way of conduct towards fellow beings, but also as a meditation which then becomes known as the meditative development of the 'Sublime States' (*brahmavihārabhāvanā*). When earnestly and methodically cultivated they lead the meditator to higher stages of mental development known as *jhāna* or meditative absorption.

In his exhortation to Rāhula, the Buddha says: 'Cultivate, Rāhula, the meditation on lovingkindness; for by cultivating lovingkindness ill-will is banished. Cultivate, Rāhula, the meditation on compassion; for by cultivating compassion harm and cruelty are banished.'[2]

From this it is clear that *mettā* and *karuṇā* are diametrically opposed to ill-will and cruelty respectively. Ill-will or hate, like sense desire (lust), is also caused by the sense faculties meeting sense objects. When a man's eye comes in contact with a visible object, which to his way of thinking is unpleasant and undesirable, then repugnance arises if he does not exercise systematic wise attention. It is the same with ear and sound, nose and smell, tongue and taste, body and contact, mind and mental objects. Even agreeable things, both animate and inanimate, which fill man with great pleasure can cause aversion and ill-will. A person, for instance, may woo another whom he loves and entertain thoughts of

1. See above, p. 20. n. i. 2.
2. *M. Mahā Rāhulovāda-sutta*, No. 62.

sensual affection, but if the loved one fails to show the same affection or behaves quite contrary to expectation conflicts and resentment arise. If he then fails to exercise systematic attention, if he is not prudent, he may behave foolishly, and his behaviour may lead to disaster, even to murder or suicide. Such is the danger of these passions.

This is a good example by which to understand the nature of wrong thoughts (*micchā-saṁkappa*), and how they operate to the disadvantage of he who hoids them. In this case uncontrolled sensual affection or lust may lead to intense ill-will which brings about injury, harm and violence resulting in death, sorrow and lamentation.

'Whatever a foe to a foe may do—
The wrathful to the wrathful—
The ill-directed mind can do it worse.'[1]

In this connection it is interesting to note the saying of Āryadeva: 'By the same thing, lust is incited in one, hatred in another, delusion in the next; therefore, the sense object is without any inherent meaning.'[2]

It is natural for the worldling to entertain evil and wrong thoughts. 'Lust penetrates an undeveloped mind, as rain an ill-thatched house.'[3] Man's passions are disturbing. The lust of blinded beings has brought about hatred and all other sufferings. 'The enemy of the whole world is lust, through which all evil comes to living beings. This lust, when obstructed by some cause, is transformed into wrath.'

Man, therefore, should try to develop and unfold good and right thoughts—the infinite possibilities—that are latent in human nature. To do this one needs training in calmness (*samādhi-sikkhā*). It is through gradual training that one can check the mind and rule it (*cittaṁ vasaṁ vattati*),[4] and not become a slave to it and be under its sway (*cittassa vasena vattati*).[5] With such training in mind-culture, one can free oneself from the influence of the objects of sense. Thus by training in virtuous conduct, developing calmness and getting at the light of truth, the sage in due course passes away and of him it

1. *Dhp*. 42.
2. '*Tatraiva rajyate kascid-kascit tatraiva duṣyati*
Kascin muhyati tatraiva-tasmāt kāmo nirarthakah'. (177).

The *Catuhśataka of* Āryadeva (Reconstructed and edited by Vidushekhara Bhattāchārya).

3. *Dhp*. 13. 4. *M*. 32. 5. *M*. 32.

can truly be said: 'He indeed is the best among conquerors who conquers himself.'[1]

'The victor creates the foe,
The defeated live in pain,
The peaceful dwell in happiness
Neither victors nor defeated.'[2]

Mettā (Skt. *maitri*) is a popular term among Buddhists, yet no English word conveys its exact meaning. Friendliness, benevolence, good-will, universal love, lovingkindness are the favourite renderings. *Mettā* is the wish for the welfare and happiness of all beings, making no restrictions whatsoever. It has the characteristic of a benevolent friend. Its direct enemy is ill-will (hatred) while the indirect or masked enemy is carnal love or selfish affectionate desire (*pema*, Skt. *prema*) which is quite different from *mettā*. Carnal love when disguised as *mettā* can do much harm to oneself and others. One has to be on one's guard against this masked enemy. Very often people entertain thoughts of sensual affection, and mistaking it for real *mettā* think that they are cultivating *mettā*, and do not know that they are on the wrong track. If one were dispassionately to scrutinize such thoughts one would realize that they are tinged with sensuous attachment. If the feeling of love is the direct result of attachment and clinging, then it really is not *mettā*.

Carnal love or *pema* is a kind of longing capable of producing much distress, sorrow and lamentation. This fact is clearly explained by the Blessed One in the discourses, and five verses of the chapter on Affection, in the *Dhammapada* (16) emphasize it thus:

'From what is beloved grief arises,
From what is beloved arises fear.
For him who is free from what he loves
There is no grief and so no fear.

'From affection, grief arises. . . .
From attachment grief arises. . . .
From lust grief arises. . . .
From craving grief arises. . . '[3]

As is well known, to love someone means to develop an attachment to the loved one, and when the latter is equally fond of you a

1. *Dhp.* 103. 2. *Dhp.* 201. 3. *Dhp.* 212–16.

bond is created, but when you are separated or when the dear one's affection towards you wanes, you become miserable and may even behave foolishly. In his formulation of the Noble Truth of Suffering, the Buddha says: 'Association with the unloved is suffering, separation from the loved is suffering, not to get what one wants is suffering. . . .'[1] *Mettā*, however, is a very pure sublime state of the human mind; like quicksilver it cannot attach itself to anything. It is a calm, non-assertive super-solvent among virtues.

It is difficult to love a person dispassionately, without any kind of clinging, without any idea of self, me and mine; for in man the notion of 'I' is dominant, and to love without making any distinction between this and that, without setting barriers between persons, to regard all as sisters and brothers with a boundless heart, may appear to be almost impossible, but those who try even a little will be rewarded; it is worth while. Through continuous effort and determination one reaches the destination by stages.

A practiser of *mettā* should be on his guard against callous folk who are egocentric. It often happens that when a person is gentle and sincere others try to exploit his good qualities for their own ends. This should not be encouraged. If one allows the self-centred to make unfair use of one's *mettā*, kindliness and tolerance, that tends to intensify rather than allay the evils and sufferings of society.

> 'Some serve and consort with one for their own gain,
> Hard is it to find disinterested friends:
> Since impure people think only of their own profit,
> Walk alone, like the horn of a rhinoceros.'[2]

The Buddha seems to have been compelled to say this though it was as unpalatable then as it is today.

As *mettā* has the characteristic of non-attachment to any beings, it is easier to cultivate it when one's mind is less inclined to carnality or sensuous attachment. *Nekkhamma*, as we saw earlier, means giving up sense pleasures, and *mettā* implies friendship without sensual affection. So we see that *nekkhamma* and *mettā* harmonize and support each other. In the early Buddhist writings we find several discourses that deal with *mettā*, but one of them, the Discourse on Loving-kindness,[3] is the most popular with most Buddhists. It is divided into two parts. The first details the standard of moral conduct

1. See above, p. 44. 2. *Sn.* 75. 3. *Metta-sutta, Sn.*

required by one who wishes to attain purity and peace, and the second the method of practising *mettā*. Thus it goes:

'He who is skilled in well-being, and who seeks to attain Peace, *Nibbāna*, should act thus: He should be able, upright, very upright, amenable to good counsel, gentle, free from arrogance.

'Contented, easily supportable, with few duties, living on little, restrained in senses, discriminating, courteous, and not greedily attached to families.

'Let him do nothing that is mean for which the wise might rebuke him. Happy and safe may all beings be, may they have happy minds!

'Whatsoever living beings there be—the quakers (seekers)[1] or the steadfast (the Attained),[2] the long, the stout, the mid-sized, the short, the small, the large.

'Those visible and those invisible, those dwelling at a distance and those nearby, those who are born as well as those seeking birth—may all beings have happy minds!

'Let none deceive nor despise another, anywhere in any way. In anger or ill-will let him not wish another ill.

'Even as a mother would cherish her only child, with her life, even thus towards all beings let him cultivate a boundless heart.

'Let him cultivate, above, below and all around boundless love towards all the world, unhindered, without anger, without enmity.

'Standing, walking, sitting or reclining let him develop this mindfulness as long as he is awake; this they say is 'the Noble Living' here (in the Buddha's Dispensation).

'Not being a follower of wrong views—being virtuous, endowed with Insight, lust in the senses discarded,—never again verily shall he enter any womb.'

In another discourse[3] the Blessed One speaks of eleven blessings which a meditator of *mettā* could expect: 'He sleeps and wakes in comfort, has no bad dreams; he is dear to both human and non-human beings, the gods guard him; no fire, poison or weapon harms him; his mind can be quickly concentrated, his countenance is happy and serene, he dies without being confused in mind. If he fails to attain Arahatship, or the Highest Sanctity, here and now, he will be born in the world of Brahma.'

1. Those who have not yet attained Arahatship.
2. The Arahats, the Perfect Ones.
3. *A.* v. 342.

Vicious thoughts of animosity and cruelty are most detrimental and harmful to those who harbour them. It is an accepted fact that both mind and body undergo certain changes when a man is angry. His heart beats faster with the result that both mental and physical energy is dissipated. How true is the old saying: 'Be not angry, anger makes one age.' Yes, 'when a man is angry he looks ugly, he is in pain, anger clouds his mind and he cannot distinguish between right and wrong. The angry man knows no meaning, he fails to see an idea, he is enveloped in darkness as if blind.'[1] This is the outcome of anger, hence the need to control it until it can be totally eliminated.

Mettā is the best antidote for anger in oneself. It is the best medicine for those who are angry with us. Let us extend loving-kindness to all who need it with a free and boundless heart.

In the discourses one often finds the following question put by the Master to his disciples on meeting them: 'How is it with you, how are you faring? I trust that you are well, that you are not short of food. I trust that you are living together on friendly terms, happy and in concord as milk and water blend, regarding one another with loving eyes.'[2]

The Buddha was an embodiment of *mettā*; an exponent of loving-kindness by precept and example. In the whole of the Buddhist Canon there is not one occasion when the Buddha showed anger or spoke an unkind word to anyone—even to his opponents and enemies. There were those who opposed him and his doctrine, yet the Buddha never regarded them as enemies. In debate he was calm and met opposition without being ruffled, without showing anger. Saccaka, the controversialist, at the end of a debate with the Master, could not help saying: 'It is wonderful, it is marvellous, good Gotama, while thus being spoken to so insistently, while thus being violently attacked with accusing words, the good Gotama's colour was clear, and his countenance happy like that of an Arahat, a perfect one, a Supremely Enlightened One.'[3]

Even when people were scurrilously offensive and reproached him in strong terms, the Buddha never lost countenance. It is often mentioned that he smiled (*mihitapubbaṅgama*). The story connected with the 320th verse of the *Dhammapada* is interesting:

On one occasion when the Buddha was staying at Rājagaha, a heartless individual bribed certain villains to revile the Master when

1. *A.* iv. 94.
2. *M.* 31, 128. *A.* i. 70 and passim.
3. *M.* 36.

he entered the city for alms. They followed him through the city shouting: 'You are a robber, a simpleton, a fool, a camel, an ox, an ass, you have no hope of deliverance from suffering.'

Hearing these words, the Venerable Ānanda, the personal attendant of the Buddha, was very grieved and said to the Master:

'Venerable sir, these people are reviling us, let us go elsewhere.'
- Where shall we go Ānanda?
- Let us go to some other city, venerable sir.
- Suppose, Ānanda, people revile us there, where then shall we go?
- Then we will go to some other city, venerable sir.
- But suppose people revile us there also. Where then shall we go, Ānanda?
- Then we will go to yet another city, venerable sir.
- Ānanda, we should do no such thing; wherever a tumult arises, even there should we remain until that tumult dies away. When these uproars have subsided then only should we go elsewhere. As an elephant on the battle-field endures the arrows shot from a bow, even so, Ānanda, shall I endure abusive speech; most people are, indeed, ill-natured.'

To what extent the Buddha tried to impress on his disciples the need to cultivate lovingkindness is abundantly clear from the following:

'Monks, if a person were to harbour ill-will even when wild bandits with a double-handed saw were to dismember him, he is not a follower of my teaching. Thus, monks, should you train yourselves: "Unsullied shall our minds remain, neither shall an ill word escape our lips, but kindly and compassionate, we will ever abide with loving hearts and not harbour hate. We will radiate lovingkindness even to them (the bandits) and then we will radiate the whole world with thoughts of infinite friendliness, without hate, without ill-will!" That is how you must train yourselves, monks.'[1]

Admonishing his disciples, the Buddha says:

'Monks, if others were to speak ill of me or ill of the *Dhamma* or ill of the *Saṅgha* (the Order) you should not on that account entertain thoughts of enmity and spite, and be worried. If, monks, you

1. *M.* 21.

are angry and displeased with them it will impede your mental development.

'If you feel angry and displeased, would you then be able to know the good and ill speech of others?'

'That would not be so, venerable sir.'

'Monks, if others were to speak ill of me, or ill of the *Dhamma* or ill of the *Saṅgha*, you should then unravel what is untrue and make it all clear, saying: "For this reason, this is false, for this reason, this is untrue, this is not in us." '[1]

The Buddha does not believe in overcoming anger by anger. He emphatically says:

'Hatred never by hatred
Is appeased in this world;
By love alone is it appeased
This is an ancient principle.'[2]

Highly developed thoughts of *mettā* seem to possess magnetic power. By radiating such sublime thoughts it is possible to influence and win over people. The power of *mettā* as illustrated by the life of the Buddha can be seen in many a story told of him. Among the best is that of Roja, the Malla. When the Mallas came to know that the Buddha was to visit their city, Kusinārā, for the first time, they all decided to see him. Roja, however, did not want to accompany them, but he consented at last though much against his will. Yet he was drawn to the Buddha as a calf to its mother even before he saw the Master. This was an instance of the psychic power of *mettā* (*mettā-iddhi*).[3] The taming of the demon Āḷavaka, the ruthless robber Angulimāla, the drunken elephant Nālāgiri and several others were all examples of the Buddha's *mettā*.

It is rather amusing to observe that some of his contemporaries, especially members of other faiths, were frightened of the Buddha and dared not send their disciples and followers to him lest they be converted to his faith. This is clear from the following:

Once Nigaṇṭha Nātaputta (the Jaina Mahāvīra) wished to send his well-known lay disciple, Upāli, to the Buddha to refute his words on a point of controversy. Then Dīghatapassin the Jaina, speaking

1. *D.* I.
2. *Dhp.* 5. *Sanantano:* An old standing principle (*porāṇiko dhammo*) followed by the Buddhas and the saints. (*Com.*)
3. *Vin. Mhvg. Khandaka* vi.

to Nātaputta said: 'To me, venerable sir, it is not at all desirable that Upāli should refute the words of the recluse Gotama. For the recluse Gotama is deceitful; he knows a magic spell by which he entices disciples of other sects (*Gotamo māyāvi āvaṭṭaniṁ māyaṁ jānāti*).'[1]

They perhaps were not aware that it was the Buddha's *mettā*, his large love and kindliness, that attracted people to him and not any 'enticing device'.

'Through love one adds to the fund of human happiness, one makes the world brighter, nobler and purer and prepares it for the good life better than in any other way. There is no ill-luck worse than hatred, it is said, and no safety from others' hostility greater than the heart of love, the heart in which hate is dead. . . .

'If one has developed a love that is truly great, rid of the desire to hold and to possess, that strong clean love which is untarnished with lust of any kind, that love which does not expect material advantage and profit from the act of loving, that love which is firm but not grasping, unshakable but not tied down, gentle and settled, hard and penetrating as a diamond but unhurting, helpful but not interfering, cool, invigorating, giving more than taking, not proud but dignified, not sloppy yet soft, the love that leads one to the heights of clean achievement, then, in such a one can there be no ill-will at all.

'Love is an active force. Every act of the loving one is done with the stainless mind to help, to succour, to cheer, to make the paths of others easier, smoother and more adapted to the conquest of sorrow, the winning of the highest bliss.

'The way to develop love is through thinking out the evils of hate, and the advantages of non-hate; through thinking out according to actuality, according to *karma*, that really there is none to hate, that hate is a foolish way of feeling which breeds more and more darkness, that obstructs right understanding. Hate restricts; love releases. Hatred strangles; love enfranchises. Hatred brings remorse; love brings peace. Hatred agitates; love quietens, stills, calms. Hatred divides; love unites. Hatred hardens; love softens. Hatred hinders; love helps. And thus through a correct study and appreciation of the effects of hatred and the benefits of love, should one develop love.'[2]

1. *M.* 56; *A.* ii. 190.
2. *The Lamp of the Law* by Soma Thera and Piyadassi Thera (Kandy Buddhist Publication Society, Ceylon), pp. 20–2.

The third aspect of right thought is *Karuṇā*, pity or compassion. *Karuṇā* (the same in Pāli and Sanskrit) is defined as: 'The quality which makes the heart of the good man tremble and quiver at the distress of others.' 'The quality that rouses tender feelings in the good man at the sight of others' suffering.' Cruelty, violence is the direct enemy of *karuṇā* while homely grief is the indirect or masked enemy. Though the latter may appear in the guise of a friend, it is not true *karuṇā*, but false sympathy; such sympathy is deceitful and one must try to distinguish true from false compassion. The compassionate man who refrains from harming and oppressing others and endeavours to relieve them of their distress, gives the gift of security to one and all, making no distinction whatsoever.

By precept and example the Buddha was the Great Compassionate One (*Mahā Kāruṇika*). He radiated his great compassion towards all living beings. His actions were never divorced from compassion. The entire Dispensation of the Buddha is permeated with this sublime quality of *karuṇā*. Goodness and violence cannot co-exist; goodness constructs while violence destroys. Compassion cannot be cultivated by one who is obsessed with thoughts of selfishness. It is the self-sacrificing man who fills his heart with pure thoughts of pity and wishes to help and serve others. The selfish cannot be of real service to others; for their selfish motives prevent them from doing good. No sooner do they become selfish and self-possessed than they fail to soften their hearts. Hard-heartedness is overcome by pity, by sympathy. If you remove *karuṇā* from the teachings of the Buddha you remove the heart of Buddhism; for all virtues, all goodness and righteousness have *karuṇā* as their basis, as their matrix.[1] All the virtues (*pāramī*) that a Bodhisatta or one bent on enlightenment cultivates, are initiated by compassion. Compassion is tenderness, a quality of the heart, while understanding or wisdom is hard and penetrative. Compassion should be guided by understanding and understanding by compassion. They go hand in hand and are the back-bone of Buddhism.

One must be careful not to confuse compassion with morbid manifestations of sadness, with feelings of mental pain and with sentimentality. At the loss of a dear one, man weeps, but that is not compassion. If we analyse such feelings carefully we will conclude that they are outward manifestations of our inner thoughts of selfish affection. Why do we feel sad? Because our loved one has passed away. He who was our kith and kin is now no more. We feel

1. *Karuṇā nidhānaṁ hi sīlaṁ.*

that we have lost the happiness and all else that we derived from him and so we are sad. Do we not see that all these feelings revolve round the 'I', 'Me' and 'Mine'? Whether we like it or not, self-interest was responsible for it all. Can we call this *karuṇā*, pity or compassion? Why do we not feel equally sad when others who are not our kith and kin pass away before our eyes? Because we were not familiar with them, they were not ours, we have not lost anything and are not denied the pleasures and comforts we already enjoy. It will now be clear that our feeling of sadness at the loss of a dear one is the outcome of our own selfishness: this is a subtle psychological affair, and all worldlings are subject to such shortcomings and weaknesses. It is the man with a highly developed mind who controls such feelings and tries to see the situation as it really is, according to *karma*, to see things as they are, and not as they appear to be.

Compassion is surely not a flabby state of mind. It is a strong enduring thing. When a person is in distress it is the truly compassionate man's heart that trembles. This, however, is not sadness; it is this quaking of the heart that spurs him to action and incites him to rescue the distressed. And this needs strength of mind, much tolerance and equanimity (*upekkhā*), another of the four sublime states.[1] Those who rush to a conclusion and declare compassion to be an expression of feebleness, because it has the quality of tenderness, do not know what they are talking about. May be according to them persecution is a sign of strength.

The past lives (*jātakas*) of the Bodhisatta tell us in moving detail how he endeavoured himself to help others, to succour the forlorn and relieve them of their distress. Life is precious to all, but the Bodhisatta, while he was preparing himself for Buddhahood, did many things that the ordinary man dare not even think of doing. He even gave his limbs and life as a sacrifice for the sake of others. The accounts of selfless giving and loving compassion of great men like the Bodhisatta are thus recorded in the books:

> 'One who to save a limb, rich treasures gave,
> Would sacrifice a limb, his life to save,
> Yea, wealth, limbs, life and all away would fling,
> Right and its claims alone remembering.'[2]

1. See p. 20, n. 2.
2. *Mahā-Sutasoma jātaka*, No. 537, *Jātaka Stories*, Vol. V., P.T.S.

To such an exceptionally high degree does a Bodhisatta cultivate *karuṇā*.

You are often moved by a sudden cry of pain, or by the sight of another's distress. Your heart melts, and you wish to act in accordance with your kind feelings. You rush to the rescue of the helpless one, you succour him and relieve him of his distress. You do not crave selfishly for some remuneration or try to exploit the situation by depriving him of his belongings. This is true *karuṇā* in the finest sense of the word. If by chance you are rewarded or honoured for your humanity, then that is a different thing.

It seems to me that it is not quite proper to help others, to be of service to the poor and the needy, with the sole intention of gaining 'merit'—reaping in return much profit and gain. If we approach a situation with such selfish motives then our good action is tarnished; we should not be too conscious of the result of our good deeds and be attached to it. The result will follow us like our own shadow; for actions have reactions, seed brings forth fruit, cause produces effect. To know the deed and its due consequence is right understanding, but to become attached to the results is to invite greed or craving which is a stumbling block to right understanding, purity and peace.

When we offer food to a starving man we need not think of a good rebirth in the heavens, a rebirth in a good state of existence, or expect to reap a good harvest in return; for that is not the Buddhist attitude, or as a matter of fact the right attitude. By such wishful thinking we only add fuel to the fire of our greedy selfish thoughts. On close analysis you will see that the only real reason for giving food to that man is that he is hungry. Hunger, as the Buddha says, is the worst ailment.[1] When we see that he has eaten, that his hunger has ceased, and that he feels happy, then we too feel happy and pleased. Such selfless actions really bring us unalloyed joy. Gladness at another's happiness is the third sublime state known as *Muditā* or sympathetic joy. You will now see how the four sublime states[2] function together supporting each other.

Thus by selfless giving, by being generous (*dāna*), we cease to be niggardly and become liberal not only with our wealth, but with our thoughts—we become more and more broad-minded.

We must thus try to understand the true significance of action (*karma*) and result (*vipāka*) in Buddhist thought.

It is very necessary to be conscious of the good and bad results of our actions, in order to know how they come to fruition, but we

1. *Dhp.* 203. See also p. 159.
2. Lovingkindness, Compassion, Sympathetic Joy and Equanimity.

should not be greedily attached to the result. A correct understanding of the law of *karma*, and how it operates, incites us to be just and compassionate.

Compassion is not limited merely to the giving of food and such material things to the poor and needy, or to giving a copper to a beggar. All actions done with a pure motive, free from greed, false views and pride, are reckoned as genuine acts of kindness. Imparting knowledge to the illiterate, guiding the muddle-headed and the uninstructed along the right path, giving strength and moral support to the weak and fearful, ministering to the sick, etc., are all humane actions.

Marvellous, for instance, was the Buddha's mode of ministering to the sick. He was the great healer. Not only did he heal the sick with the charm of his friendship but he also ministered to them out of compassion. The Commentary to the *Dhammapada*[1] records a touching story: A young man of Sāvatthi listened to the Buddha, gained confidence in him and entered the Order. He became known as Tissa. After a time he fell sick. First small pustules broke out on his body, gradually became bigger and burst, developing into ulcers. His fellow monks, being unwilling to look after Tissa, abandoned him and he was forlorn. The Buddha came to know of this, went to the fireplace and set some water to boil. Then the Blessed One went to where Tissa was and caught hold of the corner of the bed on which he was lying. The monks, realizing what the Master was trying to do, carried the patient with the bed to the fireplace. There the Master made the monks wash Tissa's garments and dry them, while he gently cleaned the ulcers and washed the sick monk. The patient was most refreshed and lay on his bed with a composed mind. Thereupon the Blessed One explained the doctrine to him. With a collected mind Tissa listened and at the end of the sermon attained the highest stage of sainthood and passed away. The funeral rites were duly performed and the Buddha caused the relics to be enshrined in a stupa.[2]

1. *Dhp*. 41.

2. 'To the north-east of the monastery of Jetavana', wrote General Alexander Cunningham in his *Archaeological Report*, 1862–3, 'there was a *stupa* built on the spot where Buddha had washed the hands and feet of a sick monk.... The remains of the *stupa* still exist in a mass of solid brick-work, at a distance of 550 feet from the Jetavana monastery. The ruined mass which is 24½ feet in height, is built entirely of large bricks 24 by 10 by 3½ inches, which is a sufficient proof of its antiquity.'

In General Cunningham's map of Sāvatthi the site of this *stupa* is marked H. in the plan. See *Archaeological Survey of India* (Simla, 1871), p. 341.

No human quality is a prerogative of a particular religion, nation, race or culture. All those who have eyes to see and minds to understand will realize that all acts of friendship, pity and large-heartedness are common to humanity. But alas, when people are misguided and misled, they speak of and plan 'just wars'—we even read of 'holy wars'. War is war, 'just' or 'holy'. It is never peace, all war is barbarous.

The books mention an incident which once brought the Buddha to the battlefield. The Sākyas and the Koliyas were on the verge of war over the waters of the river Rohini. Knowing the disaster ahead, the Master approached them and asked them which was more precious, water or human blood. They admitted that human blood was more precious. The Master spoke to them and the intended war was prevented.[1]

The Buddha is known as one who has dropped the cudgel (*nihita-daṇḍa*), one who has dropped the weapon (*nihita-sattha*). The only weapon he successfully wielded was that of love and compassion. He armed himself with truth and loving compassion. He tamed the ruthless like Ālavaka, Angulimāla and the drunken elephant Nālāgiri and many another who had harmed him by his power of love and compassion. Angulimāla who was tamed and who became a disciple of the Master and later an Arahat said in praise:

> 'Some are tamed by cudgels,
> Some by goads and some by whips.
> With neither club nor weapon,
> I by the steadfast one was tamed.'[2]

The Buddha's disciples as admonished by him wandered forth 'for the good of the many, for the happiness of the many' and spread the *Dhamma*, the doctrine, without harming any one, and without any coercive proselytism.

The Buddhist conception of *karuṇā* has no compromising limitations. All beings include even the tiniest creature that crawls at one's feet. The Buddhist view of life is such that no living being is considered as outside the circle of *mettā* and *karuṇā* which make no distinction between man, animal and insect, or between man and man, as, high and low, rich and poor, strong and weak, wise and unwise, dark and fair, brahmin and caṇḍāla or as Christian, Hindu,

1. *A. Com*: i. 341; *Sn. Com:* 357; *Therig. Com:* 141.
2. *Thg.* 878.

Muslim, Buddhist, etc.; for *mettā* and *karuṇā*, as we saw above, are boundless and no sooner do we try to keep men apart on the false basis mentioned above, than the feeling of separateness creeps in and these boundless qualities become limited which is contrary to the high ideals of the exponent of these virtues.

It was the spirit of love and compassion taught by the Buddha that touched the heart of Asoka, the great Buddhist Emperor of India in the third century B.C. Before he became a Buddhist he was a warlike monarch like his father (Bindusāra) and grandfather (Candragupta). Wishing to extend his territories he invaded and conquered Kālinga. In this war thousands were slain, while many more were wounded and taken captive. Later, however, when he followed the Buddha's creed of compassion he realized the folly of killing. He felt very sad when he thought of the great slaughter, and gave up warfare. He is the only military monarch on record who after victory gave up conquest by war (*dig-vijaya*) and inaugurated conquest by righteousness (*dharma-vijaya*). As his Rock Edict XIII says, 'he sheathed the sword never to unsheath it, and wished no harm to living beings'.

The spread of the Buddha's creed of compassion throughout the Eastern world was largely due to the enterprise and tireless effort of Asoka the Great. The Buddha-law made Asia mild and non-aggressive. Can we say that the same mildness, and non-aggressiveness still prevail in Asian countries as they did in the past? One doubts, and why? Modern 'civilization' is pressing hard on Asian lands. It is an accepted theory that with the rise and development of this so-called civilization man's culture (which is the outcome of inner development) deteriorates and he changes for the worse. With the march of modern science very many changes have taken place, and all these changes and improvements, being material and external, tend to make modern man more and more worldly-minded and sensuous with the result that he neglects, or purposely ignores, the qualities of the heart, and becomes self-interested and heartless. The waves of materialism seem to influence mankind and affect their way of thinking and living. People are so bound by their senses, they live so exclusively in the material world that they fail to contact the good within.

If only the love and compassion that throb through the teachings of the Buddha ruled man's action today we should not be living in this atmosphere of suspicion, fear, jealousy, arrogance, greed, hate and delusion that makes this world more and more an armed camp and drives us steadily to the brink of Armageddon.

It is a religious view of life, a life of love and understanding that is needed to establish complete mental harmony and well-being. Today more than at any other time we need the light of the *Dhamma*.

9

RIGHT SPEECH

(*Sammā-vācā*)

All religions and philosophies advocate morals or ethics of some kind or other for man's own well-being and for the good of the society in which he lives. These ethical codes are not of the same level or category, but they vary. What is moral to some, may not be so to others; what one condemns as immoral may be recognized as moral by another. Principles of right and wrong behaviour depend, at times, on the background of the different people of the world—their geographical, economic and social conditions, and so on. Thus the criteria of the principles of morality differ.

It looks as if with the passage of time people seem to think that some of the morals laid down by religious teachers are outdated, and in their enthusiasms for a gay life they do not hesitate to put aside principles of behaviour if they consider them a hindrance. They then adopt new modes of conduct which, later, become conventions, and once that has occurred, no one cares to speak ill of them. Nevertheless there are many moral principles which all people, irrespective of colour, race or religion, are expected to follow.

The moral code taught in Buddhism is very vast and varied and yet the function of Buddhist morality or *sīla* is one and not many. It is the control of man's verbal and physical actions, his behaviour; in other words, purity of speech and action. All morals set forth in Buddhism lead to this end—virtuous behaviour, yet *sīla* is not an end in itself, but a means, for it aids *samādhi* or concentration. *Samādhi*, on the other hand is a means to the acquisition of *paññā*, true wisdom, which in turn brings about deliverance of mind, the final goal of the teaching of the Buddha. Virtue, Concentration and Wisdom therefore is a blending of man's emotions and intellect. It is to this end that the Master directs his disciples.

The Buddha's attitude towards life is not merely rational, but a practical realization of all that is good—ethical perfection as well as mental deliverance. This implies that the Master wants us to cultivate good emotions and abandon the bad. The emotional aspect should be developed though that alone does not lead us to final emancipation. Good emotions should always be blended with right understanding. So it is clear that Virtue, Concentration and Wisdom are the three strands of the rope by the aid of which the prudent man reaches the highest goal and proclaims his achievements by saying: 'Done is what is to be done' (*kataṁ karnīyaṁ*). Thus the *Dhamma* guides the follower through pure living and right understanding to the attainment of freedom from all ill.

In this chapter we shall discuss right speech. In the next two chapters right action and right livelihood will be dealt with respectively. As these three are in the *sīla* Group, the entire Buddhist code of morality spoken of in the context of the Eightfold Path, a few words may not be out of place to explain briefly the *sīlas* as expounded in Buddhist writings.

The final emancipation, the highest goal, in Buddhism, is not attained at once. It is a gradual process, a gradual training. As the discourses often point out mental purity is gained after a thorough training in virtuous behaviour. Mental purity and attainments are not possible without moral purity. The Buddha exhorts his disciples first to establish themselves in virtue or moral habits before entering on the path of meditation and wisdom.[1] Hence the need to start from the very beginning. The starting point in the Dispensation of the Buddha is *sīla*, virtuous behaviour. Standing on the firm ground of *sīla* one should endeavour to master the fickle mind.

The Buddha points out to his disciples the ways of overcoming verbal and physical ill behaviour. Having tamed his tongue, having controlled his bodily actions and made himself pure in the way he earns his living the disciple establishes himself well in moral habits (*sīlavā*). Thus he trains himself in the essential precepts of restraint observing them scrupulously and seeing danger in the slightest fault.[2] While thus restraining himself in word and deed he tries to guard the doors of the senses,[3] for if he lacks control over his senses unhealthy thoughts are bound to fill his mind. Seeing a form, hearing a sound, and so on, he is neither attracted nor repelled by such sense objects, but maintains balance, putting away all likes and dislikes. This control of the senses he practises with zest.

1. See above, p. 82.
2. *Pātimokkhasaṁvara, M.* 107.
3. *Indriyaguttadvāra.*

He eats moderately[1] and mindfully: not for self-indulgence, not to beautify the body, but to keep it unharmed for living the holy life (*brahma cariya*). He is devoted to wakefulness[2] and cleanses his mind of taints.[3] This behaviour or mode of living applies to a monk and not to the layman.

Now if the disciple is earnest and mindful he will advance without faltering and start the more difficult task of meditation, gaining concentrative calm (*samatha*) by taking a subject that suits his temperament[4] and continuing with it without stopping. Gradually, little by little, from moment to moment[5] he purifies his mind by overcoming the hindrances[6] which obstruct meditation. Thus he who strives heedfully gains control over his fickle mind. With his speech, actions and sense organs under subjugation and his mind under control, he has now gained self-mastery. Thus training himself in Virtue and Concentration (*sīla-sikkhā* and *samādhi-sikkhā*), he now tries to gain true Wisdom or Insight by seeing all things as they really are (*yathābhūtaṁ*). Viewing things as they are implies, as we discussed above,[7] seeing the transient, unsatisfactory and no-self-nature of all conditioned and component things. To such a meditative disciple of the Buddha the 'world' is not the external or the empirical world, but the human body with its consciousness. It is the world of the five aggregates of clinging. It is this that he tries to understand as impermanent, unsatisfactory and without Self or Soul. It is to this world of body and mind that the Buddha referred when he said to Mogharāja: 'Ever mindful, Mogharāja, see the world as void (*suñña*) —having given up the notion of a Self (underlying it);[8]—so may one overcome *Māra* (death).'

Now when a disciple thus trains himself in wisdom (*paññāsikkhā*) he rightly understands, 'whatever is transient is not worth rejoicing at, is not worthy of one's regard, not worth clinging to'.[9]

He does not consider the five aggregates of clinging, the five sense organs and their corresponding sense objects as 'mine', as 'I' or 'my Self' and understands the Master's admonition:

'What is not yours, monks, put it away; putting it away will be for your good and welfare. What, monks, is not yours? Body, O

1. *Bhojane mattaññutā*. 2. *Jāgariyamanuyutto*. 3. See *A*. ii. 38.
4. For temperaments and subjects of meditations see chapter 14, p. 212.
5. *Dhp*. 239. 6. See p. 206. 7. Chapter 7, p. 95.
8. *Attānudiṭṭhimūhacca*, lit. pulling out, removing the notion of an *atta*, Self or Soul. Sn. 1119.
9. *M*. 106.

monks, is not yours, put it away; putting it away will be for your good and welfare. Feeling is not yours . . . perception is not yours . . . volitional formations are not yours . . . consciousness is not yours, put it away; putting it away will be for your good and welfare.'[1]

Thus comprehending things as they really are, thus realizing the true nature of the five aggregates of clinging, he 'lives independent, clinging to nothing in the world'[2]—the world of the aggregates and of senses—and lives experiencing the bliss of *Nirvāṇa*, the Supreme Happiness. This, in short, is the way by which the āryan (noble) disciple by gradual training attains his goal.

The reader will note that in this self-purification and self-mastery for final Deliverance, by gradual training, there is no coercion and compulsion by any external agency, there are no rewards and punishments for deeds done or left undone: no ablution by holy water,[3] neither offerings to any deity, nor worship of gods, the sun or fire. And why? Because purity and impurity depend on oneself. Things external whether animate or inanimate cannot and do not grant us purification and deliverance.

'Neither nakedness nor matted hair, nor filth, nor fasting, nor lying on the ground, nor dust and soot nor squatting can purify a being who is still perplexed.'[4]

Let us now go into details with regard to *sīla*, the Buddhist code of morality. In the first discourse of the *Digha Nikāya*,[5] we find a very long and comprehensive account of the *sīlas* which we shall not discuss here.

Among the items of right behaviour the lowest are the *pañca-sīla*, the five precepts for training, the A B C of Buddhist ethics. These are the basic principles for the lay follower.

They are:

1. I undertake the training precept to abstain from killing anything that breathes.[6]

2. I undertake the training precept to abstain from taking what is not given.

3. I undertake the training precept to abstain from sexual misconduct.

1. *S.* iii. 32; *S.* iv. 81.
2. *Satipaṭṭhāna sutta*, see chapter 13, p. 189.
3. See above, p. 30.
4. *Dhp.* 141. Even today in India one meets people who follow this kind of useless practice for purification.
5. *Brahmajāla sutta*.
6. Including oneself.

4. I undertake the training precept to abstain from speaking falsehood.

5. I undertake the training precept to abstain from liquor that causes intoxication and heedlessness.

Sir Edwin Arnold in *The Light of Asia* states the five precepts in these words:

> 'Kill not—for pity's sake—lest ye slay
> The meanest thing upon its upward way.
>
> Give freely and receive, but take from none
> By greed, or force, or fraud, what is his own.
>
> Bear not false witness, slander not nor lie;
> Truth is the speech of inward purity.
>
> Shun drugs and drinks, which work the wit abuse;
> Clear minds, clean bodies, need no Soma juice.[1]
>
> Touch not thy neighbour's wife, neither commit
> Sins of the flesh unlawful and unfit.'

These *silas* are to be kept and acted on in one's daily life, they are not for mere recitation, for lip-service or for applying to others.

> 'He who knoweth the precepts by heart, but faileth to practise them,
> Is like unto one who lighteth a lamp and then shutteth his eyes.'[2]

Buddhism does not demand of the lay follower all that a member of the Order is expected to observe. But whether monk or layman, moral habits are essential to the upward path. One who becomes a Buddhist by taking the three refuges[3] is expected, at least, to observe the five basic precepts which is the very starting point on the path. They are not restricted to a particular day or place, but are to be practised throughout life everywhere, always. There is also the possibility of their being violated by all save those who have

1. *Soma*, 'name of the plant *avestan haoma*, the juice of which was the most important ingredient in Vedic sacrificial offerings and formed the beverage of the gods'.

2. Quoted in *Tibetan Yoga and Secret Doctrine* edited by W. Y. Evans-Wentz (London, 1935), p. 65.

3. For the formula see p. 20.

attained at least the first stage of sanctity (*sotāpatti*). Nevertheless when a transgression occurs it is useless to repent of one's weaknesses and shortcomings, for repentence will not do any good to or help oneself or others. It will only disturb one's mind. Again it may be observed that according to Buddhism wrongdoing is not regarded as a 'sin', for that word is foreign to the teaching of the Buddha. There is no such thing as 'breaking the Buddha's laws', for he was not a lawgiver or an arbitrator who punished the bad and rewarded the good deeds of beings, hence there is no repentance, sorrow or regret for 'sin'. The doer of the deed is responsible for his actions; he suffers or enjoys the consequences, and it is his concern either to do good, or to be a transgressor. It must also be stated that all actions, good or ill, do not necessarily mature. One's good *karma* may suppress the evil *karma* and vice versa.

As the formula clearly shows, there are no laws or commandments. Voluntarily you promise to observe the training precepts and there is no compulsion or coercion; you yourself are responsible for your actions. If you violate what you have undertaken to keep, it is very necessary then to make a firm determination not to repeat but to correct your weakness and try hard not to lapse again. A careful thinker ought to realize that the sole purpose of keeping these precepts is to train oneself to control one's impulses, evil inclinations and wrong acts, and thus pave the path to purification and happiness, give security to society and promote cordiality. On close analysis we know that the observance of these precepts is the only way to lessen our lust (greed), hate and delusion, the root causes of all evil in society. For instance, the first precept cannot be transgressed without entertaining thoughts of hate and cruelty; in the case of the third it is specifically lust, the second and the fourth may be due to both greed and hate, and the fifth to greed, while delusion is behind all the five precepts.

It is important to note that to take intoxicating liquor causes delusion. It prevents clear thinking, lessens one's power of reasoning and brings about negligence, infatuation and a host of other evils. A drunkard is not responsible for his actions and may commit any crime. Hence the violation of this one precept may lead a man to break all the others. Says the Buddha:

> 'Give up this base of all evil
> Which lead to madness,
> To abuse of mind'.[1]

1. *Sn.* 399.

Now one may argue that to drink in moderation is harmless, but there is a saying:

'First a man takes a drink,
Then the drink takes a drink,
Then the drink takes the man.'

And so it is always better to bear in mind the Buddha's warning: 'Be mindful, self-controlled and serene.' Let us shun drugs and drinks which blind one to both the truths of life and the path to deliverance.

Remember that the third and fifth precepts have an affinity, they support each other and both bring 'enjoyment' (*rasassāda*). Sometimes in the Pāli canon the fifth precept is omitted thus including it in the third as in the case of the moral code mentioned in the Eightfold Path. Then there are the ten 'precepts, or items for training' which are meant for the novices (*sāmaṇeras*).[1] They are formed by adding five to those already mentioned.[2] They are:

6. I undertake the training precept to abstain from untimely eating.

7. I undertake the training precept to abstain from dancing, singing, music and unseemly shows.

8. I undertake the training precept to abstain from the use of garlands, perfumes, beauty creams and embellishment.

9. I undertake the training precept to abstain from the use of high and luxurious couches.

10. I undertake the training precept to abstain from accepting gold and silver.

There are also the eight training precepts observed by lay followers on special days, that is on full moon or the new moon days, etc. They are formed by combining the seventh and eighth, and omitting the tenth precept.

A person who keeps the precepts is, in the Buddha's phrase, a

1. A *sāmaṇera* is one who has entered the Order, but is not yet a *bhikkhu*, a full-fledged monk, who observes the essential (*pātimokkha*) precepts which are 220 (227) in number. See *Vin. suttavibhaṅga*, or *Book of the Discipline*, I. B. Horner, Parts 1, 2, 3, P.T.S. A novice also does not observe the *vassa*, the rains of three months, July–October, which a *bhikkhu* is expected to observe. A novice is given *bhikkhu* or higher ordination when he has reached the age of twenty. But sometimes age alone would not do. If he lacks in intelligence, has not studied the *Dhamma* and *Vinaya* sufficiently to lead a *bhikkhu*'s life, etc., he is not a fit candidate. See also preceding chapter, p. 107.

2. The third precept, however, is changed into: 'I undertake the training precept to abstain from unchastity (*abrahmacariyā*).'

good or worthy man (*sappurisa*), and if in addition he encourages another to observe them, he is still more worthy.[1]

In the Noble Eightfold Path, under the factor of right speech, four abstentions are mentioned: Abstention from falsehood, slander, harsh speech and idle chatter.

Though these training precepts are worded negatively, it should not be thought that the Buddhist code of conduct is a mere negative prohibition. It is necessary first to remove the weeds and prepare the field before sowing. Similarly it is very necessary for man first to strive to purify his speech and bodily actions and then to do good. We must admit that our mind is often tainted with unwholesome thoughts. It burns with the three fires of greed, hate and delusion and is in an unhealthy state. Naturally the manifestations of such unhealthy thoughts in the form of verbal and physical acts, cannot be healthy, hence the need first to check the evil, to abstain from loose behaviour. Abstention urges a man to do good, to be pure in speech and deed. Often people who are fond of doing much good to others, find it difficult to abstain from doing certain unbecoming things. This needs great strength of mind, effort and determination. On the other hand, it is because of one's pity and sympathy, which are not negative virtues, that one abstains from harming others and from lying because of one's love for truth, and so on.

A careful reader of the Buddha's discourses will find that the Master has also stated the precepts in positive terms thus:

'Giving up killing, he abstains from taking the life of any living being; laying aside stick and sword, modest and merciful, he lives kind and compassionate to all living beings. Abstaining from taking what is not given, taking (only) what is given . . . he dwells purified from thievish tendencies. Giving up slander . . . he lives reconciling those at variance, and strengthening those who are friendly, delighting and rejoicing in concord he speaks words conducive to reconciliation. Giving up harsh speech, he says what is gentle, pleasing to the ear, affectionate. . . . Giving up idle chatter, he speaks at the right time in accordance with facts, to the purpose, in agreement with the doctrine (*Dhamma*) and discipline, words worthy of treasuring (in the heart) seasonable, appropriate, discriminating and to the point.'[2]

Thus we see how the Master has also stressed the positive aspect in

1. *A.* ii. 217. 2. *M.* 27, 38, 51; *D.* 1. and passim.

unmistakable language. The striving one, earnestly bent on the path of purification, however, wastes no time in profitless speculation, but 'admonishing and inciting himself he follows the sign-posted path'.[1]

There is nothing vague in the teaching of the Buddha. Knowing evil as evil and good as good, why should one hesitate to avoid the wrong and tread the right path? For the Buddhist to give up evil and do good is ineluctable if he has understood his Master's teaching:

'The giving up of all evil,
The cultivation of the good
The cleansing of one's mind
This is the Buddha's teaching.'[2]

As this very important verse indicates, before doing good, it is essential to cease from evil. When a man has done both, and has thus strengthened himself in moral behaviour, he can then, if he likes, try the more difficult task of disciplining his mind through meditation. The attempt, however, so to train the mind without a background of morality, without regulated behaviour, is a mere hope and imagination that can never be realized.

The Noble Eightfold Path, in Buddhism, is the one and only way for purification. Says the Buddha:

'Action,[3] knowledge,[4] *Dhamma*[5] and noble moral life, by these are beings purified, not by lineage nor by wealth.'[6]

'Whatsoever there is of evil, connected with evil, belonging to evil—all issue from the mind. Whatsoever there is of good, connected with good, belonging to good—all issue from the mind.'[7]

'When the mind or thought is guarded, bodily action also is guarded; verbal action is also guarded.'

'When the mind is unguarded, bodily action is also unguarded, verbal action also is unguarded.'[8]

1. *Thg*. 637. 2. See p. 77, n. 2.

3. Action or *kamma* here means volition or the will for the Path (*maggacetanā*), *Com.*

4. *Vijjā*, that is wisdom for the Path, *Com.*

5. *Dhamma* here indicates concentration (*samādhi*), *Com.* This stanza in brief speaks of the threefold division of the Path: Virtue, Concentration and Wisdom through which mankind gains true purification.

6. *S.* i. 34; *M.* 143. 7. *A.* i. 11. 8. *A.* i. 261 *sutta* 105.

The origin of all these actions is either greed, ill-will and delusion or non-greed, non-ill-will and non-delusion. Actions done under the influence of the first trio are not profitable, they are blameworthy, they result in pain and they lead to further actions, not to the cessation of action. Actions done under the influence of the second trio are profitable and praiseworthy, they bring happiness and lead to the ending of further action, not to the arising thereof.[1]

Thus there are three ways of doing good and evil conditioned by three different mental factors, and they bring about results or reactions in accordance with the deed done. In this case the mind may be compared to a reservoir which needs attention to keep the water intact and pure. If the reservoir is neglected and the water becomes contaminated, the man who drinks it from the tap is in trouble. If, knowing that the water is bad, he keeps the tap turned off, he will not suffer even though the reservoir is polluted. As he cannot keep the tap closed for ever, it is his duty to see that the reservoir is cared for so that he can turn on the tap and drink the water. Man's mind, which is like a reservoir, has two outlets, speech and physical action. What is in the mind escapes through these outlets. If the thoughts are pure, their possessor experiences good results; if they are impure he experiences unwholesome results. If he refrains from allowing evil thoughts to escape through the two channels, his speech and bodily actions will not be polluted, for those two channels are securely closed, nevertheless the mind, the reservoir, is unprotected. He must make a genuine effort to watch his mind so that its contents are not polluted, and for this he needs meditation or concentration. Though his mind is thus concentrated, collected and guarded, still it is not in a state of security, so he needs wisdom, insight knowledge, to keep it free from pollution. Once this has been achieved his mind is rendered immune from all taints, defilements and pollution.

From this simile it is possible to understand that though *sīla* or virtuous behaviour which guards verbal and physical actions is the starting point of the Path, it is nonetheless so essential to man's development and purification.

With this brief general introduction to the Buddhist moral code, let us now consider Right Speech. What a wonderful thing is speech, for just a word can change a man's whole outlook towards

1. *A.* i. 263, *sutta* 107, 108.

good and evil. Are we not really fortunate in this gift which is denied to animals? Yet how few of us care to use it for our own and others' welfare. Much trouble and misunderstanding could be avoided if only people would be more thoughtful and gentle in what they say and more accurate and sincere in what they write.

Speech is a gift of great value since through it we can express thoughts and ideas which can be shared with others. But if the tongue, which is boneless and pliable, is allowed to become unruly, it can play havoc. Is it not responsible for much strife and trouble from squabbles between families to wars between nations? If man could but tame his tongue, would not the world be a far better place to live in?

Speech should not be dominated by unwholesome thoughts—by greed, anger, jealousy, pride, selfishness and so on. Much talk certainly prevents calmness and right thinking, and a glib tongue leads to all four types of wrong talk. Says the Buddha: 'Monks, there are these five disadvantages and dangers in garrulous speech: the glib talker utters falsehoods, slanders, speaks harsh and idle words, and after death is reborn in an evil state of existence.'[1]

1. In the context of right speech the first virtue is to abstain from falsehood and speak the truth. Such a person, as the *Metta sutta* says, is straight, nay transparently straight (*uju, sūju*).[2] He is sincere, upright and dependable. He does not stray from the truth to win fame, or to please another. He may seem strict, but 'truth is one, for there is no second'.[3] 'The Buddha did not say one thing one day and the contrary the next.'[4] 'Because he speaks as he acts and acts as he speaks, he is called Tathāgata.'[5] The Master is also known as *Saccanāma*, 'he whose name is Truth'.

The Buddha was so emphatic with regard to this evil of lying, that his first lesson to little Rāhula, the seven-year-old novice,[6] seems to have been on the worthlessness of falsehood (we know that children of tender age, wittingly or not, often speak falsely).

Once the Blessed One visited little Rāhula. The latter got a seat ready and water for washing the feet. The Master washed his feet and sat down. Little Rāhula paid obeisance to the Blessed One and sat at one side. Then the Master, having poured a little water into a vessel, said:

1. *A.* iii. 254. 2. See above, p. 115. 3. *Sn.* 884.
4. '*Advejjhavacanā Buddhā*' *Bv.* p. 12, verse 110: cf. *A.* iii. 403 'How, when I have definitely declared it, can there be an alternative (*dvejjhaṁ*)?'
5. *D.* iii. 135, *sutta* 29.
6. He joined the Order at the age of seven.

– Do you see, Rāhula, this little quantity of water left in the vessel?
– Yes, venerable sir.
– Even so, Rāhula, insignificant is the recluseship of those who are not ashamed to lie.

Then the Master having thrown away the water addressed the novice:

– Do you note, Rāhula, that little quantity of water thrown away?
– Yes, venerable sir.
– Even so, Rāhula, discarded, indeed, is the recluseship of those who are not ashamed to lie.

Then the Master overturned the water vessel and addressed the novice:

– Do you, Rāhula, see this vessel that has been overturned?
– Yes, venerable sir.
– Even so, Rāhula, overturned, indeed, is the recluseship of those who are not ashamed to lie.

Then the Master having uprighted the vessel addressed the novice:

– Do you, Rāhula, see this water-vessel that is void, empty?
– Yes, venerable sir.
– Even so, Rāhula, void and empty is the recluseship of those who are not ashamed to lie. . . . Even so, Rāhula (citing the simile of a king's elephant)? of anyone who is not ashamed to lie, I say that there is no evil that he cannot do. Wherefore, Rāhula, thus, indeed, should you train yourself: 'Not even for fun will I tell a lie.'[1]

2. Slander or tale-bearing (*pisuṇāvācā*) is the next evil that the tongue can commit. The Pāli word means literally 'breaking up of fellowship'. To slander another is most wicked for it entails making a false statement intended to damage someone's reputation. The slanderer often commits two crimes simultaneously, he says what is false because his report is untrue and then he back-bites.

In Sanskrit poetry the back-biter is compared to a mosquito which

1. *M.* 61.

though small is noxious. It comes singing, settles on you, draws blood and may, if a female, give you malaria. Again the tale-bearer's words may be sweet as honey, but his mind is full of poison.

Let us then avoid tale-bearing and slander which destroy friendships. Instead of causing trouble let us speak words that make for peace and reconciliation.[1] Instead of sowing the seed of dissension, let us bring peace and friendship to those living in discord and enmity. 'Be united; wrangle not,' said the Buddha. 'Concord alone is commendable' was inscribed by Asoka on stone. Since we depend on one another, we must learn to live together in peace, friendship and harmony.

3. The next virtue is to abstain from harsh words and be pleasant and courteous. What we say can bring gain or loss, praise or blame, good repute or ill, misery or happiness. A gentle word can melt the hardest heart, while a harsh word can cause untold agony.

We should think twice before we speak ill of anyone, for it is an attempt to damage his character, his good name. But it does not matter if, when praising another, we slightly overpaint the picture, for this does not lead to unpleasantness and heart-burning. As the Buddha says:

> 'In man's mouth a hatchet grows
> With which fools will cut themselves
> When they utter evil words.'[2]

In the Buddha's day a festival called 'Simpletons' Holiday'[3] was sometimes held in which only the simple minded took part. For a week they smeared their bodies with ashes and cowdung and wandered about abusing and shouting coarsely at people. Even friends, relatives, ascetics and monks were not spared. People would fling them a few coppers to be rid of them. The devout followers of the Buddha besought the Master not to enter the city until the festival was over. But the Buddha said: 'Foolish and uninstructed dolts are offensive like that, but the wise cultivate mindfulness and attain the Deathless *Nibbāna*.'[4]

Man's speech often indicates his character. A harsh word, an unpleasant gesture, a crooked smile, may turn a good-natured man into a criminal, a friend into a foe.

1. *M.* 27, 38 and passim. 2. *S.* i. 149. 3. *Bālanakkhatta.*
4. *Dhp. Com.* I. 256.

'Speak not harshly to anyone,
For those accosted will retort;
Painful is vindictive talk,
You may receive blows in exchange.'[1]

One of the past stories of the Bodhisatta tells how he weaned his otherwise good mother from harsh speech. It is said that she was rude and ill-tongued, but that her son, aware of the weakness, did not want to hurt her by speaking too plainly. One day the Bodhisatta, who was then king of Benares, went to a park with his mother and retainers. On the way a blue jay screeched so discordantly that all covered their ears and cried: 'What a harsh call, what a screech! Don't let us hear that again.' Now it happened later that when the Bodhisatta was strolling in the pleasance with his mother and retainers, an Indian cuckoo called so sweetly that the people were happy and hoped that it would sing again.

This was the moment for which the Bodhisatta had been waiting. He said: 'Mother dear, the jay's cry was dreadful and we covered our ears rather than listen to it. No one delights in a coarse language. Though dark and without beauty the cuckoo won the love and attention of all with its pleasing call. One's speech, therefore, should be friendly and restrained, calm and full of meaning. . . .' Thus exhorted by her son, the mother became refined in speech and elegant in manners.[2]

Pleasant and courteous speech attracts and is an asset to society, yet how often is beauty marred by rude talk. 'The language of the heart, the language that comes from the heart, is always simple, graceful and full of power.'[3]

4. The fourth and last virtue concerned with right speech is to abstain from frivolous talk or gossip which brings no profit to anyone, anywhere. People are too fond of idle talk, of maliciously disparaging others. The papers in their gossip columns are just as bad. Men and women with time on their hands indulge in endless chatter, amusing themselves at the expense of others. As J. L. Hollard says: 'Gossip is always a personal confession either of malice or imbecility. It is a low, frivolous and too often a dirty business in which neighbours are made enemies for life.' The Buddha's golden advice is: 'When, monks, you have gathered together there are two things to be done, either talk about the *Dhamma* (the Doctrine) or keep nobly silent.'[4]

1. *Dhp.* 133. 2. *Jāt.* no. 269. 3. C. N. Bovee.
4. *M.* 26; *Ud.* p. 31.

The Buddha was very critical of idle chatter, scandal and rumour for they disturb serenity and concentration. 'Better than a thousand sentences—a mere jumble of meaningless words—is one sensible phrase on hearing which one is pacified.'[1]

A sage is sometimes called by the Pāli word *muni* which means one who keeps silent. Yes, 'silence is golden' so 'do not speak unless you are sure you can improve on silence'.

> 'Much talking is a source of danger,
> Through silence misfortune is avoided.
> The talkative parrot in a cage is shut,
> While birds that cannot talk fly freely.'[2]

'One does not become a wise man just by talking a lot;[3] neither is he versed in the doctrine (*Dhammadhara*) because he speaks much.'[4] And lest one should misunderstand the silence of the *muni*, the Buddha also says: 'To keep silent does not turn a foolish ignoramus into a sage (*muni*).'[5]

In conclusion let us listen to the discourse on 'Good Speech':[6]

> 'The good say: 1. Noble speech is apt;
> 2. Speak the *Dhamma*[7] not *a-dhamma*:
> 3. Say what is pleasant, not unpleasant;
> 4. Speak what is true, not lies.
> Speak only words that do not bring remorse
> Nor hurt another. That is good speech, indeed.
> Truth is immortal speech, it is an ancient law.
> In truth, weal and *Dhamma* the sages are established.
> The Buddha's words of peace to *Nibbāna* lead,
> To suffering's end. Such words are good indeed.'

1. *Dhp.* 100.
2. See *Tibetan Yoga and Secret Doctrine*, p. 61.
3. *Dhp.* 258.
4. *Dhp.* 259.
5. *Dhp.* 268.
6. *Subhāsita-sutta, Sn.*
7. *Dhamma* here implies speech full of meaning and free from gossip; *a-dhamma* is its opposite.

10

RIGHT ACTION

(*Sammā-kammanta*)

RIGHT action is the second member of the morality group in Buddhism. It is abstinence from three wrong actions: killing, stealing and sexual misconduct. As we discussed in the preceding chapter, it inculcates compassion to all living beings; the taking only of things that are given; and living a pure and chaste life. These then are the first three of the five basic precepts, the other two being abstinence from lying and intoxicants. Not much science is needed to understand that these basic training precepts, while moulding the character of the individual who observes them, promote harmony and right relations with oneself and others. By such moral conduct one gives others fearlessness, security and peace. All morality, or the good life, is founded on love and compassion, *mettā* and *karuṇā*, which we discussed at length in the chapter on Right Thought. A person without these two salient qualities cannot really be called a man of morals. Verbal and physical acts not tinged with love and compassion cannot be regarded as good and wholesome. Surely one cannot kill, steal and so forth with thoughts of love and a good conscience, but one is driven by thoughts of cruelty, greed and ignorance.

It is necessary to cultivate a certain measure of mental discipline, because the untamed mind always finds excuses to commit evil in word or deed. 'When the thought is unguarded, bodily action also is unguarded; so are speech and mental action.'[1]

Says the Buddha:

'A fool is known by his actions and so is a sage. By conduct is knowledge made bright.

'One endowed with three qualities should be known as a fool. With what three? With wrong bodily behaviour, wrong speech and

1. *A.* i. 261.

wrong thought. A fool should be known as one endowed with these three qualities.

'One endowed with three qualities should be known as a sage. With what three? With right bodily behaviour, right speech and right thought. A sage should be known as endowed with these three qualities

'So, monks, you should train yourselves thus: We shall live having given up the three things endowed with which a man is known as a fool, and shall practise three things endowed with which a man is known as a sage. Thus, monks, should you train yourselves.'[1]

Conduct builds character. No one can bestow the gift of a good character on another. Each one has to build it up by thought, reflection, care, effort, mindfulness and concentrated activity. Just as in the mastery of an art one has to labour hard, so to master the art of noble conduct on which a good and strong character depends, one must be diligent and on the alert. As William Hawes says: 'A good character is, in all cases, the fruit of personal exertion. It is not inherited from parents, it is not created by external advantages, it is no necessary appendage of birth, wealth, talents or station; but it is the result of one's own endeavours.' If we would acquire a sterling character we ought to remember the Buddha's words of warning against negligence and day-dreaming: 'Be vigilant, be ever mindful.'

In the training of character the first thing necessary is to practice restraint (*saṁyama*). If, instead, a man gives himself up to sense pleasures, his good conduct and character will fall away—on this all teachers of religion and psychology agree. Those who are intoxicated with pleasures and are driven by the urge to enjoy themselves, cannot be properly educated until they have learned to control their minds.

Restraint comes through reflection on virtue and its advantages. The young especially should develop a love of virtue, for it nourishes mental life. An unrestrained mind dissipates itself in frivolous activity. Character is something we have to build up, to forge on the anvil of our resolution.

The training precepts, however, are in no sense commandments. The Buddha was no arbitrary law-giver. There is no coercion or compulsion in Buddhism. The acceptance of the precepts by laymen or monk is voluntary.

1. *A.* i. 102.

It is interesting to see how the Buddha trained his disciples. Kesi, a horse-trainer, once visited the Blessed One, and the following dialogue ensued:

– You, Kesi, are a trained man, a trainer of horses to be tamed. How do you train a horse to be tamed.
– I train a horse to be tamed, venerable sir, by mild ways and harsh ways, also by both ways.
– Suppose, Kesi, a horse to be tamed, does not submit to your training, then what do you do with that horse?
– In such a case, venerable sir, I kill him. For what reason? Lest he bring discredit to my teacher's clan. Now, venerable sir, the Blessed One is a peerless trainer of men to be tamed. How, venerable sir, does the Blessed One train a person to be tamed?
– I too, Kesi, train a person to be tamed by mild ways and harsh ways, also by both ways. This, Kesi, is the mild way: Thus is good conduct in body; thus is the result of good conduct in body. Thus is good conduct in speech; thus is the result of good conduct in speech. Thus is good conduct in thought; thus is the result of good conduct in thought. Thus are the *devas* (deities) and thus are the humans.

And this, Kesi, is the harsh way: Thus is evil conduct in body; thus is the result of evil conduct in body. Thus is evil conduct in speech; thus is the result of evil conduct in speech. Thus is evil conduct in thought; thus is the result of evil conduct in thought. Thus is hell, thus the realm of animals, thus is the realm of the *petas* (ghosts).

And this, Kesi, is the way of both the mild and the harsh: . . . (as above) . . . .

– But suppose, the person does not submit to your way of training, then what do you, venerable sir, do to that person.
– In that case, Kesi, I kill him.
– But surely the Blessed One does not deprive another of his life! Nevertheless, the Blessed One says: 'I kill him, Kesi!'
– It is true, Kesi, that the Tathāgata does not deprive another of his life, nevertheless, if the person does not submit to the training by mild ways and harsh ways, and both ways, then the Tathāgata thinks that he needs not be spoken to and admonished by his fellow monks who are wise. It kills a man in the Āriyan Discipline, Kesi, when both the Tathāgata and his fellow monks think that he need not be spoken to and admonished.'[1]

1. *A.* ii. 111, *sutta* 111.

This dialogue clearly tells us that the Buddha did not believe in imposing commandments on his followers, but as a compassionate teacher he pointed out to them what was right and what was wrong and the consequences.

'I say: "Monks, do ye give up evil." Evil can be abandoned. If it were not possible to give up evil, I would not say so. Since it can be done, I say unto you: "Monks, do ye give up evil."

'If this giving up of evil led to loss and pain, I would not say: "Give up evil."

'Monks, do ye cultivate the good. Good can be cultivated. If it were not possible to cultivate good, I would not say so. Since it can be done, I say unto you: "Monks, do ye cultivate the good."

'If cultivation of the good led to loss and pain, I would not say: "Cultivate ye the good." But since it leads to welfare and happiness, therefore do I say: "Monks, do ye cultivate the good."'

It is left to the individual to make the necessary effort to translate into action the precepts he has undertaken voluntarily. The training administered and the support that others give by way of precept and example, are of no avail if he is indifferent and slothful. The responsibility lies in his own hand.

> 'According to the seed that's sown,
> So is the fruit ye reap therefrom.
> The doer of good (will gather) good,
> The doer of evil, evil (reaps).
> Sown is the seed and planted well.
> Thou shalt enjoy the fruit thereof.'[1]

1. The first precept to abstain from killing and to extend compassion to all beings does not entail any restriction. 'All beings', in Buddhism, implies all living creatures, all that breathe. It is an admitted fact that all that live, human or animal, love life and loathe death. As life is precious to all, their one aim is to preserve it from harm and to prolong it. This applies even to the smallest creatures that are conscious of being alive. As it is said: 'Whoever in his search for happiness harasses those who are fond of happiness, will not be happy in the hereafter.'[2]

1. *S.* i. 227: *The Kindred sayings*, I, p. 293.
2. *Dhp.* 131.

The happiness of all creatures depends on their being alive. So to deprive them of that which contains all good for them, is cruel and heartless in the extreme. Is it therefore surprising that those who would kill others bring on themselves the hate and ill-will of those they seek to slay?

'All fear punishment,
Life is dear to all;
Comparing one with others
Kill not nor cause to perish.[1]

'As I am so are they
As they are so am I;
Comparing one with others
Neither slay nor cause to kill.'[2]

Not to harm and kill others is the criterion of a Buddhist and of all who feel. Those who develop the habit of being cruel to animals are quite capable of ill treating people as well when the opportunity occurs. When a cruel thought gradually develops into an obsession it may well lead to sadism. As the Buddhist books point out: 'Those who kill suffer often in this life and may come to a terrible end. After this life the *karma* of their ruthless deeds will for long force them into states of woe. Should such destroyers of life be born in prosperous families with beauty and strength and other happy bodily attributes, still their *karma* will dog them to an early grave.'

On the other hand: 'Those who show pity towards others and refrain from killing will be born in good states of existence and if reborn as humans, will be endowed with health, beauty, riches, influence, intelligence, etc.'[3]

Right Action—*sammā-kammanta* is no other than *sammā-kamma*. The doctrine of *kamma* is one of the principal tenets of Buddhism. It is our own volitional actions that we call *kamma*. If one understands the operation of *kamma* and the result of volitional acts (*kamma-vipāka*) one may not be tempted to evil and unwholesome actions which will come home to roost so that 'suffering follows as the wheel the feet of the ox'.

It is interesting to note that during the last few years investiga-

1. *Dhp*. 130.
2. *Sn*. 705.
3. See *A*. iii. 40 and *M*. 135 (*Cūlakammavibhaṅga-sutta*).

tions have been made into *karma* and rebirth. Many convincing accounts can be found in two most interesting books by Miss Gina Cerminara. Here is an extract from her *Many Mansions* (p. 50).[1]

'The Cayce life readings are fascinating because they trace human affliction and limitations of the present to specific conduct in the past and thus bring the abstract notion of karma into sharper and more immediate focus. . . . A College professor who had been born totally blind, heard about Cayce . . . and applied for a physical reading . . . which outlined four previous incarnations. . . . It was in Persia that he had set in motion the spiritual law which resulted in his blindness in the present. He had been a member of a barbaric tribe whose custom was to blind their enemies with red-hot irons and it had been his office to do the blinding.'

Yes, the world seems to be imperfect and ill-balanced. Amongst us human beings, let alone the animal kingdom, we see some born in misery, sunk in deep distress and supremely unhappy; others are born into a state of abundance and happiness, enjoy a life of luxury and know nothing of the world's woe. Again a chosen few are gifted with keen intellect and great mental capacity, while many are wrapt in ignorance. How is it that some of us are blessed with health, beauty and friends, while others are pitiful weaklings, destitute and lonely? How is it that some are born to enjoy long life while others pass away in the full bloom of youth? Why are some blessed with affluence, fame and recognition, while others are utterly neglected? These are intricate problems that demand a solution.

If we inquire we will find that these wide differences are not the work of an external agency or a superhuman being, but are due to our own actions and reactions, so that we are responsible for our deeds whether good or ill. We make our own *karma*.

Thus it is incumbent on all men of understanding to stop hurting and harming others and to cultivate a boundless heart full of pity and benevolence. Killing is killing whether done for sport, or food or—as in the case of insects—for health. It is useless to try to defend oneself by saying 'I did it for this good reason or that'. It is better to call a spade a spade. If we kill we must be frank enough to admit it and regard it as something unwholesome.

Then, with regard to the vexed question of vegetarianism, meat

1. *Many Mansions; The World Within* by Gina Cerminara (William Sloane Associates, Inc. New York, 1950).

eating is not prohibited in Buddhism. If you have neither seen, heard, nor suspect that an animal was killed especially for you, then its meat is acceptable, but not otherwise. There is no rule or injunction in the teaching of the Buddha that a Buddhist should live wholly or even principally on vegetables. Whether or not meat is eaten is purely an individual concern, but those who consume fertilized eggs, however, break the first precept.

2. The second training precept under Right Action is to abstain from stealing and to live honestly taking only what is one's own by right. To take what belongs to another is not so serious as to deprive him of his life, but it is still a grave crime because it deprives him of some happiness. As no one wants to be robbed, it is not difficult to understand that it is wrong to take what is not one's own. The thought that urges a person to steal can never be good or wholesome. Then robbery leads to violence and even to murder.

This precept is easily violated by those in trade and commerce, for all kinds of fraud and dishonesty come under the second precept. A man can use both his pen and his tongue with intent to steal. There can be no peace or happiness in a society where people are always on the look-out to cheat and rob their neighbours.

Sometimes it is thought that poverty leads to theft. There is some truth in it, but if people are lazy and workshy, or if they misuse their talents, they become poor. They are then tempted to rob the rich, while others may consider theft an easy means to living a gay life. And so crime increases. It is the duty of governments to reduce poverty by removing unemployment.

Theft may take many forms. For instance, if an employee slacks or works badly and yet is paid in full, he is really a thief, for he takes money he has not earned. And the same applies to the employer if he fails to pay adequate wages. So, as Carlyle said: 'Make yourself an honest man, and then you may be sure that there is one less rascal in the world.'

3. The final training precept here of Right Action is to abstain from wrong sexual behaviour. What is needed is more self-control rather than sermons and books on the subject. In the chapter on Right Thought we discussed at length sense indulgence with reference to renunciation. Here we shall try to understand in brief what, according to Buddhism, sexual wrong is. Let us first listen to the opening discourse of the *Aṅguttara Nikāya*, another original collection in Pāli:

'Monks, I know not of any other single form by which a man's heart is attracted as it is by that of a woman. Monks, a woman's form fills a man's mind.

'Monks, I know not of any other single sound. . . .
I know not of any other single smell. . . .
I know not of any other single flavour. . . .
I know not of any other single touch . . . by which a man's heart is attracted as it is by that of a woman. A woman's sound, smell, flavour, and touch fill a man's mind.

'Monks, I know not of any other single form, sound, smell, flavour and touch by which a woman's heart is attracted as it is by the form, sound smell, flavour and touch of a man. Monks, a woman's mind is filled with these things.'

Here is a sermon on sex explained in unmistakable language, the truth of which no sane man dare deny. Sex is described by the Buddha as the strongest impulse in man. If one becomes a slave to this impulse even the most powerful man may turn into a weakling; even the sage may fall from the higher to a lower level. The sexual urge, especially in youth, is a fire that needs careful handling. If one is not thoughtful and restrained, it can cause untold harm. 'There is no fire like lust.'[1] 'Passions do not die out: they burn out.'

Since the Buddha was a practical philosopher he did not expect his lay followers to lead ascetic lives. Indeed, he called them 'enjoyers of sense pleasures' (*gihī kāmabhogī*). Being well aware of man's instincts and impulses, his appetites and urges, the Master did not prohibit sexual relations for the laity as he had done for monks. But he warned man against wrong ways of gratifying the sexual appetite. He went a step further and recommended the observation of the eight precepts[2] with special emphasis on the third one for the laity during days of retreat (*uposatha*) or as the occasion demanded.

If a person makes up his mind to live an unmarried life he should make a real effort to be chaste in body, speech and thought. If he is not strong enough to remain single, he may marry, but he should refrain from such sexual relations as are wrong and harmful. As the Buddha explains in the discourse on 'Downfall':[3]

'If a person is addicted to women (given to a life of debauchery), is a drunkard, a gambler, and squanders all his earnings—this is a cause of his downfall.

1. *Dhp.* 262. 2. See above, p. 133.
3. *Parābhava-sutta, Sn.* 16, 18, 20.

'Not satisfied with one's own wives, if one has been with whores and the wives of others—this is a cause of one's downfall.

'Being past one's youth, to take as wife a girl in her teens, and to be unable to sleep for jealousy—this is a cause of one's downfall.'

Speaking of women the Buddha says tersely: 'Loose or immoral behaviour is the taint of a woman.'[1] 'Best among wives is she that pleases the husband.'[2] 'The wife is the comrade supreme.'[3] Goldsmith writes: 'The perfect wife is much more serviceable in life than petticoated philosophers, blustering heroines, or virago queens. She who makes her husband and her children happy is a much greater character than the ladies described in romance whose whole occupation is to murder mankind with shafts.'

Bhikkhu Sīlācara (Mr. McKechnie) writing on the third precept says:

'At every moment it is our minds that make us what we are. And in this matter of sex, mind plays a very important part; indeed, we might say that if the mind were completely under our control here, there would be little or no need for vigilance elsewhere.

'If we look about us we can see to what a pass lack of mental control in this matter of sex has brought the human race. Consider the "lower animals" as we are pleased to call them, and their sexual behaviour. Which really is lower here, the animal, or the man? Which acts in a normal, regular manner as regards sexual behaviour? And which runs off into all manner of irregularities and perversities? Here it is the animal that is the higher creature, and man that is the lower. And why is this? It is simply because man who possesses the mental capacity which, rightly used, could make him master over his sexual impulsions, has actually used his mental powers in such deplorable passion as to make himself more a slave to those impulsions than are the animals.'[4]

The Buddha's explanation of the third precept in the forty-first discourse of the *Majjhima Nikāya* and elsewhere, is interesting and important. The discourse deals with all the ten wholesome and unwholesome actions. What follows is a slightly condensed version of it.

Answering a question of the brahmin householders of Sāla as to why some beings after their death are born in an evil and others in a good state of existence, the Master said: 'Householders, some beings

1. *Dhp.* 242. 2. *S.* p. 7. 3. *S.* i. 37.
4. *The Five Precepts* (Colombo).

after death go to a state of woe owing to their not having lived a life of *Dhamma*, a life of righteousness, and harmony.'

Now when the brahmins did not fully understand what the Buddha said and asked him to explain in detail, the Master replied:

'Householders, some are cruel and merciless to living beings. Some take what is not given. Some abuse the pleasures of the senses, having sexual relations with those (virgins) protected by a mother, father, parents, a brother, sister or relations, with those who have a husband, with those whose use (in this way) deserves punishment and even with those who are engaged.'[1]

Such, householders, is the threefold practice of *a-dhamma*, of unrighteousness and disharmony in regard to the body.

The Buddha went on to describe the fourfold practice of *a-dhamma* in speech, namely lying, slandering, harsh words and idle chatter. He then said:

'Householders, some are covetous; they covet another's property thinking: "O that what belongs to others might be mine"; some are malevolent, polluted in mind, and think: "let these beings be killed, slaughtered, annihilated or destroyed, or let them not even live"; and some are of wrong view, of perverted outlook and think: "There is no (result) from gifts and offerings; no result from deeds well or ill done; there is neither this world nor a world beyond. (To those in the world beyond there is not this world, to those here, there is not a world beyond, *Com.*) There is no (result from good or bad behaviour to) mother and father; there are no beings who spontaneously arise (this denies the existence of *devas* or deities); there are no recluses and brahmins who are of good conduct, who live righteously and proclaim this world and the world beyond, having realized super-knowledge (this denies the existence of omniscient Buddhas)." Such, householders, is the three-fold practice of *a-dhamma*, of unrighteousness and disharmony in regard to thought.'

Then the Buddha went on to explain the threefold practice of *Dhamma*, of righteousness and harmony in regard to body, speech and thought—the opposite of all that is mentioned above.

It is good to bear in mind that as a religious teacher, the Buddha pointed out to Indian society the right and wrong way in ethics and

1. Lit. 'adorned with the garland of engagement'.

morals, and the evil consequences of immoral and loose behaviour, but he never interfered in sexual matters, neither did he meddle with institutions or policies because these were the concern of a government. In his own kingdom, that is in his Dispensation, however, the attitude of the Buddha was different; at times he was strict with his disciples. As guide and teacher, he often advised the members of the Order to be of good conduct, seeing terror even in minute faults, and to be decent, quiet and modest so that the displeased might have pleasure and the happiness of those who were already pleased might be increased.[1]

To those who joined him and entered the Order to lead an ascetic life, the Buddha gave special admonition. To the monks, sexual relations of any kind are forbidden, with good reason. But a monk is at liberty to put away the robes and return to lay life if that of a monk is too trying, and he finds it hard to delight in renunciation. In such cases the Master gave advice and explained things like an affectionate father, but never compelled his followers to lead the ascetic life against their wishes because these are psychological problems and must be so treated. One of the benefits obtained from meditation and other practices recommended by the Buddha to the members of the Order, is for the purpose of sublimation—the elimination of pathological conditions that may spring up as a result of abstinence from indulging in the senses.

Two verses in the *Dhammapada* (246, 247) enumerate the training precepts and in a word make plain the evil consequence of their violation:

'Whoever in this world takes life,
Speaks what is not truth,
Takes what is not given,
Goes to other's wives,

Indulges in drinking
Intoxicating liquors,
He even in this world
Digs up his own root.'[2]

In this and in the preceding chapter we have discussed in detail the five precepts (*pañca-sīla*), the minimum moral obligation

1. *Vinaya; A.* iii. 67.
2. Of prosperity and happiness.

expected of a layman who becomes a Buddhist by taking as his refuges the Buddha, the *Dhamma* and the *Saṅgha.*[1] In conclusion, it may not be out of place to mention briefly the advice given by the Buddha to little Rāhula, the novice, who was his own son:

- What do you think, Rāhula, for what purpose is a mirror?
- For the purpose of reflecting, venerable sir.
- Even, so, Rāhula, after repeated reflection should bodily actions be done; after repeated reflection should verbal and mental actions be done.

Then the Buddha goes on to say that if, on reflection, one realizes that a bodily act tends to harm oneself, others or both then it is unwholesome and productive of pain, and should on no account be performed. If on reflection one realizes that a bodily act tends to harm neither oneself, nor others nor both it is wholesome and productive of happiness, and should be performed. Similarly with regard to one's verbal and mental actions.

Continuing the Master says:

'Whosoever, Rāhula, in the distant past—recluses or brāhmaṇas—purified their bodily, verbal and mental actions—they all did so after repeated reflection. Whosoever, in the distant future—recluses or brāhmaṇas—shall purify their bodily, verbal and mental actions—they all too, will do so after repeated reflection. And whosoever, in the present time—recluses or brāhmaṇas—purify their bodily, verbal and mental actions—they all do so after repeated reflection.

'Therefore, Rāhula, thus must you train yourself: "We will purify bodily action after repeated reflection; we will purify verbal action after repeated reflection: we will purify mental action after repeated reflection"—thus must you train yourself, Rāhula.'[2]

The careful reader of this condensed account of the discourse will understand how well the Buddha brings out the psychological importance of man's actions, his *karma*, which in the ultimate sense is volition or *cetanā* and the Buddhist view of self and others. 'As I am, so are they' is the criterion to be adopted in all we do.

The tendency in man to give way to his desires, his longings and inclinations, is very strong. But too often he does not reflect enough

1. See p. 20. 2. *M.* 61.

before taking action, so that the results turn out to be not what he intended. In this discourse, reflection, thinking arising from meditation, is stressed by the Master. The advice to Rāhula, the novice, though given twenty-five centuries ago, is indeed apt today. Space and time are no impediment to good counsel when it embodies eternal principles.

11

RIGHT LIVELIHOOD

(Sammā-ājīva)

THE third and the last member of the morality group is right livelihood which entails not dealing in arms and lethal weapons, animals for slaughter, human beings, intoxicating drinks, and poison. Though the Buddha mentioned only these five, there are, as we know, many other wrong ways of earning a living. We must bear in mind that the Buddha was addressing Indian society in the sixth century B.C., which consisted for the most part, even as it does today, of farmers, herdsmen and traders. It is interesting to note that there are, in the Buddhist Canon, sections which graphically depict the life of the farmer and the herdsman. The second and fourth discourses of the *Sutta-nipāta* (Discourse Collection, The Harvard Oriental Series, vol. 37) bear ample testimony to this fact. India was an agricultural land and its government was not 'democratic'. Most of the states were feudal being under a rājā as in the case of the Buddha's own clan, the Sākyans, but there were also republics such as that of the Licchavīs which were governed by a senate of elders and leading men. In the kingdoms, the rājā was the ruler to whom all were subservient and owed their allegiance. Life seems to have been quiet compared with that in many lands today. Since the ways of earning a living were limited, the Buddha only warned against five of them.

We must not think that the Buddha spoke only to the common people on the evil consequences of wrong and the advantages of right living. In the *Nikāyas*, notably in the *Dīgha* and *Aṅguttara*, we find sermons on the life that the ruler or administrator ought to lead. It is stated categorically that the king should rule righteously (*dhammena*) and not unrighteously (*a-dhammena*). Rulers in addition to keeping the same precepts as their subjects were expected to possess all the wholesome qualities that go to make a good head of the state. The Buddhist books mention Ten Duties or Principles of a king (*dasa-rājā-dhamma*): Generosity in giving, morality, self-sacrifice or unselfishness, honesty, gentleness, not being given to luxurious living, self-restraint, no anger, no violence, patience and agreeability.[1] As the Buddha points out, it is the ruler who should first establish himself in *Dhamma*, in piety and righteousness, avoiding the vices, and so give the lead to his subjects. He says: 'If he who is reckoned best among men does not live righteously, need we speak of the others? They will follow suit. If the rājā is unrighteous the whole realm lives in woe. . . . If he lives aright, the others emulate him and the whole realm lives in happiness.'[2]

Never resting on his laurels, the king or ruler is expected to be kind and dutiful to his subjects: 'like a benevolent father to his children'.[3] The king given to self-indulgence, and intoxicated with the thought of authority (*issariyamadamatta*), is not praised, but looked down upon.[4] In order to be just, honest and upright to all, without partiality or favouritism, the ruler is expected to avoid the four wrong ways of treating people: that is with desire, anger, fear and delusion.[5]

In this respect, Asoka the Great of India, who, because of his exemplary life, later became known as *Dhammāsoka*, or Asoka the Righteous, may be regarded as one of the most just, wise and benevolent rulers of all time. This is shown by his edicts:

'All men are my children.'

'Just as I want my own children to enjoy all prosperity and happiness in this life and the next, so I want the same for all men.'

'The world should be comforted by me. From me the world should receive happiness not sorrow.'[6]

'There is no duty higher than to promote the happiness of the whole world.'

'Work I must for the good of the whole world.'[7]

It can be said without a trace of doubt that King Asoka, who followed the advice of the Buddha for the righteous administration of a country, was a model ruler and, as H. G. Wells wrote: 'amidst

1. *Dāna, sīla, pariccāga, ajjava, maddava, tapa, akkodha, avihiṁsā, khanti, avirodha. Jāt.* I, 260.
2. *A.* ii. 74. 3. *D.* ii. 178. 4. *S.* i. 100.
5. *Chanda, dosa, bhaya, moha.* These four are called *agati* or wrong ways of treating people.
6 *Edict* I. 7. *Edict* II.

the tens of thousands of monarchs . . . that crowd the columns of history the name of Asoka shines, and shines almost alone, a star'.[1]

That was twenty-three centuries ago. Since then things seem to have changed for the worse and people to care less and less for the welfare of their fellows. They do not hesitate to use any means to grab the things they crave for even to the extent of depriving others of life itself.

'In this modern world right livelihood can be one of the most difficult rules to obey. So many kinds of work are harmful to society and are unworthy of a true Buddhist. There are the arms and nuclear warfare industries; the drink trade; occupations involving the slaughter or vivisection of animals; yellow journalism; dishonest advertising and publicity; and business that includes usury. Buddhism is not a narrow-minded religion. It regards human frailties with understanding and sympathy. Yet the sincere Buddhist cannot profess one code of morality and earn his livelihood in an occupation with another, debased code.'[2]

The precept about right livelihood was designed to bring true happiness to the individual and society and to promote unity and proper relations among people. Unjust and wrong ways of living apply to individuals, families and nations. A wrong and unrighteous way of life brings in its train much unhappiness, disharmony and trouble to the whole society. When a person or community succumbs to the evil of exploiting others, it interferes with the peace and harmony of society. It is sheer selfishness and greed that prompt a man to adopt wrong and unlawful ways of life. Such folk are utterly indifferent to the loss and pain caused to their neighbours and to society. Therefore says the Buddha: 'Neither for one's own nor for others' sake should one do any evil. One should not covet a son, wealth or a kingdom, nor wish to succeed by unjust means. Such a man is indeed virtuous, wise and righteous.'[3]

The Buddha was not unaware of the burdens borne by a layman with a wife and children, hence he did not expect from him the same ethical conduct as he did from the monks. But he emphatically stressed that the layman should strive hard to observe at least the five training precepts, the minimum moral obligation of the ordinary person, and that he should try to earn a living by right means, by

1. *The Outline of History* (Cassell & Co., London, 1934), p. 402.
2. *Mind Unshaken*, John Walters (Rider and Company, 1961), p. 47.
3. *Dhp*. 84.

right conduct (*dhamma-cariyā*) and thereby support his wife and children. What is earned by unjust and unrighteous means—by killing, stealing, cheating, through dishonesty and deceit, cannot be regarded as right living. Ethically it is unrighteous living (*a-dhamma-cariyā*), an uneven life, a life of disharmony (*visama-cariyā*).

The Buddha does not disparage the layman, but sympathizes with his frailties and shortcomings. Society after all consists not only of ascetics and recluses who have left home to be homeless, but of lay men and women who form the bulk of society, which ultimately is an assemblage of 'sociological units' so that the welfare or ill-fare of society depends on the individuals. If the individuals are good and lead a decent life, society naturally cannot be bad.

Some of the discourses like *Sigāla-sutta*[1] which is rightly called the layman's code of discipline (*gihi-vinaya*), *Vyagghapajja-sutta*,[2] etc., given by the Buddha especially for the laity, clearly show the Master's concern for both the material welfare and spiritual development of his lay disciples. In the discourse to young Sigāla the Master explains in plain language the full duties of a layman to all with whom he has relations: The reciprocal duties of parents and children; teacher and pupil; husband and wife; friends and relatives; master and servant; and duty to the religious, that is to recluses and brahmins. In this way the Buddha encourages the layman to live a righteous life, doing his duty to the best of his ability and leaving nothing undone.

Mrs. C. A. F. Rhys Davids, commenting on the *Sigāla-sutta*, says:

'The Buddha's doctrine of love and good-will between man and man is here set forth in a domestic and social ethics with more comprehensive detail than elsewhere. . . . And truly we may say even now of this Vinaya, or code of discipline, so fundamental are the human interests involved, so sane and wide is the wisdom that envisages them, that the utterances are as fresh and practically as binding today and here as they were then at Rājagaha. "Happy would have been the village or the clan on the banks of the Ganges, where the people were full of the kindly spirit of fellow-feeling, the noble spirit of justice which breathes through these naïve and simple sayings."[3] Not less happy would be the village or the family on the banks of the Thames today, of which this could be said.'[4]

1. *D.* 31. 2. *A.* ii.
3. T. W. Rhys Davids, *Buddhism* (London, 1907), p. 148.
4. *Dialogues of the Buddha*, part iii, p. 168.

As we well know, after attaining full enlightenment the Buddha did not all the time confine himself to a cell, but wandered from town to town and village to village through the highways and byways of India. He moved more with the commoner than with the aristocrat. Kings and princes came to him for guidance and instruction, but the Master went to the poor, lowly and lost to help them. He knew the people, from the lowliest walks of life to the highest, and was well aware of the political, social and economic conditions of India during his time. That being so he did not restrict his sermons and discussions to matters of high philosophy and advanced psychology. As a practical teacher of infinite compassion and understanding he was mindful of the social and economic wellbeing of the masses and always wished by his advice to alleviate the misery of people, and see that they lived without too much unhappiness. It is true that real happiness is derived from a life of purity and peace; but it is obvious that without a certain degree of material and economic security no moral and spiritual progress can be achieved.

So far as a monk is concerned there are four requisites (*catu paccaya*) for progress on the path to purity and freedom. They are robes, food, a lodging and medicine. These are the bare necessities without which no human being can live. Basically they are also the fundamental needs of a layman.

It was the Buddha's custom to ask the monks on meeting them: 'How is it with you; how are you faring? I trust you are well, and that you are not short of food.'[1] There is the touching tale[2] of a herdsman who in looking for a lost ox, missed his midday meal. On his way back, fatigued and hungry, he went to the Buddha to listen to him preaching. The Blessed One however, knowing that the man had not eaten all day, inquired from the people if he could first be fed. The Buddha knew that it was profitless to preach to any man without first satisfying his hunger. It was on that occasion that the Master said:

> 'Hunger is the greatest malady,
> The aggregates are the greatest ill,
> Knowing this as it is (the wise know)
> *Nibbāna*, the bliss supreme.'[3]

Although the Buddha did not attach much importance to material

1. *M.* 31, *A.* i. 70 and passim. See above p. 116.
2. *Dhp. Com.*
3. *Dhp.* 203.

progress in the modern sense, nor to mundane welfare, he did not entirely ignore it, because it is the basis for man's mental or spiritual progress as pointed out above. So the Buddha was very outspoken with regard to certain aspects of material conditions and social welfare.

It is an admitted fact that poverty is the main cause of crime. If people are deprived of the four requisites mentioned above, the bare necessities, or if these are scarce, especially food, people's minds are not at rest. They cannot and do not think of moral behaviour, or give a thought to righteous living. Necessity has no law, and they stoop to unjust and unrighteous ways of gaining a subsistence. Owing to lack of economic security, and of money, people are led to commit theft and other crimes. The *Kūṭadanta-sutta*[1] states how in order to raise the social and economic conditions of a country, the farmers and traders should be given the necessary facilities to carry on their farming and business, and that people should be paid adequate wages. Thus when they have enough for their subsistence and are economically secure, crime is lessened and peace and harmony prevail.

In another discourse the Buddha explains to Anāthapiṇḍika, the banker who founded for him the Jetavana monastery, the four kinds of happiness a layman ought to enjoy. The first is ownership, or economic security, so that he has sufficient means (*atthi-sukha*) acquired lawfully by his own efforts, without resorting to the five trades detailed above; the second is the joy of wealth (*bhoga-sukha*) or happiness gained by the judicious expenditure of lawful wealth; the third is the bliss of not being in debt (*aṇana-sukha*), the joy and satisfaction that comes with the thought: 'I owe nothing to anyone'; the fourth is the bliss of being without blame (*anavajja-sukha*), which is the satisfaction derived from the thought: 'I am blessed with blameless acts of body, speech and mind.'[2]

All these discussions and sermons in Buddhism go to show that the layman as a member of society should work hard to earn a living and strengthen his economic and social position lest he becomes a burden to himself and others, but at the same time he should avoid wrong and unrighteous ways of living and not deviate from the path of duty and rectitude.

The Buddha's instructions and advice on right livelihood are addressed both to the layman and to the members of the *Sangha.* He has clearly explained to his disciples that the monk's life should

1. *D.* 5. 2. *A.* ii. 69, *sutta* 62.

be absolutely pure and free from fraud. The Master is indeed very emphatic on this matter, for he says:

'Monks, whatsoever monks are cheats, stubborn, babblers, cunning, passionate, proud, uncalmed—such monks are no followers of mine. They have fallen away from this *Dhamma-vinaya* (Doctrine and Discipline), nor do they grow, increase and prosper in this *Dhamma-vinaya*.'[1] Further says the Master: 'Monks, this holy life (*brahmacariyaṁ*) is lived neither to cheat people nor for scheming, nor for profit and favour, nor for the sake of honour. It is not for gossiping and prattling, nor with the intention: "let people know me as so-and-so." But, monks, this holy life is lived for the sake of restraint, for abandoning, for dispassion, for cessation.'[2]

As the discourse on 'Going Forth'[3] points out, the Buddha himself gives the lead and example to his disciples when he says:

'Leaving home I gave up
All evil words and acts,
Pure was my livelihood.'

The question of abstention from the five kinds of wrong trades does not arise in the case of the monk, for he should not be in business, and he has not the responsibility and care of a family life. He has left home and is simple in his ways, with few wants. As the Buddha says, it is the duty of the devout layman to provide him with the four requisites: Robes, food, lodging and medicine.[4]

The monk, as one who has entered upon the holy life, should avoid all wrong means of living, for if he is not clean and pure in this he cannot follow the path of purification with any degree of confidence and satisfaction. Hence the Buddha says:

'Verily one path is for gain, but that which leads to *Nibbāna* is quite another. Let the monks, the disciples of the Buddha, having understood it thus, not delight in worldly favours and honours, but cultivate detachment.'[5]

With this chapter we close the discussion on the Morality (*sīla*) Group of the Noble Eightfold Path. In the two immediately preceding chapters we dealt with Right Speech and Right Action which with Right Livelihood form the Buddhist Moral Code or Ethics. This fact is again made clear in a succinct statement of the Buddha in the seventy-eighth discourse of the *Majjhima Nikāya*:

1. *A.* ii. 26, *sutta* 25.
2. *A.* ii. 26, *sutta* 26.
3. *Pabbajjā-sutta*, sn. v. 407
4. *A.* ii. 65, *sutta* 60.
5. *Dhp.* 75.

'Which, householder, are the wholesome moral habits (*kusalasīlaṁ*)? Wholesome deeds of body; wholesome deeds of speech; and, I declare that included in moral habits, is complete purity of livelihood. These are called wholesome moral courses. And what is the origin of these courses? . . . It is in the mind (thought, *citta*). . . . Which mind? For there are many different minds (thoughts). That mind (thought) which is free from attachment, anger and delusion. From this are the wholesome Moral Courses derived. . . .'

Words and acts are thoughts manifested. In Buddhism both motive and effect should be taken into consideration. However good the motive may be, if the effect is not going to be healthy, we should refrain from such misguided words and deeds.

12

RIGHT EFFORT

(*Sammā-vāyāma*)

MODERN man is involved in much more rush and tension than in the past. His expression, speech and movements seldom show calm or relaxation. If you stand at the corner of a busy street and scan the faces of the people hurrying feverishly by, you will notice that many of them are restless. They carry with them an atmosphere of stress, are mentally disturbed and not calm. Is it wrong to say that this rush and tension are mainly due to modern civilization? When the external world is so busy, man's 'world within' also tends to be restless so that his inner calm and peace are lost. He seems to seek happiness outside instead of inside himself, but happiness does not depend on the external world, on modern civilization. Yet history has proved again and again, and will continue to prove, that nothing in this world is lasting. Nations and civilizations rise, flourish and die away, and thus the scrolls of time record the passing pageant, the baseless vision and the fading flow that is human history. Man has brought the external world under his sway, while science and technology seem to promise that they can turn this world into a paradise. But man cannot yet control his mind, he is no better for all his scientific progress.

Man is born with impulses that make him swerve from the path of peace and rectitude, and modern civilization stimulates many of these impulses strongly. As the Buddha says:

'All is burning, all is in flames. And what is the "all" that is in flames, that is burning? The eye is burning. Visible objects are burning. Eye-consciousness is burning. Eye-contact is burning. Feeling whether pleasant or painful or neither pleasant nor painful that arises with eye-contact as its condition, that too is burning.

'With what are they burning? With the fire of craving, with the fire of hate, with the fire of delusion. They are burning with birth, ageing and death, with sorrow, lamentation, pain, grief and woe. Similarly,

'The ear is burning. . . .
The nose is burning. . . .
The tongue is burning. . . .
The body is burning. . . .

'The mind is burning. . . . Mental objects are burning. Mind-consciousness is burning. Mind-contact is burning. Feeling . . . is burning. . . .

'Seeing thus the wise become dispassionate towards the eye, visible objects, eye-consciousness, eye-contact and feeling . . . become dispassionate towards ear, nose, tongue, body and the mind; become dispassionate towards mental objects, mind-consciousness, mind-contact and feeling. . . . Through dispassion greed fades away. With the fading away of greed, his mind is liberated. When his mind is liberated, there comes the knowledge that it is liberated. . . .'[1]

A fire keeps burning so long as there is fuel. The more fuel we add, the more it burns. It is the same with the fire of life. We keep on feeding our senses to satisfy their appetite. It is true that our senses need food, that they should not starve, but it is vital to give them the proper food and to lessen the greed of each sense faculty. Unless this is done there will be no control of conflicts, no harmony and peace of mind. If we want mental progress we must make the necessary effort to guard our thoughts; for evil thoughts are ever ready to creep in and overwhelm the lazy man. As the *Dhammapada* says: 'The man who lives brooding over pleasures, unrestrained in the senses, immoderate in food, lazy and inert—him verily *Māra*[2] overthrows as wind a weak tree.'[3]

The control of thoughts and senses is not easy. It is hard to deprive the mind of unwholesome thoughts, to check evil inclinations and curb impulses, but we must do this difficult thing if we wish to ease the tension and the mental itch that is ever ready to sap the mind until man and mind are destroyed.

Like the tortoise that promptly draws in all its limbs on sensing

1. *Vinaya Mahāvagga, khandaka.*

2. The word *Māra* is used in the sense of passions (*kilesa*). *Māra* often implies the Buddhist personification of all that is evil; i.e. all that bind man to the round of existence.

3. *Dhp.* 7.

danger, so should the sage try to guard and control his sense doors and sexual appetite.

But how does a person control his senses? Is it by shutting his eyes and ears, by not sensing the sense objects? Certainly not. The Buddha once talked with a certain brahmin youth, Uttara, a pupil of Pārāsariya:

– Uttara, does Pārāsariya, the brahmin, teach control of (lit. the development of) the senses[1] to his disciples?
– Good Gotama, the brahmin Pārāsariya does teach control of the senses to his disciples.
– But in what way does Pārāsariya, the brahmin, teach control of the senses to his disciples?
– As to this, good Gotama, one should not see material form with the eye, nor hear sounds with the ear. It is thus, good Gotama, that the brahmin Pārāsariya teaches control of the senses, to his disciples.
– In that case, Uttara, the blind and the deaf must have controlled their senses. For a blind man, Uttara, does not see material form with his eyes, nor a deaf man hear a sound with his ears.

The brahmin youth was silent, and knowing this the Master said to the Venerable Ānanda:

'In one way, Ānanda, does the brahmin Pārāsariya teach control of the senses. In the noble (*ariya*) discipline, however, Ānanda, the incomparable control of the senses (is taught) differently.

'And what, Ānanda, is the incomparable control of the senses? Herein, Ānanda, to a monk seeing form with the eye, there arises liking and disliking, and both liking and disliking. He knows thus: "Arisen in me has liking and disliking, and both liking and disliking. That too is conditioned, gross and causally dependent. But whatever equanimity there is, that is peaceful and sublime." So the liking and disliking and both the liking and disliking that arose in him are extinguished and equanimity remains. As if a man who has opened his eyes should close, or having closed should open them, even so with the same speed and ease do the liking and disliking and both the liking and disliking vanish, so that equanimity remains.

1. *Indriya-bhāvanaṁ.*

'Hearing a sound with the ear. . . .

Smelling an odour with the nose. . . .

Tasting a flavour with the tongue. . . .

Feeling some tangible thing with the body. . . .

Cognizing a mental object with the mind there arise (in him) liking and disliking and both liking and disliking . . . (as before) . . . and equanimity remains.'[1]

The mental force that plays the greatest havoc today is *taṇhā,* the strong, excessive greed which is ever driven by ignorance. This lust, this thirst of blinded beings, has caused hatred and all other suffering. It is not nuclear weapons but lust, hatred and delusion that are most destructive to man. Bombs and weapons are created by his lust to conquer and possess, by his hatred that leads to killing, by his delusion both to conquer and destroy. The thirst for fame, power and domination has brought untold agony to mankind. If man makes no effort to check the longings that are ever ready to sway his mind, he will become a slave to that mind. He is then no longer superior to the beast, for they both eat, sleep and satisfy their sexual appetite. The beast cannot, however, develop spiritually, but man is otherwise. He possesses latent qualities which can be developed, brought to the conscious level and used for his own and others' welfare. If a man lacks this quality of examining his own mind, of developing wholesome thoughts and discarding repulsive ones, his life lacks drive and inspiration. Hence the Buddha's constant advice to his followers to be vigilant and alert in controlling evil thoughts and cultivating healthy ones.

'Arise! Sit up! Train yourself strenuously for peace of mind.'[2]

'This doctrine, monks, is for the energetic, strong and firm in purpose, and not for the indolent.'[3]

'Monks, what is there that the sincerely zealous cannot achieve?'

'Verily, let skin, sinews and bones remain; let flesh and blood in the body dry up; yet shall there be no decrease of energy till that which is to be won by manly strength, energy and effort is attained.'[4]

Thus did the Buddha rouse his disciples to action.

The verses of the Elder Abhibhū, later approved by the Buddha, give great encouragement and strength to strivers:

1. *M.* 152. 2. *Sn.* 332. 3. *A.* iv. 234. 4. *M.* 70. I. 481.

'Bestir yourselves and make an effort,
Work hard in the Dispensation;
(Then) sweep away the hosts of *Māra* (the passions),
As an elephant a reed-thatched shed.

'Whoso in this Doctrine and Discipline
Shall live in vigilance and heedfulness
Repeated rebirth renounces
And puts an end to suffering.'[1]

Effort (*vāyāma*) in Buddhism implies mental energy and not physical strength. The latter is dominant in animals whereas mental energy is so in man, who must stir up and develop this mental factor in order to check evil and cultivate healthy thoughts. A follower of the Buddha should never give up hope or cease to make an effort, for even as a Bodhisatta the Buddha never ceased to strive courageously. He was the very picture of energy (*vīra*). As an aspirant for Buddhahood he was inspired by the words of his predecessors: 'Be ye full of zealous effort. Falter not! Advance!'[2] And in his endeavour to gain final enlightenment, he spared no effort. With determined persistence he advanced towards his goal, his enlightenment, caring naught even for life.

'Fie on this life! It is better for me to die in this fight (with passions) than to live defeated.'[3] The Master's right effort reached its climax when he sat under the Bodhi Tree for the deep meditation which ended in Full Enlightenment. From that moment as his life clearly shows, he was never subject to moral or spiritual fatigue. From the hour of his enlightenment to his passing away, he strove tirelessly to elevate mankind, regardless of the bodily fatigue involved, and oblivious to the many obstacles and handicaps in his way. Though physically he was not always well, mentally he was ever watchful and vigorous. By precept and example the Buddha taught a strenuous life.

The foregoing conveys the outstanding characteristic of the Buddha and his disciples. The Master has been very emphatic about this sixth factor of the Path, right effort, because it was not in his power to save people. He was no saviour, and gave no guarantee that he would save others from the shackles of *saṁsāra*, but he was ever ready to guide them on the upward path, to encourage them and give them moral support. The idea that one man can raise

1. *S.* i. 157. 2. *Bv.* Verse 107; *Jāt. Com.* 3. *Sn.* 440.

another from lower to higher levels and ultimately rescue him tends to make man weak, supine and foolish. It degrades him and smothers every spark of his dignity.

This emphasis on right effort by the Buddha explains in unmistakable language that Buddhism is not a doctrine of pessimism, a teaching for the feeble-minded who look at things from the most unfavourable point of view, but that it is a true warrior's religion.

The right effort spoken of by the Buddha is instrumental in eliminating evil and harmful thoughts, and in promoting and maintaining good and healthy thoughts.

As a market gardener pulls up weeds before he sows his seed, so the meditator tries to remove unwanted weeds from his mental field. If he fails in his weeding nothing worthwhile can be sown successfully. He then manures the field and protects it from animals and birds. So should the meditator watch over his mental field and nourish it appropriately.

The function of right effort is fourfold, to prevent, abandon, develop and maintain.[1]

1. What is the effort to prevent?

'Herein a monk puts forth his will to prevent the arising of evil, of unwholesome thoughts that have not yet arisen. He strives, develops energy and strengthens his mind (to this end).

'Herein, a monk, seeing a form, hearing a sound, smelling an odour, tasting a flavour, feeling some tangible thing or cognizing a mental object, apprehends neither signs nor particulars (that is, he is not moved by their general features or by their details). Inasmuch as coveting and dejection, evil and unwholesome thoughts break in upon one who dwells with senses unrestrained, he applies himself to such control, he guards over the senses, restrains the senses. This is called the effort to prevent.'

2. What is the effort to abandon?

'Herein a monk puts forth his will to abandon the evil, unwholesome thoughts that have already arisen. He strives, develops energy and strengthens his mind (to this end).

'Herein a monk does not admit sense desires that have arisen, but abandons, discards and repels them, makes an end of them and

1. *Saṁvara, pahāna, bhāvanā, anurakkhaṇa.*

causes them to disappear. So also with regard to thoughts of ill-will and of harm that have arisen. This is called the effort to abandon.'

3. What is the effort to develop?

'Herein a monk puts forth his will to produce and develop wholesome thoughts that have not yet arisen. He strives, develops energy and strengthens his mind (to this end).

'Herein a monk develops the Factors of Enlightenment based on seclusion, on dispassion, on cessation that ends in deliverance, namely: Mindfulness, Investigation of the *Dhamma*, Energy, Rapturous Joy, Calm, Concentration and Equanimity.[1] This is called the effort to develop.'

4. What is the effort to maintain?

'Herein, a monk maintains a favourable object of concentration (meditation). . . . This is called the effort to maintain.'

These then are the four efforts:

'To prevent, abandon, develop and maintain
These are the four efforts that he taught,
The Kinsman of the Sun. Herein a monk
With strenuous effort reaches suffering's end.'[2]

The unwholesome thoughts referred to here are the three root causes of all evil, namely: thoughts of lust (craving), hate and delusion. All other passions gather round these root causes, while wholesome thoughts are their opposites.

The sole purpose of this fourfold effort is success in meditation. The four right efforts are the requisites for concentration. As we saw above[3] right effort is included in the group of *samādhi* or Concentration. As such, right effort is interrelated and interdependent. It functions together and simultaneously with the other two factors of the group, namely right mindfulness and right concentration. Without right effort the hindrances[4] to mental progress cannot be overcome. Right effort removes the evil and unhealthy thoughts that act as a barrier to the calm of absorption, and promotes and

1. *Sati, dhamma-vicaya, viriya, pīti, passaddhi, samādhi, upekkhā.*
2. *A.* ii. 15 *suttas* 13, 14. 3. *P.* 84. 4. See p. 206.

maintains the healthy mental factors that aid the development of concentration.

When the meditator's mind slackens, it is time for him to summon courage, whip up effort and overpower indolence. Obduracy of mind and mental factors is a dangerous enemy of meditation; for when a man's mind is inert, slackness arises. This leads to greater slackness which produces sullen indifference.

The Buddha warns against this flabbiness of character:

> 'Who fails to strive when it's time to strive
> Who though young and strong is full of sloth
> Who is loose in thoughts[1] and inactive
> He does not by wisdom find the path.'[2]

'Monks, I know not of any other single thing of such power to prevent the arising of sloth and torpor, if not already arisen: or, if arisen, to cause its abandonment, as effort. In whom there is strenuous effort, sloth and torpor arises not; or, if arisen, is it abandoned.'[3]

Mind culture through these four great efforts is not something that can be gained overnight. It needs time and the regular practice of mental exercises. An athlete or body-builder does not stop training after a day or two, but goes on with his programme. Regular exercises without unnecessary strain are the key to physical fitness. If he only practises by fits and starts, he will never be a good athlete. When training the mind, the same golden rule should be applied—regular work and constant pressing on.

One need not struggle with evil thoughts when doing mental exercises. It should all be natural. If we try to fight our evil thoughts we shall not succeed. Instead we should note and watch our thoughts as they rise, analyse them, and try to ease the tension. The technique is like that of swimming. If you do not move your limbs you will sink; if you whirl about, you will not swim; or like the sleeper—if you struggle with the thought of sleep, you will never fall off; it will only be a mental torment to you. You must not make any effort to sleep. It must come naturally, and you should only relax any tense muscles.

Again, self-torment is one of the two extremes that the Buddha

1. That is entertaining thoughts of lust, hate, harm, etc.
2. *Dhp.* 280. 3. *A.* I. 4.

wants the meditator to avoid as profitless. It is useless to torture the body in order to stop the rise of evil thoughts, for such torment often ends in aversion and frustration. When the mind is frustrated, callous indifference to meditation follows. All our mental exercises should be natural and performed with awareness. 'Zeal without prudence is like running in the night.'

As the Buddha points out extremes should be avoided everywhere by those who wish to gain deliverance through enlightenment—they should keep to the middle path. In the practice of right effort, too, one has to follow the same median way.

A horseman, for instance, watches the speed of his mount and whenever it goes faster than he wants, he reins it back. On the other hand whenever the horse shows signs of slowing down he spurs it on and thus keeps to an even speed. Even so should one cultivate right effort, not overdoing it lest one be flurried, and avoiding slackness lest one becomes slothful. Like the horseman one should always be balanced. The following illustrates this well.

There is the story[1] of a monk, the venerable Soṇa-kolivisa, who was making a violent but unsuccessful effort to exert himself physically and mentally. Then the following thought occurred to him while in solitude: 'The disciples of the Blessed One, live with zealous effort and I am one of them. Yet my mind is not free of taints. My family has wealth; I can enjoy my riches and do good; what if I were to give up the training and revert to the low life, enjoy the riches and do good?'

The Blessed One reading his thoughts approached him and asked:

- Soṇa, did you not think: 'The disciples of the Blessed One live with zealous effort . . . (as before) . . . and do good'?
- Yes, venerable sir.
- And what do you think, Soṇa, were you not skilful at the lute before, when you were a layman?
- Yes, venerable sir.
- And what do you think, Soṇa, when the strings of your lute were over strung was it then in tune and playable?
- No, indeed, venerable sir.
- And what do you think, Soṇa, when the strings of your lute were too slack was it then in tune and playable?
- No, indeed, venerable sir.

1. *Vinaya Texts*, ii. 1 ff; *A.* iii. 374–5 *sutta* 55.

– But when, Soṇa, the strings of your lute were neither overstrung nor too slack, but keyed to the middle pitch, was it then in tune and playable?
– Surely, venerable sir.
– Even so, Soṇa, effort when too strenuous leads to flurry and when too slack to indolence. Wherefore, Soṇa, make a firm determination thus: Understanding the equality of the faculties,[1] I shall grasp at the aim by uniformity of effort.
– Yes, venerable sir.

The venerable Soṇa followed the instructions of the Blessed One and in due course attained perfection and was numbered among the Arahats.'[2]

The twentieth discourse of the *Majjhima Nikāya* gives practical instructions on how to keep away distracting thoughts and is indispensable to a meditator. The gist of it is as follows. The Buddha addressing his disciples said:

'Monks, the monk who is intent on higher thought should reflect on five things from time to time. What five?

'1. If through reflection on an object, evil, unwholesome thoughts associated with desire, hate and delusion arise in a monk, he should (in order to get rid of them) reflect on another object which is wholesome. Then the evil unwholesome thoughts are removed; they disappear. By their removal the mind stands firm and becomes calm, unified and concentrated within (his subject of meditation).

'As a skilled carpenter or his apprentice knocks out and removes a coarse peg with a fine one, so should the monk get rid of that evil object by reflecting on another object which is wholesome. Then the evil unwholesome thoughts associated with desire, hate and

1. The faculties are five in number: Faith, energy, mindfulness, concentration and wisdom (*saddhā, viriya, sati, samādhi* and *paññā*) *M.* 70, 77 and passim. On these faculties see *S.*v. 377.

2. This episode occurs in the Commentary to the *Thera-gāthā*: 'He received a subject of study from the Master, but was unable to concentrate, owing to his meeting people while he stayed in Cool Wood. And he thought: "My body is too delicately reared to arrive happily at happiness. A recluse's duties involve bodily fatigues." So he disregarded the painful sores on his feet got from pacing up and down, and strove his utmost but was unable to win. And he thought: "I am not able to create either path or fruit. Of what use is this religious life to me? I will go back to lower things and work merit." Then the Master discerned, and saved him by the lesson on the Parable of the Lute, showing him how to temper energy with calm. Thus corrected, he went to Vulture's Peak, and in due course won arahatship.' *Psalms of the Brethren* by Mrs. Rhys Davids (P.T.S., London), p. 275.

delusion are removed, they disappear. By their removal the mind stands firm . . . within.

'2. If the evil thoughts still arise in a monk who reflects on another object which is wholesome, he should consider the disadvantages of evil thoughts thus: "Indeed, these thoughts of mine are unwholesome, blameworthy, and bring painful consequences." Then his evil thoughts are removed, they disappear. By their removal the mind stands firm . . . within.

'3. If the evil thoughts still arise in a monk who thinks over their disadvantages he should pay no attention to, and not reflect on those evil thoughts. Then the evil thoughts are removed, they disappear. By their removal the mind stands firm . . . within.

'4. If the evil thoughts still arise in a monk who pays no attention to and does not reflect on evil thoughts, he should reflect on removing the root of those thoughts. Then the evil unwholesome thoughts are removed, they disappear. By their removal the mind stands firm . . . within.

'5. If evil thoughts still arise in a monk who reflects on the removal of their root, he should with clenched teeth, and tongue pressed against his palate, restrain, overcome, and control the (evil) mind with the (good) mind. Then the evil thoughts are removed, they disappear. By their removal the mind stands firm . . . within.

'If through a monk's reflection on a wholesome object; thinking over the disadvantages of evil thoughts; paying no attention and not reflecting on evil thoughts; reflecting on the removal of their root; restraining, overcoming, and controlling the (evil) mind with the (good) mind with clenched teeth and tongue pressed against his palate; evil thoughts are removed, and the mind stands firm and calm, becomes unified and concentrated within (its subject of meditation), that monk is called a master of the paths along which thoughts travel. He thinks the thought that he wants to think; he thinks not the thought that he does not want to think. He has cut off craving and removed the fetter fully; mastering pride he has made an end of suffering.'[1]

It is not only during an hour of serious meditation that we need this all-important quality of right effort. It should be cultivated always wherever possible. In all our speech, actions and behaviour, in our daily life, we need right effort to perform our duties whole-

1. For a detailed account see *The Removal of Distracting Thoughts* by Soma Thera (Buddhist Publication Society, Kandy, Ceylon). For brevity's sake I omitted all the similes but one.

heartedly and successfully. If we lack this quality of zealous effort, and give in to sloth and indolence we cannot proceed with any degree of confidence in the work we have undertaken.

To refrain from greed, anger, jealousy and a host of other evil thoughts to which people are subject, we need strength of mind, strenuous effort and vigilance. When free from the rush of city life, from nagging preoccupation with the world, we are not tempted to lose control: it is only in society that it becomes an effort to check such lapses. Any meditation we may have done is of immense help to enable us to face all this with calm.

When developing right effort we must be sincere about our thoughts. If we analyse them we find that they are not always good and wholesome. At times they are unwholesome and foolish, though we may not always express them in words and actions or both. Now if we allow such thoughts to rise repeatedly, it is a bad sign; for when an unhealthy thought is allowed to recur again and again, it tends to become an obsession. It is, therefore, essential to make a real effort to keep unwholesome thoughts at bay. When they occur they should be ignored. Not to notice them is far from easy, but until we succeed unhealthy thoughts will always be taking possession of our minds.

There is, however, one thing to remember. A person bent on curbing harmful impulses avoids, as far as possible, people who are obsessed by those impulses, and all talk that leads to them. Try to avoid people and things that tend to colour your sane and sober thoughts. Modern society is in danger of being swamped by distractions and temptations which can only be controlled if we undertake the difficult task of steadily training our minds.

Since worldly progress, gain and profit depend largely on our own efforts, surely we should strive even harder to train our minds and so develop the best that is in us. Since mental training requires the greatest effort, strive on now. 'Do not let your days pass away like the shadow of a cloud which leaves behind it no trace for remembrance.'

As Plotinus says:

'Withdraw into yourself and look. And if you do not find yourself beautiful as yet, do as does the creator of a statue that is to be made beautiful; he cuts away here, he smooths there, he makes this line lighter, this other purer, until he has shown a beautiful face upon the statue. So do you also; cut away all that is excessive; straighten all that is crooked, bring light to all that is shadowed, labour to make all glow with beauty, and do not cease chiselling your statue until there shall shine out on you the splendour of virtue, until you shall see the final goodness surely established in the stainless shrine.'[1]

Man's mind influences his body profoundly. If allowed to function viciously and entertain unwholesome thoughts, mind can cause disaster, can even kill a being; but it can also cure a sick body. When mind is concentrated on right thoughts with right effort and understanding the effect it can produce is immense. A mind with pure and wholesome thoughts really does lead to healthy relaxed living.

'Recent research in medicine, in experimental psychology and what is still called parapsychology has thrown some light on the nature of mind and its position in the world. During the last forty years the conviction has steadily grown among medical men that very many causes of disease, organic as well as functional, are directly caused by mental states. The body becomes ill because the mind controlling it either secretly wants to make it ill, or else because it is in such a state of agitation that it cannot prevent the body from sickening. Whatever its physical nature, resistance to disease is unquestionably correlated with the psychological condition of the patient.'[2] That even so grossly 'physical' a complaint as dental caries may be due to mental causes was maintained in a paper read before the American Dental Congress in 1937. The author pointed out that children living on a perfectly satisfactory diet may still suffer from dental decay. In such cases, investigation generally shows that the child's life at home or at school is in some way unsatisfactory. The teeth decay because their owner is under mental strain.

'Mind not only makes sick, it also cures. An optimistic patient has more chance of getting well than a patient who is worried and unhappy. The recorded instances of faith healing include cases in which even organic diseases were cured almost instantaneously.'[3]

In this connection it is interesting to observe the prevalence, in

1. Plotinus on the Beautiful, translated by Stephen MacKenna. Reproduced in *Meditation for Beginners* by J. I. Wedgwood.

2. For the physical basis of resistance, see *The Nature of Disease* by J. E. R. McDonagh, F.R.C.S.

3. Aldous Huxley, *Ends and Means* (London, 1946), pp. 258, 259.

Buddhist lands, of listening to the recital of the *Dhamma* for protection and deliverance from evil, and for promoting welfare and well-being. The selected discourses for recital are known as *Paritta-suttas*. '*Paritta*' in Pāli and '*paritrāṇa*' in Sanskrit mean, principally protection. They are used to describe certain suttas or discourses (spoken by the Buddha) that are regarded as affording protection and deliverance from evil. The practice of reciting and listening to the *paritta-suttas* began very early in the history of Buddhism. It is certain that their recital produces mental well-being in those who listen to them with intelligence and are confident in the truth of the Buddha's words. Such mental well-being can help those who are ill to recover, and it can also help to induce the mental attitude that brings happiness and to overcome its opposite. Originally in India those who listened to *paritta* sayings of the Buddha understood what was recited and the effect on them was correspondingly great.

According to the *Dhamma* the mind is so closely linked with the body that mental states affect the body's health and well-being. Some doctors even say that there is no such thing as a purely physical disease. Unless, therefore, these bad mental states are caused by previous evil acts (*akusala kamma-vipāka*), and so are unalterable, it is possible so to change them that mental health and physical well-being follow.

How can bad influences springing from evil beings be counteracted by recital of *paritta-suttas*? Well, they are the result of evil thinking. They can, therefore, be destroyed by the good states of mind caused by listening intelligently and confidently to *paritta* sayings, because of the power of concentration that comes into being through attending whole-heartedly to the truth of the sayings. *Paritta-sutta* recital is a form of *saccikiriya*, of depending on the truth for protection, justification or attainment. This means complete establishment in the power of truth to gain one's end. The saying: 'The power of truth protects a follower of the truth' (*Dhammo have rakkhati dhammacāriṁ*) is the principle behind these *sutta* recitals. If it is true that virtue protects the virtuous, then a person who listens to these sayings with complete confidence in the Buddha's words, which spring from complete enlightenment, will acquire so virtuous a state of mind that he will conquer any evil influence.

The recital of *paritta-suttas* also brings material blessings through the mental states caused by concentration and confidence in listening intelligently to the recital. According to the Buddha right effort is a necessary factor in overcoming suffering.[1] Listening to one of these recitals in the proper way can also generate energy for the purpose of doing good and following the path of worldly progress with diligence.

It is undoubted that listening to these *paritta-suttas* must produce in the intelligent and confident listener only wholesome states which can cure and prevent illness. There is no better medicine than truth (*Dhamma*) for both mental and physical ills, which are the cause of all suffering and misfortune. So the recital of *paritta-suttas* may, when they are listened to rightly, bring into being mental conditions of health necessary for material progress, physical welfare and well-being.

1. See *S.* i. 214.

13

RIGHT MINDFULNESS

(*Sammā-sati*)

It is no exaggeration to say that for us the most important thing in the universe is ourselves. If, on the other hand, we hold that some other thing, whether animate or inanimate, is as wonderful, it is our mind that is responsible for the opinion. In us the most wonderful and important thing is our mind, our consciousness. If the so-called individual is compared to a magnet, his mind represents the magnetic force which, though imperceptible and intangible, can work wonders. Man's mind too is like that; it manifests in diverse ways. It is dominant, pre-eminent and supersedes all existing forces, for it is beyond the laws of chemistry and physics.

Now if we consider ourselves the most important thing in the world, it behoves us to protect ourselves and others at the same time.

'If you hold yourself
Dear, watch yourself well.'[1]

The following discourse of[2] the Buddha illustrates the point.

'Once upon a time, monks, an acrobat climbed his bamboo pole and called to his pupil: "Now, boy, climb the pole and stand on my shoulders." When the pupil had done so the master said: "Now, boy, protect me and I will protect you; by thus looking after each other, we will show our tricks, earn money and come down safe from the pole."

'The pupil, however, said: "No, master, that won't do. You protect yourself, and I will protect myself. Thus self-protected and self-guarded we will show our tricks, earn money, and come down safe from the pole. That is the method!" '

1. *Dhp.* 157. 2. *S.* v. 168.

The Blessed One continued:

'Now, monks, just as the pupil said to his master: "I will protect myself", so should you practise the Arousing of Mindfulness[1] (i.e. mindfulness should be practised for self-protection). "I will protect others", thus the Arousing of Mindfulness should be practised (i.e. mindfulness should be practised to protect others). By protecting oneself, one protects others; by protecting others one protects oneself. And how, monks, by protecting oneself does one protect others? By repeated practice, by developing, by frequent occupation with it.

'And how, monks, by protecting others, does one protect oneself? It is by forbearance, by harmlessness, by lovingkindness and by compassion. . . . Monks, you must practise arousing of mindfulness, saying: "I will protect myself," "I will protect others."'

What this discourse indicates is clear to the thoughtful reader. The emphasis is on mindfulness. The Buddha exhorts us to cultivate the Arousing of Mindfulness for our own and others' protection.

Forbearance, harmlessness, lovingkindness and compassion are virtues through which one brings protection and security to others. None of these virtues can be cultivated without mindfulness. The person who is mindful is conscious of his thoughts, words and acts.

Right mindfulness guards a man from deviating from the path of righteousness, and encourages him to do that which is good. Thus through arousing mindfulness, by repeated practice, by frequent occupation with it, one protects oneself and others.

To protect oneself is not egoism, not selfish security, but self-discipline, self-training, both moral and mental training. To the extent that we are mentally strong and confident, so can we help others. If we are weak and diffident we can help neither ourselves nor others. Altruism, as a principle of action, is based on our character and mental development.

The saying: 'By protecting oneself one protects others; by protecting others one protects oneself,' removes the dual misconception that the followers of original Buddhism, of the *Theravāda*, are selfish and pessimistic. Many in their enthusiasm think that the genuine meditator who strives to train himself, or the man who tries to guard himself from evil, is self-centred, but this is not justifiable. One must train, must guard oneself to be of service to others.

1. *Satipaṭṭhāna*.

Such silent folk are often invisible helpers. A person may be large-hearted, but if his private life is questionable, and leads to no good, from the standpoint of the Buddha he neglects himself very badly, and cannot really serve others; he is no real helper of society.

We should also be on our guard against taking the latter part of the saying and overemphasizing it in our enthusiasm to serve others. The two parts of the sentence should be taken together if we are to be balanced.

The Bodhisatta,[1] as is evident from the scriptures, first trained himself, cultivated the *Pārami*, the Perfections, to the full, before he attained supreme enlightenment. Then exercising wisdom and compassion, the two cardinal virtues of his teachings, he guided others on the right path and became a true helper of mankind. As a Bodhisatta while giving a helping hand to others, he did not fail to help himself. We ought always to serve others, while at the same time never forgetting ourselves and training ourselves in mindfulness. That is the right method leading to the welfare and well-being of oneself and others.

In another context the Buddha says: 'One should first establish oneself in what is proper; then instruct others. Such a wise man will not become stained (will not be remorseful).'[2]

In the Buddhist texts we often come across the word *appamāda*, heedfulness, which is very close to the word *sati*, mindfulness. It is difficult to translate *appamāda* adequately. Literally it means the non-neglect of mindfulness. *Pamāda*, its opposite, is negligence, which in this context means allowing one's mind to wander among objects of sense pleasure. *Appamāda* implies, therefore, ever-present watchfulness or heedfulness in avoiding ill and doing good. The word is definitely used to denote mindfulness.

It is significant that the Buddha emphasizes the importance of *appamāda* in his final admonition to his disciples: 'Strive on with heedfulness (*appamādena sampādetha*).' It is equally significant to note that the last words of the Venerable Sāriputta, the foremost disciple of the Buddha, who predeceased the Master, also advocate the value of *appamāda*: 'Strive on with heedfulness, this is my advice to you.'

Mindfulness, complete awareness, and clear comprehension—these are the ways with which one brings meditation to fulfilment. He who is mindful and aware of himself at all times, is already at the gates of the Deathless.

1. See p. 14, n. 2. 2. *Dhp.* 158.

Meditation is the life-blood of Buddhism, as heedlessness is of death. Says the Buddha:

'Heedfulness is the way to the Deathless;[1] heedlessness is the way to death. The heedful do not die;[2] the heedless are like the dead.

'Clearly understanding this (difference)[3] the wise in heedfulness, delighting in the pasture[4] of the Noble Ones (*ariyas*) rejoice in (their own) heedfulness.

'Ever meditative, ever strenuously striving, those wise ones realize *Nibbāna*, the supreme security from bondage.'[5]

The importance of heedfulness is emphasized by the Master in these words:

'As the footprint of every creature that walks the earth can be placed in the elephant's footprint which is the largest of all—even so heedfulness is the one quality by which one acquires welfare both here and hereafter.'[6]

'Heedfulness causes wholesome thoughts that have not yet arisen to rise. It also causes unwholesome thoughts that have already risen to wane. In him who is heedful, good thoughts, not yet arisen, arise, and evil thoughts, if arisen, wane.'[7]

The man with presence of mind, who surrounds himself with watchfulness of mind (*satimā*), the man of courage and earnestness —passes the lethargic and the heedless (*pamatto*) as a race-horse a decrepit hack.

'Heedful among the slothful
Awake among the sleepy,
The sage outstrips them all
As the racehorse a hack.'[8]

Constant mindfulness and vigilance is necessary to avoid ill and do

1. *Amata* = *Nibbāna*, *com.*

2. This does not mean that the heedful are immortal, far from it, all beings are mortal; the idea implied is that the heedful who realize the deathless *Nibbāna* are beyond both birth and death. The heedless are regarded as dead; for they are subject to repeated births and deaths, *saṁsāra*.

3. The fact that there is an escape from *saṁsāra* for the heedful, but not for the heedless.

4. *Gocara*, i.e. Arousing of Mindfulness (*satipaṭṭhāna*).

5. *Dhp.* 21–23. 6. *S.* i. 86. 7. *A.* i. 11.

8. *Dhp.* 29. Lit. 'As a swift horse a weak one.'

good. Our thoughts and emotions need constant care and watchfulness to direct them to the path of purification. It is through such persevering watchfulness that mental progress is realized.

Much learning is of no advantage to its possessor if he lacks mindfulness without which he cannot make the best use of his learning. Even learned men fail to see a thing in its proper perspective when they lack this all-important quality of mindfulness. Men of good standing, owing to words spoken thoughtlessly and without due consideration to their consequences, are often subject to severe and justifiable criticism. There is a saying: 'The spoken word, the lost opportunity, and the sped arrow can never be recalled.' Mindfulness, in a sense, is the chief characteristic of all good and wholesome actions that tend to one's own and another's profit.

Let us listen to these words of the Buddha: 'O monks, I know of no other single thing that brings such great loss as heedlessness. I know of no other single thing that brings such great profit as heedfulness. Heedfulness, verily, brings great profit.'[1]

The Master warns his followers against heedlessness because it is so detrimental to man's progress, both worldly and spiritual. 'Be on the alert; be mindful', is a warning that he gave to his disciples whenever he detected them lacking in earnestness. Exhorted by a single saying of this nature many a man changed his whole life. The books record instances where this happened after some brief reminder such as:

'Be vigilant, be mindful,
Be well-disciplined, O monks,
With thoughts well collected
Keep watch over your mind.'[2]

Further says the Blessed One:

'I, monks, do not say to each and every monk that he should strive on with heedfulness; neither do I say that he should not strive on with heedfulness. Those monks who are Arahats, taint-extinguished, who have lived the holy life, done what was to be done, laid down the burden, who have attained their goal by stages and utterly destroyed the fetters of becoming, who are freed by perfect knowledge—to such monks, I do not say "strive on with heedfulness". For what reason? Perfected are they through heedfulness, it

1. *A.* 3. 2. *D.* 16.

is not possible for them to be heedless. But, those monks who are training, and have not attained mental perfection, but live aspiring for the supreme security from bondage—to such I say "strive on with heedfulness". For what reason? It is good, if these monks, living in suitable quarters, associating with good friends, restraining their sense faculties, would realize and live by attaining here and now, by their higher knowledge, that supreme consummation of the noble life for the sake of which sons of (good) family rightly leave home for homelessness. Seeing this fruit of heedfulness for these disciples, monks, I say "strive on with heedfulness".'[1]

As we discussed in the preceding chapter, meditation is fulfilled by the conjunction of the three last factors of the path: effort, mindfulness and concentration. These form the three strands of the rope; they are intertwined and interrelated. Mindfulness, however, is considered as the strongest strand, for it plays an important role in the acquisition of both calm and insight. Mindfulness which is awareness is a certain function of the mind and, therefore, a mental factor. Without this all-important factor of mindfulness one cannot cognize sense objects, one cannot be fully aware of one's behaviour. It is called right mindfulness because it avoids misdirected attention, and prevents the mind from paying attention to things in a false way. Mindfulness guides its possessor on the right path to purity and freedom.

Now this right mindfulness should be applied to each and every thing one does. In all our movements we are expected to be mindful. Whether we walk, stand or sit, whether we speak, keep silent, eat, drink or answer the calls of nature—in all these and in all other activities we should be mindful and wide awake. 'Mindfulness, O monks, I declare, is essential in all things everywhere.'[2]

In this context it must be noted that in the Buddhist scriptures the word mindfulness (*sati*) is often used with another word of equal significance, 'Clear Comprehension' (*sampajañña*). The compound word *sati-sampajañña* occurs frequently in the discourses. Mindfulness and clear comprehension are co-operative.

As a man going from the open into a dark room gradually discerns the objects in it, so does a man when fully awake and mindful comprehend things better and bring their true nature to light. The true nature of things is shrouded by ignorance, is camouflaged by nescience; but mindfulness of the right type, which we shall discuss

1. *M.* 70. 2. *S.* v. 115.

in this chapter, aids man to right understanding and deliverance of mind.

'Just as in a gabled house, monks, whatever rafters there are all converge on the ridge-pole, resort equally to the ridge-pole, are fixed in the ridge-pole and join together there, even so, whatever wrong states there are, all are rooted in ignorance, are fixed in ignorance and join together there. Wherefore, monks, you must train yourselves: "We will live together with heedfulness".'[1]

Ignorance is to experience that which is unworthy of being experienced, namely evil. Further it is the non-perception of the conglomerate nature of the aggregates; non-perception of sense organ and object in their nature as organ and object; non-perception of the emptiness or the relativity of the primaries; non-perception of the dominant nature of the sense-controlling faculties and of the thus-ness, the infallibility, of the Four Truths.[2]

And the five hindrances nourish (or condition) this ignorance. They hinder the understanding of the way to release from suffering. And what nourishes these hindrances? The three evil modes of life: bodily, verbal and mental wrong-doing. This threefold nutriment is in turn nourished by non-restraint of the senses. The food of non-restraint is shown to be lack of mindfulness and clear comprehension (*asati asampajañña*). In this context non-restraint is caused by the object (*dhamma*) drifting away, by the mind lapsing and forgetting the characteristics of existence (impermanence, unsatisfactoriness and voidness of Self) and the true nature of things.

It is when one does not bear in mind the impermanency and other characteristics of things that one allows oneself liberties in speech and deed, and gives rein to imagination of an unwholesome kind. Lack of clear comprehension means no clear comprehension of purpose, suitability, resort and non-delusion.[3] When one does something without a right purpose; when one considers or does things which do not help the good, or which prevent improvement; when one forgets the *Dhamma*, which is the true resort of those who strive; when one lays hold of things believing in one's delusion that they are pleasant, permanent and substantial, then non-restraint is encouraged.

And behind this lack of mindfulness and clear comprehension lies unwise or unsystematic attention, which the books call atten-

1. *S.* ii. 263. 2. *Sv.* p. 134.
3. *Sāttha sampajañña, sappāya-s, gocara-s, asammoha-s.*

tion that is off the right course. For it takes the impermanent as permanent, the unsatisfactory as satisfactory, the Soulless as Soul, the offensive as beautiful or the bad as good.[1]

When unsystematic attention increases it fulfils two things: ignorance and thirst for becoming. Ignorance being present, the arising of the entire mass of suffering comes to be. Thus a person of unwise or unsystematic attention revolves endlessly in the cycle of existence (*saṁsāra*); like a ship drifting at the wind's will, like a herd of cattle in a whirlpool or like an ox yoked to a cart.

The word *sati* (Skt. *smṛti*) also means 'memory' or 'remembrance; for instance terms such as '*anussati*', calling to mind; *paṭissati*, remembrance, indicate memory, but in the doctrine, mindfulness in the sense of 'attention' or 'awareness' is most significant. As with any other factor of the Eightfold Path, there are two mindfulnesses, one wrong and the other right. The former is mindfulness directed towards things evil and unwholesome while the latter is directed towards things good and wholesome. Now right mindfulness in the Noble Eightfold Path is explained as the fourfold 'Arousing of Mindfulness' (*Satipaṭṭhāna*). The word *paṭṭhāna*, which is the shortened form of *upaṭṭhāna*, means literally 'placing near (one's mind),' i.e. remaining aware, establishing or arousing, as in the expression *satiṁ upaṭṭhapetvā*, literally 'having kept present' (his mindfulness).

'To raise up the person to a keen sense of awareness in regard to an object and to bring into activity, to call forth, and stir up the controlling faculty, the power, the enlightenment factor, and the way factor of mindfulness is the Arousing of Mindfulness designed.

'Every Arousing of Mindfulness in regard to body, feeling, consciousness or a mental object can be considered as a beginning of the road to insight. And so these "Arousings" are, in a sense, "starting points". Further with the Arousing of Mindfulness one wakes up heedfulness, intentness and carefulness, and is in a state of mental preparedness in regard to any work in hand.

'These Arousings of Mindfulness are many as regards objects, but are one in the sense of taking place in a single way of quietude charged with insight that leads to *Nibbāna*.'[2]

The discourse on the Arousing of Mindfulness (*Satipaṭṭhāna-sutta*, Skt. *Smṛti-upasthāna sūtra*), which may be called the most important

1. See also p. 96.
2. *The Way of Mindfulness*, Bhikkhu Soma (Lake House, Colombo, 1949), p. xviii.

discourse by the Buddha on mental development or meditation, occurs twice in the Buddhist Canon, as the tenth discourse of the *Majjhima Nikāya* and as the twenty-second of the *Dīgha Nikāya.* The latter, which is called the *Mahā-satipaṭṭhāna-sutta*, i.e. the Great Discourse, deals with the Four Noble Truths at length, and it is only in this respect that it differs from the former. The discourse which is reproduced at the end of this chapter is the shorter version.

There is no other single discourse in the entire Buddhist Canon that is regarded with so much reverence and high esteem by those who follow the original teachings of the Buddha. In Ceylon this *sutta* is recited by the lay devotees when they observe the eight precepts on a full moon day, and spend the time at a monastery. Even if they do not understand the full meaning of the discourse they listen attentively with deep devotion thus concentrating their minds on the Buddha-word. It is a common sight to see a monk reciting this *sutta* by the bedside of a dying man so that his mind may be directed towards, and concentrated on, the Buddha-word and that his last thoughts may be purified.

If we read and try to understand this discourse it becomes clear that it covers the principal tenets of Buddhism, and that mindfulness has to be applied to all—the world within and without—always, everywhere during our waking life.

One may think that the contents of this discourse are rather obsolete and impracticable. That is because man has adapted himself to his environment and lives subserviently in a rut. Our character depends upon our habits which with most of our longings and inclinations do not lead to right thinking and understanding, but to detesting anything that might drag the mind from its customary channels.

The ordinary layman in the midst of life's turmoil may wonder how a busy man can practise *satipaṭṭhāna*, the Arousing of Mindfulness, as described in the discourse. It is true that the practice of some of the *sati* methods mentioned in the *sutta* needs time and a cloistered atmosphere: but surely it can be cultivated during our daily work. For instance there is no need to go into seclusion to curb hindrances. It is while we are in society that we are often confronted with disagreeable sights and sounds, etc., which tend to evoke harmful and unhealthy thoughts, and it is then that we need mindfulness to restrain ourselves from entertaining them. While we are at work, sense desire, ill-will, jealousy, pride and other unwholesome thoughts are sure to arise and upset our balance of mind.

It is then that we need meditation to check such harmful elements. If we are not slaves to our passions, if we are strong-willed, we can restrain ourselves and curb the conflicts in us.

Further, time spent in secluded contemplation is not wasted: it goes a long way to strengthen a man's character. It is an asset to our daily work and progress if we can find the time to cut ourselves off from routine and spend a day or two in quiet contemplation. This is surely not escapism or living in idleness, but the best way to strengthen our minds and mental qualities. It is a beneficial introspection; it is by examining one's thoughts and feelings that one can probe into the inner meaning of things, and find the power within.

'A certain aloofness, a withdrawing of the mind at times from the busy-ness of life is a requisite to mental hygiene.'

Right mindfulness is a mental factor that sharpens the power of observation, and assists right thinking and understanding. Orderly thinking and reflection is conditioned by man's right mindfulness or awareness. The five senses used by the conscious mind as instruments provide food for thought. The suitability or not of the food we take depends on our mindfulness. If, for instance, what we take in is conditioned by wrong mindfulness and unsystematic attention, then it tends to make our mind sick, and often deludes us.

The discourse states clearly how a man takes heed of his thoughts, mindfully watching and observing each and every one, good or ill, salutary or otherwise. The whole of the discourse warns us against negligence and day-dreaming and urges us to be mentally alert and watchful. As a matter of fact, the earnest student will note that the very reading of the discourse, at times, makes him watchful, earnest and serious-minded. It goes without saying that right mindfulness is a quality that no sensible man treats with contempt. Truly it is essential to cultivate mindfulness in these distracted times when so many people are unbalanced.

Right mindfulness is instrumental not only in bringing concentrative calm, but in promoting right understanding and right living. It is an essential factor in all our actions both worldly and spiritual. 'Mindfulness is as salt is to curry.'[1]

Unwholesome thoughts interfere with concentration, and the function of right effort, as we saw above, is to put aside such thoughts and promote and maintain healthy ones; but this is not possible if we lack mindfulness or constant watchfulness. Right effort and right

1. *Satipaṭṭhāna Com.*

mindfulness go arm in arm to check the arising of evil thoughts and to develop and promote good thoughts. As the Master points out at the very beginning of the *sutta*, the fourfold Arousing of Mindfulness is the one and only way along which the liberated ones have safely gone. Therefore it is said:

> 'Ever virtuous and wise, with mind collected,
> Reflecting on oneself and ever mindful,
> One crosses the flood so difficult to cross.'[1]

Let us now turn to that one and only way.

The Discourse on the Arousing of Mindfulness[2]

Thus have I heard:

At one time the Blessed One was living among the Kurus, at Kammāsadhamma, a market-town of the Kuru people.

Then the Blessed One addressed the monks thus: 'Monks', and they replied: 'Venerable sir.' The Blessed One spoke as follows:

This is the only way, monks, to purify beings, surmount sorrow and lamentation, destroy pain and grief, reach the right path and realize *Nibbāna*, it is the way of the four Arousings of Mindfulness. What four? Herein (in this Dispensation), a monk[3] lives practising body contemplation on the body, ardent, clearly comprehending and mindful (of it), having overcome covetousness and grief concerning the world (of the body); he lives practising feeling-contemplation on feelings, ardent, clearly comprehending and mindful, having overcome covetousness and grief concerning the world (of feeling), he lives practising mind-contemplation on the mind, ardent, clearly comprehending and mindful, having overcome covetousness and grief concerning the world (of the mind); he lives practising mind-object contemplation on mind objects, ardent, clearly comprehending and mindful, having overcome covetousness and grief concerning the world of (mental objects).

1. *Sn.* 174.

2. I have slightly condensed the discourse without deleting the essentials, but have dropped the similes.

3. Whosoever undertakes this practice is meant by the term monk (*bhikku* Skt. *bhikshu*) *Com.*

I. THE CONTEMPLATION OF THE BODY

1. *Mindfulness on Breathing*

And how, monks, does a monk live practising body-contemplation on the body. Herein, a monk having gone to the forest, to the foot of a tree, or to a lonely place[1] sits down crosslegged[2] keeping the body erect and his mindfulness alert, mindful he breathes in, mindful he breathes out. When breathing in a long breath, he knows: 'I breathe in a long breath'; when breathing out a long breath, he knows: 'I breathe out a long breath'; when breathing in a short breath, he knows: 'I breathe in a short breath'; when breathing out a short breath, he knows: 'I breathe out a short breath'. 'Conscious of the entire process[3] I will breathe in', thus he trains himself: 'Conscious of the entire process I will breathe out', thus he trains himself.

Thus he lives practising body-contemplation on the body internally or externally or both internally and externally (that is contemplating his own breathing and another's breathing, and contemplating his own and another's breathing alternatively).... Thus he lives independent clinging to nothing in the world.

Thus indeed, a monk lives practising body-contemplation on the body.

2. *The Postures of the Body*

And again, when going, he knows: 'I am going'; when standing, sitting, lying down, he knows (i.e. he is aware of the posture); he knows any other position of the body. Thus he lives practising body-contemplation on the body . . . (as before). . . . He lives independent, clinging to nothing in the world.

1. Your own bedroom, or your 'shrine room' if you are fortunate in having one, may be a lonely and more personal place for you.

2. This posture, like an isosceles triangle and practised by most of the easterners, may not be practicable to some, especially those of the western world, but they can adopt a posture that does not bring them discomfort. They may sit on a chair, but for this particular meditation, unlike the others, the body should be 'erect' without unnecessary rigidity, hands may be relaxed on the lap, or the right palm may be placed on the left. Eyes may be shut or they may gaze at the tip of the nose without straining themselves; lips should be closed, the tongue touching the upper palate. All these indicate that a person bent on this meditation should also try to have his body 'collected', which is an asset to his mental concentration.

3. *Sabba-kāya*. Literally, 'the whole (breath) body'. According to the *Visuddhi Magga*, '*kāya*' here does not mean the physical body, but the whole mass of in-breathing and out-breathing.

3. *The Fourfold Clear Comprehension*

And again, in going forward and in going backward, he applies clear comprehension; in looking straight forward and in looking elsewhere, he applies clear comprehension; in bending and in stretching he applies clear comprehension; in wearing the robes, carrying the alms bowl, in eating, drinking, chewing, savouring, in answering the calls of nature, he applies clear comprehension; in walking, in standing, in sitting, in sleeping;[1] in waking, in speaking and in keeping silence, he applies clear comprehension.

Thus he lives practising body-contemplation on the body. . . .
He lives independent clinging to nothing in the world.

4. *The Reflection on the Repulsiveness of the Body*

And again, he reflects on this very body encased by the skin and full of impurities from the soles up and from the hair of the head down, thinking thus: 'There are in this body, hair of the head, hair of the body, nails, teeth, skin, flesh, sinews, bones. . . .'

Thus he lives practising body-contemplation on the body. . . .
He lives independent clinging to nothing in the world.

5. *The Reflection on the Material Elements*

And again, he reflects on this very body . . . thinking thus: 'There are, in this body, the elements of solidity, fluidity, temperature and motion[2] . . .'

Thus he lives practising body-contemplation on the body. . . .
He lives independent clinging to nothing in the world.

6. *The Nine Cemetery Contemplations*

And again, if he sees a dead body . . . he contemplates on his own body thus: 'Verily, this body of mine too is of the same nature, it will become like that and will not escape from it.'

Thus he lives practising body-contemplation on the body. . . .
He lives independent clinging to nothing in the world.

(The discourse explains nine different stages of the corpse. In each case the meditator contemplates on his own body thus: 'Verily,

1. 'Who, after lying down falls asleep, and then, after getting up from his sleep, reflects: "The bodily and mental things which existed during the time of sleep ended just during sleep," is called a doer of clear comprehension in sleeping and waking.

'The non-occurrence of processes which make action or are made of action is sleep: the occurrence, waking.' *The Way of Mindfulness*, Bhikkhu Soma (Colombo, 1949), p. 95.

2. See above, p. 45.

this body of mine too is of the same nature, it will become like that and will not escape it.')

II. THE CONTEMPLATION OF FEELINGS

And, how does a monk live practising feeling-contemplation on feelings? Herein, a monk when experiencing a pleasant feeling, knows: 'I experience a pleasant feeling'; when experiencing a painful feeling, he knows: 'I experience a painful feeling'; when experiencing a neutral feeling, he knows: 'I experience a neutral feeling.' When experiencing a pleasant worldly feeling, he knows: 'I experience a pleasant worldly feeling'; when experiencing a pleasant unworldly feeling, he knows: 'I experience a pleasant unworldly feeling'; when experiencing a painful worldly feeling, he knows: 'I experience a painful worldly feeling'; when experiencing a painful unworldly feeling, he knows: 'I experience a painful unworldly feeling'; when experiencing a neutral worldly feeling, he knows: 'I experience a neutral worldly feeling'; when experiencing a neutral unworldly feeling, he knows: 'I experience a neutral unworldly feeling.'[1]

Thus he lives practising feeling contemplation on feelings internally or externally . . . (as before). . . . He lives independent clinging to nothing in the world.

III. THE CONTEMPLATION OF MIND

And how does a monk live practising mind contemplation on the mind? Herein a monk knows the mind with lust, as being with lust; the mind without lust, as being without lust; the mind with hate, as being with hate; the mind without hate, as being without hate; the mind with delusion as being with delusion; the mind without delusion, as being without delusion; the shrunken state of mind as the shrunken state (that is an inert state of mind); the distracted state of mind as the distracted state (that is a restless state of mind); the developed state of mind as the developed state (the consciousness of *rūpa* and *arūpa jhāna*, i.e. meditative absorptions of the form and formless sphere); the undeveloped state of mind as the undeveloped state (the ordinary consciousness of sensuous existence);

1. Worldly (*sāmisa*) feelings are those 'bound up with home life'; and unworldly (*nirāmisa*) feelings are those 'bound up with renunciation'. Unworldly pleasant feeling is happiness brought about by the meditation while unworldly painful feeling is due to the awareness of one's imperfections and slow progress on the Path to Deliverance. Unworldly neutral feeling is equanimity resulting in insight. *M.* 137.

the surpassable mind as surpassable (the consciousness of sensuous existence); the unsurpassable mind as unsurpassable (the consciousness of the form and formless sphere); the concentrated mind as concentrated; the unconcentrated mind as unconcentrated; the liberated mind as liberated; the unliberated mind as unliberated. Thus he lives practising mind-contemplation on the mind internally or externally . . . (as before). . . .

He lives independent clinging to nothing in the world.

IV. THE CONTEMPLATION OF MIND-OBJECTS

And how does a monk live practising mind-object-contemplation on the mind-objects?

1. *The Five Hindrances*

Herein a monk lives practising mind-object contemplation on the mind-objects of the five hindrances.[1] And how does he practise mind-object contemplation on the mind-objects of the five hindrances?

Herein, when sense desire is present in him, the meditator knows: 'There is sense desire in me,' or when sense desire is absent, he knows: 'There is no sense desire in me.' He knows how the abandoning of arisen sense desire comes to be; and he knows how the non-arising in the future of the abandoned sense desire comes to be. (The same with regard to ill-will, sloth and torpor, restlessness and worry and sceptical doubt.)

Thus he lives practising mind-object contemplation on mind-objects internally or externally. . . .

He lives independent clinging to nothing in the world.

2. *The Five Aggregates of Clinging*

Herein a meditator thinks: 'Thus is material form, thus is the arising of material form, thus is the passing away of material form. (Similarly with regard to feeling, perception, mental formations and consciousness.) Thus he lives practising mind-object contemplation on mind-objects internally or externally. . . . He lives independent clinging to nothing in the world.

3. *The Six Internal and the Six External Sense-bases*

Herein a meditator knows the eye, knows material (visible) forms

1. For a detailed account of the Hindrances see p. 206.

and the fetter[1] that arises dependent on both (the eye and forms); he knows how the arising of the non-arisen fetter comes to be; he knows how the abandoning of the arisen fetter comes to be, and he knows how the non-arising in the future of the abandoned fetter comes to be.

He knows the ear and sounds . . . the nose and smells . . . the tongue and savours . . . the body and tactile objects . . . the mind and mind-objects, and knows the fetter arising dependent on both; he knows how the arising of the non-arisen fetter comes to be; he knows how the abandoning of the arisen fetter comes to be; and he knows how the non-arising in the future of the abandoned fetter comes to be.

Thus he lives practising mind-object contemplation on mind-objects internally or externally. . . .

He lives independent clinging to nothing in the world.

4. *The Seven Factors of Enlightenment*

Herein, when the enlightenment-factor of mindfulness is present in him, the meditator knows: 'The enlightenment-factor of mindfulness is in me'; or when the enlightenment-factor of mindfulness is absent, he knows: 'The enlightenment-factor of mindfulness is not in me.' He knows how the arising of the non-arisen enlightenment-factor of mindfulness comes to be; and he knows how the consummation of the development of the arisen enlightenment-factor of mindfulness comes to be. (Similarly with regard to the other six factors of enlightenment: Investigation of *dhammas*,[2] energy, rapture, calm, concentration and equanimity.)

Thus he lives practising mind-object contemplation internally or externally. . . .

He lives independent clinging to nothing in the world.

5. *The Four Noble Truths*

Herein a monk knows according to reality: 'This is suffering; this is the arising of suffering; this is the cessation of suffering; this is the path leading to the cessation of suffering.'

Thus he lives practising mind-object contemplation on mind-objects internally or externally or both internally and externally. . . .

He lives contemplating origination-factors in mind-objects, or he lives contemplating dissolution-factors in mind-objects, or he lives contemplating both origination-and-dissolution factors in mind-objects.

1. See below, p. 210.
2. *Dhamma* here stands for mind and matter.

Or his mindfulness is established with the thought, 'mental objects exist', to the extent necessary for just knowledge and mindfulness, and he lives independent clinging to nothing in the world.

Thus indeed, monks, a monk lives practising mind-object-contemplation on the mind-objects of the Four Noble Truths.

Verily, O monks, should any person practise these four Arousings of Mindfulness in this manner for seven years, then he should expect one of two results: Knowledge (of final Deliverance, i.e. Arahatship or Sainthood) here and now, or, if there be yet a remainder of clinging, the state of Non-return (*anāgāmitā*, the penultimate stage of sainthood).[1]

Let alone seven years, should any person practise these four Arousings of Mindfulness in this manner for seven months . . . six months . . . five months . . . three months . . . two months . . . a month . . . half-a-month—then he should expect one of two results: Knowledge here and now, or, if there be yet a remainder of clinging, the state of Non-return.

Let alone half-a-month, should any person practise these four Arousings of Mindfulness in this manner for seven days, then he should expect one of two results: Knowledge here and now, or, if there be yet a remainder of clinging, the state of Non-return.

Because of this it was said: 'This is the only way, O monks, for the purification of beings, for the surmounting of sorrow and lamentation, for the destroying of pain and grief, for reaching the right path, for realizing *Nibbāna*, namely the four Arousings of Mindfulness.'

Thus spoke the Blessed One. Glad at heart, the monks welcomed the words of the Blessed One.[2]

The careful reader will note that in this discourse mindfulness is specially concerned with just four things: Body, feeling, mind and mind-objects, all pertaining to the human being. The contemplation of the body makes us realize its true nature, without any pretence, by analysing it right down to its ultimates, into its fundamental elements. This mental scrutiny of our own bodies helps us to realize what kind of a phenomenon the human body is, to realize that it is a

1. As at *M.* 70.

2. When translating this discourse from the Pāli, I have closely followed: *The Way of Mindfulness*, being a translation of the *Satipaṭṭhāna Sutta* of the *Majjhima Nikāya:* its Commentary. . . . By Bhikkhu Soma (Colombo, 1949); and *The Heart of Buddhist Meditation*, a handbook of mental training, based on the Buddha's Way of Mindfulness, by Nyānapoṇika Thera (Rider and Company, 1962), p. 117.

process without any underlying substance or core that may be taken as permanent and lasting.

The in-breathing and out-breathing discussed here, we know, is spontaneous. Normally no one tries to breathe consciously, but when practising mindfulness on breathing we try to do it consciously and to be aware of the breath. What is aimed at is to cultivate and increase the power of concentration, and to acquire tranquillity of body and mind. It is interesting to note that modern psychologists have recognized the value and importance of conscious breathing as tending to ease the tension and restlessness of man's mind.

Again the exercising of clear comprehension in connection with the postures of the body and its actions like walking, etc., aids us to remove discursive thoughts, improve our power of concentration and develop awareness and heedfulness.

Then the contemplation of feeling which is the second type of mindfulness mentioned in the discourse is purely subjective, a 'doing in the mind'. We are expected to analyse our feelings or sensations and decide whether they are pleasant, unpleasant or neutral. Generally, people are depressed when they have to entertain unpleasant sensations, they dislike such feelings, but are elated over pleasant sensations. This mental exercise of mindfulness, however, helps a man to experience all feelings with a detached outlook, and to avoid becoming a slave to sensations. He also learns gradually to realize that there is only a feeling and that too is a passing phenomenon; there is no 'Self' that feels.

The contemplation of mind which is the third type of mindfulness speaks to us of the importance of studying our own mind, of becoming aware of our diverse thoughts—in this case, thoughts of lust, hate and delusion, the root cause of all wrong-doing, and their opposites that counteract those unwholesome thoughts. This kind of dispassionate discernment of mind and its thoughts makes a man understand the real function of his mind, its real nature and behaviour, how it can be used for both useless and profitable actions. The man who practises contemplation of the mind learns to control it and not be under its sway.

The books tell us the interesting story of the elder Mahā Phussa. Practising mindfulness he was always watching his thoughts. If while walking an evil thought were to occupy his mind, he would stop and not continue until the evil thought had been got rid of. People who noticed this used to wonder whether he had lost his way, or lost something on the way. Later through constant practice of mindfulness he became an Arahat, a man without taints. This indicates that the ancients were aware of their thoughts not only when seated in a given posture at a particular time, for meditation, but always.

This contemplation of the mind also makes us realize that what we call mind is only an ever-changing process consisting of equally changing mental factors, and that there is no abiding entity called Ego, Self or Soul.

The fourth and last type of mindfulness covers all the essential *Dhamma*, the teachings of the Master, most of which are discussed in detail in the present work.

The description of each type of mindfulness in the *sutta* ends with the words: 'he lives independent clinging to nothing in the world'. This is the result aimed at by the meditator, an achievement for the earnest and ever zealous. Hard indeed it is to live clinging to nothing in the world, and our efforts to reach such high levels of mental life may not be crowned with success. Yet it is worth while striving again and again. Some day, if not in this life, in another birth, we may reach the summit that all who really strive have reached. 'Sow a thought,' someone has said, 'and you reap a deed. Sow a deed, and you reap a habit. Sow a habit, and you reap a character. Sow a character, and you reap a destiny—for character is destiny.'

14

RIGHT CONCENTRATION

(*Sammā-samādhi*)

ALL religious systems teach some kind of meditation or mental exercise for man's inner development. It may take the form of silent prayer, reading individually or collectively from some 'holy scripture' or concentrating on some sacred object, person or idea. And it is believed that these mental exercises, at times, result in seeing visions of saints, or holy men, in conversing with them or hearing voices, or some similar mysterious occurrences. Whether they are illusions, imaginations, hallucinations, mere projections of the sub-conscious mind, or real phenomena, one cannot say with certainty. Mind is an invisible force and is quite capable of producing all these phenomena. Trance is carried so far by certain yogis and mystics, that it becomes anaesthetic and they do not feel anything.[1] The present writer has seen people in 'meditation' postures who have fallen into a kind of coma and seem to be lost in thought. Others witnessing such occurrences wrongly think that this is a kind of meditation (*bhāvanā*).

The Buddhist books tell us that through *jhāna* (Skt. *dhyāna*), meditative absorption, and through the development of mental faculties, man is capable of gaining psychic powers which enable him to see things far away, even beings on various planes of existence; to hear sounds at a distance and see past births, etc. But it is very important to bear in mind that the Buddhist *jhāna* is not a state of auto-hypnosis, unconsciousness or coma. It is a state of mental purity where disturbing passions and impulses are subdued and calmed down, so that the mind becomes unified and collected, and enters into a state of clear consciousness and mindfulness.

It is interesting to observe that recent research in para-psychology has gained some acceptance of these phenomena. Interest in the

1. *With Mystics and Magicians in Tibet* by Alexandra David Neel (Penguin 1940), gives interesting accounts of Tibetan mystics.

subject of extra-sensory perception in experimental psychology is slowly gaining ground and the results obtained seem to be beyond ordinary comprehension.[1]

These are, however, only side-products which are of minor significance when compared with man's final deliverance, his release from bonds. At times, these para-normal happenings may even act as bonds and retard realization. The meditation taught in Buddhism is neither for gaining union with any supreme being nor for manifesting any mystical experiences nor is it for any self-hypnosis, it brings calm and insight for the sole purpose of attaining unshakable deliverance of mind and supreme security from bondage through the total extirpation of all the mental defilements.

Man is an ever-changing process of mind and body, in which the most important element is the mind. In Buddhism, therefore, the greatest importance is attached to the human mind. Once a monk asked the Master: 'Pray, venerable sir, by what is the world led? By what is the world drawn along? Under the sway of what one *dhamma* have all gone?'

'Well, monk, the world is led by mind (thought); by mind the world is drawn along; all have gone under the sway of the mind, the one *dhamma*.[2]

While some of his contemporaries like Nātaputta (Jaina Mahāvīra) considered actions to be the most important, the Buddha gave mind the foremost place.[3] To control and clean the mind is the heart of the Buddha's teaching. Happiness has to be found and perfection won through the mind. But so long as mind is defiled, polluted and uncontrolled, nothing worthy can be achieved through it. Hence the Buddha stressed mental purity as essential for true happiness and deliverance from suffering.

Many a man today thinks that freedom and unrestraint are synonyms, and, due to the materialistic trend of modern culture, which is predominantly sensual, thinks that the taming of the self (mind) hinders self-development. In the teaching of the Buddha, however, it is quite different. The self must be subdued and tamed on right lines if it is really to become well. To guard the mind from

1. For information read works of J. B. Rhine of Duke University, Ian Stevenson of Virginia University and papers contributed to scientific publications by these Professors, the books of Gina Cerminara and the Cayce Reports, and *The Case for Rebirth* by Francis Story (Buddhist Publication Society, Kandy, Ceylon, 1959).

2. *A.* ii. 177. This is put in verse at *S.* i. 39. There the question came from a deity.

3. See *Upāli sutta, M.* 56.

actions of lust, hate and delusion and train it to perform actions freed from lust, hate and delusion is the way to true weal and happiness in the dispensation of the Buddha.

It is only when the mind is controlled and is kept to the right road of orderly progress that it becomes useful for its possessor and for society. A disorderly mind is a liability both to its owner and to others. All the havoc wrought in the world is wrought by men who have not learned the way of mind control, balance and poise.

Rank, caste, colour and even wealth and power cannot necessarily make a man a person of value to the world. Only his character makes a man great and worthy of honour. 'It is character that illumines wisdom.'[1] As the Buddha says: 'Radiant is the mind at birth, it is polluted only by chance defilements.'[2] It is indeed hard to curb the impulses and control evil inclinations, to give up what lures and holds us in thrall and to exorcise the evil spirits that haunt the human heart in the shape of unwholesome thoughts. These thoughts are the manifestations of lust, hate and delusion, the three-fold army of Death (*Māra*), which cannot be routed until one has attained real purity by constant training of the mind.

Control of the mind is the key to happiness. It is the king of virtues and the force behind all true achievement. It is owing to lack of control that various conflicts arise in man's mind. If he is to control them he must learn not to give free rein to his longings and inclinations and should try to live self-governed, pure and calm.

Calmness is not weakness. A calm attitude at all times shows a man of culture. It is not too hard for a man to be calm when things are favourable, but to be composed when things are wrong is hard indeed, and it is this difficult quality that is worth achieving; for by such calm and control he builds up strength of character. It is quite wrong to imagine that they alone are strong and powerful who are noisy, garrulous and fussily busy.

> 'Yes; emptiness is loud, but fullness, calm;
> The fool's a half-filled crock; the sage, a lake.'[3]

The man who cultivates calmness of mind rarely gets upset when confronted with the vicissitudes of life. He tries to see things in their proper perspective, how things come into being and pass away. Free from anxiety and restlessness, he will try to see the fragility of

1. *A.* i. 102. 2. *A. i. 10.*
3. *Sn.* 721. (Lord Chalmers' translation.)

the fragile. 'Quiet minds . . . go on, in fortune or misfortune, at their own private pace, like a clock during a thunderstorm.'[1]

No amount of argument about calming the mind and perfecting life leads us to our desired aim. But each act of genuine renunciation of and detachment from the objects that incite passion, that lead us deeper into the night of ignorance and enslave us with their lure, leads to calmness and final deliverance.

Often our attempts to reach perfection are not crowned with success. But failure does not matter so long as we are sincere and pure in our motives, and strive again and again without stopping. No one reaches the summit of a hill at once. One rises by degrees. Like the skilful smith who removes the dross in gold bit by bit man must try to purge his life of its impurities. The path pointed by the Buddha for inner growth and development is that of meditation. Let us now turn to that path.

It is an admitted fact that when a man's mind is too engrossed in worldly affairs, in material things, his inclination for spiritual development is less. On the other hand, he who is genuinely bent on meditation or mental training cares less for worldly things. The yogi or the serious thinker is less attached to the material, is less concerned with worldly affairs.

Although the great majority of mankind delights in sensual pleasures, is attached to things that are seemingly important and agreeable, still there are people both in the East and West 'with little dust in their eyes', 'with keen faculties', seeking something quite different from the worldly-wise, different from the pre-occupation of the world.

In recent times people have been busy examining and investigating psychic phenomena the study of which seems to reveal hidden channels of the human mind, and the urge in man to seek spiritual guidance. Man's need for inner development is on the increase, which is a good sign.

It goes without saying that thoughts that are of real importance can only grow as the result of long periods of quiet. It is in and through solitude that the human mind gains in strength and power. The greatest creative energy works in silence, but people seem to like noise better than silence. The vast majority are so burdened with everyday affairs, so engrossed in things seemingly very important, that they overlook the importance of silent contemplation. When we withdraw into the silence, we are absolutely alone to see

1. R. L. Stevenson.

ourselves as we really are; we stand face to face with actuality, and then we can learn to overcome the weaknesses and limitations of ordinary experience. But we seem so often to be busy like a squirrel in a revolving cage which, though very active, merely turns the cage. The hen on her eggs, though seemingly inactive and lethargic, is doing something useful, she is warming the eggs so that the chicks hatch out.

We should try to put in at least half an hour every day being busy like the hen on her eggs. When our mind is calm and quiet it is time to take advantage of it by engaging in silent communication with our own mind in order to understand our true nature without pretence. Now the ordinary layman may ask: 'How can we householders, living a life of toil and need, with so many duties to perform, find the time to meditate?' Man, however, finds time to indulge in things that delight him. If he has the will surely he can devote a short period every day to meditation, whether it be at dawn, just before sleep, or when the mind is ready—some time, however brief, wherein to collect his thoughts and concentrate.

If a man thus tries to practise a little quiet contemplation day by day, he will be able to perform his duties better and in a more efficient way, he will have the courage to face tribulations and worries with a brave heart and will find contentment more easily. It is worth trying. Only one must have the determination and the urge to make the effort.

All types of meditation discussed in Buddhism lead to mental health and never to sickness; for each and every type of meditation is an effort to control and ease the tension of mental states that tend to sicken the mind. Ills of the body are not difficult to cure, but ailments of the mind are truly hard to remedy, hence the need and the effort to cleanse the mind of its impurities. This may be the most difficult thing that a man can do, but it is just what he ought to do. 'Rare in this world are those who can claim freedom from mental illness even for one moment save those in whom the taints have been wiped out (the Arahats).'[1]

When Nakulapitā, who was old, weak and ailing, approached the Master to pay his respects and hear something to his cheer and comfort, the Buddha said: 'It is true that you are weak and ailing. For a person carrying this body about to claim but a moment's health would be foolish. For this reason, thus you should train yourself: "Though my body is sick, my mind shall not be sick." Thus must you train yourself.'[2]

1. *A.* ii. 143. 2. *S.* iii. 2.

It must be stated emphatically that meditation is not a voluntary exile from life, or something practised for the hereafter. Meditation should be applied to the daily affairs of life, and its results are obtained here and now. It is not something separated from the work-a-day life. It is part and parcel of our lives. If we ignore it life lacks meaning, purpose and inspiration.

In Buddhism meditation[1] occupies the highest place; for it is in and through meditation that enlightenment and supreme security from bondage, spoken so highly of in the teachings of the Buddha, are attained.

Expositions of meditation as it is handed down in the early Buddhist writings are more or less based on the methods used by the Buddha for his own attainment of enlightenment and *Nirvāṇa* and on his personal experience of mental development.

Meditation as practised and experienced by the Buddha, before and after his enlightenment, is divided into two forms or systems: Concentration of mind or *samādhi* (*samatha*), that is unification of the mind (*cittekaggatā*, Skt. *cittaikāgratā*), and 'Insight' (*vipassanā*, Skt. *vipaśyanā* or *vidarśanā*). Of these two forms, *samādhi* or concentration has the function of calming the mind, and for this reason the word *samatha* or *samādhi*, in some contexts, is rendered as calmness, tranquillity or quiescence. Calming the mind implies unification or, if you like, 'one-pointedness' of the mind. Unification is brought about by focussing the mind on one salutary object to the exclusion of all others.

'What is concentration? What are its marks, requisites and development?

'Whatever is unification of mind, this is concentration; the four arousings of mindfulness[2] are the marks of concentration; the four right efforts[3] are the requisites for concentration; whatever is the exercise, the development, the increase of these very things, this is herein the development of concentration.'[4]

This statement clearly indicates that the three factors of the

1. The word meditation really is no equivalent of the Buddhist term *bhāvanā* which literally means 'development' or 'culture', i.e. development of mind or culture of mind. *Bhāvanā,* in Buddhism, means cultivation in the true sense of the word. It is the removal of all evil and unwholesome mental factors, and developing or cultivating all good and wholesome mental factors in order to produce a calm, concentrated mind that sees the true nature of all phenomenal things and realizes *Nirvāṇa*, the supreme security from bondage.

2. See above, p. 185.

3. See above, pp. 84, 168.

4. *M.* i. 301, *sutta* 44.

samādhi group, namely, right effort, right mindfulness and right concentration function together in support of each other. They comprise real concentration.

Many 'subjects of meditation' (*kammaṭṭhāna*)[1] are mentioned in the texts and commentaries, and some of them when carefully developed enable the meditator to reach very high mental concentration and attainments known as *jhāna*, meditative absorptions which lead to 'the Sphere of Nothingness' or 'the Sphere of Neither-Perception-nor-Non-Perception'. However high and lofty these mental attainments may be, they cannot, and do not, bring about realization of truth and supreme security from bondage.

It is evident from the texts that neither Ālāra Kālāma nor Uddaka Rāmaputta, two of the most advanced meditation masters of the day to whom the Bodhisatta Gotama went for instruction and guidance, nor his contemporary yogis, could show him the way to the highest truth and security from bondage. This was because all their mystical experiences which culminated in 'the Sphere of Neither-Perception-nor-Non-Perception', were insufficient to probe into the true nature of all conditioned things, that is to see Reality, to see things as they really are. These *jhānic* experiences undoubtedly bring about a very high concentration of mind which leads to absolute calm and tranquillity resulting in unalloyed feelings of rapturous joy and happiness in this life (*diṭṭhadhammasukha-vihāra*). Now this happiness is caused by mental calm which is the natural result of subduing the five special hindrances mentioned in the books, which we will discuss presently.

It must be mentioned here that the development of concentrative calm (*samatha bhāvanā*) as taught in Buddhism is not exclusively Buddhist. Yogis before the advent of Buddha practised different systems of meditation as they still do now. India has always been a land of mysticism, but the yoga then prevalent never went beyond a certain point. The Bodhisatta was not satisfied with mere *jhāna* and mystical experiences, his one and only aim was to attain Reality, *Nirvāṇa*. With this end in view he probed into the deepest recesses of his mind in search of a method of meditation that would bring him complete peace and deliverance.

As we saw above,[2] the Bodhisatta finally sat under a tree at Gayā and practised concentration applying himself to mindfulness of in-and-out breathing (*ānāpānasati*). Having thus gained perfect

1. *Kammaṭṭhāna* means literally a basis for concentration, some salutary object on which to concentrate.

2. See p. 15 ff.

calm, he was able to develop Insight (*vipassanā*), or true wisdom that enables a person to see things as they really are, to see the three characteristics or signs of conditioned things: impermanence, suffering or unsatisfactoriness and not-Self. It was by this 'Insight', this penetrative wisdom, that the Bodhisatta was able to burst through the hard shell of ignorance to Reality, to comprehend, in all their fullness, the Four Noble Truths, the *Dhamma* 'not heard (by him) before'.[1]

The word *vipassanā* (*vi+ passanā*) means by derivation, seeing in an extraordinary way—from the word *passati* to see and the prefix *vi* denoting, special or particular. *Vipassanā*, therefore, means, seeing beyond what is ordinary, clear vision. It is not surface seeing or skimming, not seeing mere appearances but things as they really are, which means seeing the three characteristics of all phenomenal existence.[2] It is this insight, with calm concentration of mind as its basis, that enables the yogi to purge his mind of all defilements and see Reality—*Nirvāṇa*. Insight meditation (*vipassanā-bhāvanā*), therefore, is a typical doctrine of the Buddha himself, a unique experience of the Master, exclusively Buddhist, and was not in existence prior to the advent of the Buddha.

Thus calm and insight (*samatha-vipassanā*) go together and 'they occur simultaneously (*yuganaddha*)'[3] One brings meditation to fulfilment by yoking calm and insight together so that they pull evenly. On the one hand is calming of the mind, on the other keen investigation.

'Here the development of penetrative Insight (*Vipassanā*) combines with that of tranquillizing concentration (*Samatha*), and each functions in a way that does not outstrip the other. Both gain uniformity of force. Through the overdoing of analysis there can be flurry. And indolence creeps in through too much tranquillity.'[4]

And the Buddha says: 'Develop calm, O monks, the monk who has gained calm sees things as they are.'[5]

The development of concentrative calm, however, is never an end in itself. It is only a means to something more sublime which is of vital importance, namely insight (*vipassanā*). In other words, a means to the gaining of Right Understanding, the first factor of the Path. Though only a means to an end, it plays an important role in the Noble Eightfold Path. It is also known as *citta-visuddhi*, purity of mind, which is brought about by stilling the hindrances. And

1. *S.* v. 421 (First Sermon).
2. See pp. 95, 210.
3. *M.* 149; III, 289 *Yuganaddhā ti ekakkhaṇikayuganaddhā, Com.*
4. *The Way of Mindfulness* by Bhikkhu Soma (Lake House, Colombo, 1949), p. xvii.
5. *S.* iii. *sutta* 5.

no purity of mind, no concentrative calm, can be expected from a person who is oppressed with painful feelings. It is plain and clear that so long as a man's body or mind is afflicted with pain no concentration worth the name can be obtained. The Buddha makes this point clear: 'The mind of him who suffers is not concentrated.'[1]

'Two things (*dhammā*), monks, should be developed for the understanding of lust, hate and delusion. . . . What two? Calm and insight. These two things should be developed for the abandonment, extinction and cessation of lust, hate and delusion. . . .'[2]

Further says the Buddha:

'Two things, monks, partake of knowledge (*vijjā-bhāgiyā*); calm and insight; when calm is developed, so is mind; through developed mind lust is abandoned. When insight is developed, so is wisdom (right understanding); through developed insight, ignorance is abandoned. The mind polluted with lust is not liberated. When there is pollution through ignorance wisdom is not developed. Thus deliverance of the mind (*ceto vimutti*) is due to the mind being cleansed from lust. Deliverance of wisdom (*paññā vimutti*) is due to the mind being cleansed from ignorance.'[3]

From the foregoing it is obvious that calm and insight, in other words, Right Concentration and Right Understanding of the Path, cannot be separated; together they support each other. Without a certain measure of concentrative calm no insight can be developed and without some measure of insight, some knowledge of the nature of life, no concentration can be developed. This fact is explained by the Buddha thus:

> 'No concentration is there for the unwise,
> No wisdom in one who lacks concentration;
> In whom there is concentration and wisdom,
> He truly is in *Nibbāna*'s neighbourhood.'[4]

The seeker of highest purification who is well established in virtue, practises true asceticism (*tapas*), burns out his passions and develops the path of meditative absorption (*jhāna magga*) by overcoming the many obstacles that confront a meditator. But there are five particular hindrances that obstruct concentration and the path to deliverance. In the texts they are called '*pañca nivaraṇāni*, the five hindrances'. Referring to them the Buddha says: 'There

1. *S*. v. 398. 2. *A*. i. 100. 3. *A*. i. 61. 4. *Dhp*. 372.

are, monks, these five hindrances which cause blindness, loss of vision, and non-knowledge which take away one's insight, are associated with pain and do not lead to *Nibbāna*.'[1]

Nīvaraṇāni means that which hinders and obstructs mental development. They are called hindrances because they completely close in, cut off and obstruct. They close the door to deliverance. What are the five?

1. Sense desire (*kāmacchanda*).
2. Ill-will (*vyāpāda*).
3. Sloth and torpor (*thīna-middha*).
4. Restlessness and worry (*uddhacca-kukkucca*).
5. Sceptical doubt (*vicikicchā*).

1. *Kāmacchanda* is lust for sense objects. Sensual thoughts definitely retard mental development. They disturb the mind and hinder concentration. Sensuality is due to non-restraint of the senses, which when unguarded give rise to thoughts of lust so that the mind-flux is defiled. Hence the need for the yogi to be on his guard against this hindrance which closes the door to deliverance.[2]

2. The next is ill-will. As in the case of sense desire, it is unwise or unsystematic attention that brings about ill-will, which when not checked propagates itself, saps the mind and clouds the vision. It distorts the entire mind and its properties and thus hinders awakening to truth, and blocks the path to freedom. Lust and ill-will based on ignorance, not only hamper mental growth, but act as the root cause of strife and dissension between man and man and nation and nation.

3. The third hindrance, *thīna* and *middha*, is sloth or a morbid state of the mind and mental properties. It is not, as some are inclined to think, sluggishness of the body; for even the Arahats, the Perfect Ones, who are free from this ill also experience bodily fatigue. This sloth and torpor, like butter too stiff to spread, makes the mind rigid and inert and thus lessens the yogi's enthusiasm and earnestness for meditation so that he becomes mentally sick and lazy. Laxity leads to greater slackness until finally there arises a state of callous indifference.

4. The fourth hindrance is restlessness and worry, another disadvantage that makes progress difficult. When the mind becomes restless like flustered bees in a shaken hive, it cannot concentrate. This mental agitation prevents calmness and blocks the upward path. Mental worry is just as harmful. When a man worries over one thing and another, over things done or left undone and over misfortunes, he can never have peace of mind. All this bother and

1. *S.* v. 97. 2. For details see above, p. 60.

worry, this fidgeting and unsteadiness of mind prevents concentration. Hence these two drawbacks, restlessness and worry, are included in the five hindrances that retard mental progress.

5. The fifth and the last hindrance is sceptical doubt. The Pāli word *vi* + *cikicchā* means literally: without (*vi* = *vigata*) medicine (*cikicchā*). Yes, one who suffers from perplexity is really suffering from a dire disease, and unless he sheds his doubts, he will continue to worry over and suffer from this illness. As long as man is subject to this mental itch, this sitting on the fence, he will continue to take a sceptical view of things which is most detrimental to mental development. The commentators explain this hindrance as the inability to decide anything definitely; it also includes doubt with regard to the possibility of attaining the *jhānas*. Thus these five hindrances both individually and collectively prevent the attainment of concentrative calm.

The mind that is obsessed by such detrimental forces cannot concentrate successfully on any object of a wholesome nature. It is true that a man can, however, concentrate on an object with thoughts of lust or ill-will, etc., but then, that is wrong concentration (*micchā samādhi*). It is obvious that as long as impurities or passions (*kilesa*) exist in man, evil and unwholesome thoughts will continue to arise. The meditator who practises *samādhi*, however, is incapable of committing any evil; for the hindrances are under control.

One has to develop five psychic factors known as *jhānaṅga* or factors of *jhāna* to overcome the hindrances. They are: *vitakka*, *vicāra*, *pīti*, *sukha* and *ekaggatā* which are the very opposites of the five hindrances. It is these psychic factors that raise the yogi from lower to higher levels of mental purity. The consciousness that is associated with them becomes known as *jhāna*. These psychic factors, in order, step by step, subdue the hindrances that block the path of concentration.

Sense desire, for instance, is subdued by *ekaggatā*, that is, unification of the mind; ill-will by joy (*pīti*); sloth and torpor by applied thought (*vitakka*); restlessness and worry by happiness (*sukha*) and doubt by sustained thought (*vicāra*). When they are placed side by side they stand thus:

kāmacchanda	—	ekaggatā
vyāpāda	—	pīti
thīna-middha	—	vitakka
uddhacca-kukkucca	—	sukha
vicikicchā	—	vicāra

Now a person who is really bent on meditation seeks a secluded spot and avoids people as much as possible. Calm that is gained through meditation in solitude will help a prudent man to return to the world and carry on in a better, more methodical and efficient way without falling a prey to the pleasures of city life.

A sincere student bent on deep study cuts himself off from sense attractions, seeks a congenial atmosphere, works hard and passes his examination. In the same way the meditator retires to some suitable place and fixes his mind on a subject of meditation. He has now ventured on a most difficult task. He sees how his mind really works, how his thoughts come and go, how they appear and reappear. He lives contemplating mental objects. Now when sense desire is present, he knows: 'I have sense desires'; and when they are not present, he knows: 'I have no sense desires. . . .' In this way the meditator understands the remaining four hindrances.[1] Thus with the aid of right effort and right mindfulness, the two other factors of the path that comprise *samādhi*, he first gains proximate concentration (*upacāra samādhi*); then by subduing the hindrances and washing out the impurities of his mind-flux, he gradually reaches the first *jhāna*. This is called ecstatic or attainment-concentration (*appanā samādhi*). By stages, in due course, he attains the three other *jhānas*.[2] At this *jhānic* stage the intense steadiness of his mind can be compared to the unflickering flame of a lamp on a windless day. This deep concentration fixes the mind aright and causes it to be unmoved and undisturbed. The mind and its properties are

1. See above, p. 206.

2. The four *jhānas* (meditative absorptions) are formulated in the discourses as follows:

(a) 'Herein, monks, a monk, aloof from sense desire, aloof from unwholesome thoughts, attains to and abides in the first *jhāna* which is detachment-born and accompanied by applied thought, sustained thought, joy and bliss.

(b) 'Again by allaying applied and sustained thought, he attains to and abides in the second *jhāna* which is inner tranquillity, which is unification of mind, devoid of applied and sustained thought and which has joy and bliss.

(c) 'Again by detachment from joy he dwells in equanimity, mindful and with clear comprehension and enjoys bliss in body, and attains to and abides in the third *jhāna* which the noble ones (*ariyas*) call: "Dwelling in equanimity, mindfulness and bliss."

(d) 'Again and by the giving up of bliss and suffering, by the vanishing already of joy and sorrow, he attains to and abides in the fourth *jhāna* which is neither suffering nor bliss and which is the purity of equanimity-mindfulness.'

D. ii. 186; *M.* i. 159, 181 and passim.

maintained in a state of balance like a pair of scales held in a steady hand. As long as he is in this meditative absorption, in this highest type of concentration, he cannot be disturbed under the most adverse conditions. After attaining the fourth *jhāna*, he can develop supernormal powers, read the mind of others, probe into the distant past and see former births, etc.

It may, however, be noted that even this higher practice of *samādhi* does not place the meditator in a position of security; for the underlying or latent tendencies are not removed. They are in abeyance and at any moment may reappear when circumstances permit, and plague his mind if right effort and right mindfulness wane. As he still has the impurities, unwholesome impulses, latent in his make-up, he is not yet in a state of absolute security. He has only gained calm of mind through concentration which is a very necessary means to insight. It is through insight that the latent tendencies are rooted out of his mind. When these tendencies lie dormant in the recesses of man's mind they are called latent or underlying (*anusaya*). They are dormant so long as they are not fed. The five sense organs, with the mind as the sixth, provide the necessary food in the form of visible objects, sounds, smell, taste, touch and mental objects. These foods are either agreeable or offensive. In either case sense objects act as stimulants, and no sooner are the latent tendencies thus stimulated than they rise to the surface. This rising of the tendencies is known as *pariuṭṭhāna* or *samudāgata*. When they are thus awakened and roused, they tend to escape, and seek an outlet. If man fails to exercise wise attention and to control the risen tendencies, they escape either through the doors of speech or deed or both, and that is called transgression or going beyond (*vītikkama*).

Of these three stages of the tendencies, the third, that is the 'transgression stage', is coarse, the second, the 'risen stage', is fine, and the first, or the 'latent stage', is still finer. The three weapons to overcome and deliver mind from these three stages are Virtue, Concentration and Wisdom. Through Virtue or *sīla* all bodily and verbal ill actions are brought under control, and the transgression stage is checked. It is true that even for taming verbal and physical acts a certain measure of mental discipline is needed, but not necessarily intense and serious meditation. Man may, through *sīla*, be calm and composed verbally and physically, but not in mind; he lacks Concentration, *samādhi*. Virtue cannot control the mind, though it is an asset to mental calm. Concentration with the aid of wise attention subdues the second stage of the tendencies thus preventing them from escaping. Concentration, however, is incapable of removing the latent tendencies, but wisdom, or *paññā* does so. Through wisdom, which is insight, all impulses, all tendencies, with their roots are removed and abolished. And this is deliverance (*nissaraṇa*).

It is *vipassanā bhāvanā*, Insight-meditation,[1] that removes the latent tendencies. So the meditator, establishing himself in concentrative calm, develops insight:

> '*Sabbe saṁkhārā aniccā. . . .*
> *Sabbe saṁkhārā dukkhā. . . .*
> *Sabba dhammā anattā. . . .*'[2]

> 'All conditioned things are impermanent;
> All conditioned things are *dukkha*, unsatisfactory.
> All *dhammā* (things) are without a Self, a Soul.'

The development of insight means the attempt to understand the five aggregates of clinging as impermanent, unsatisfactory and without Self. So the meditator, ardent and wise, continues with his Insight-meditation, until one day, for the first time, he gains insight into the true nature of himself, that is of his aggregates, and partially experiences *Nirvāṇa* thus attaining the first stage of realization. This achievement breaks the three fetters[3] (1) self-illusion, i.e. the delusion of an 'I' presiding over the aggregates, (2) doubt and (3) indulgence in (wrong) rites, rituals and ceremonies, so that he becomes a *Sotāpanna*, a Stream Enterer.[4] As his dross is not fully burnt he is reborn seven times at most but never below the human plane.[5] His words and acts are perfectly moral and he abstains from killing, stealing, adultery, lying and the use of intoxicants.

Continuing zestfully his 'Insight-meditation', he weakens two more fetters, (4) sense desire and (5) ill-will. With a clearer vision of *Nirvāṇa* he attains the second stage of realization and becomes

1. See chapter 7 on Right Understanding, p. 95.
2. *Dhp.* 277–9.
3. There are ten fetters (*dasa saṁyojanāni*) 1. *sakkāya-diṭṭhi*, 2. *vicikicchā*, 3. *sīlabbata-parāmāsa*, 4. *kāma-rāga*, 5. *vyāpāda*, 6. *rūparāga*, 7. *arūparāga*, 8. *māna*, 9. *uddhacca*, 10. *avijjā*. (*Saṅgīti-sutta*, *D.* 33.)
4. 'Stream' is a synonym for the Path. *Com.*
5. The same idea is conveyed in the tenth verse of the *Ratana-sutta* or 'Jewel Discourse', *Sn.* For a detailed commentarial explanation of the verse and the technical terms, see *Minor Readings* and *Illustrator* by Bhikkhu Ñāṇamoli (Pāli Text Society, London, 1960), p. 204.

known as *Sakadāgāmi*, a Once-Returner; for if he fails to attain Arahatship he is reborn on earth only once more.

Finally breaking the weakened fetters of sense desire and ill-will,[1] he then attains the third stage of realization, sees *Nirvāṇa* with a still clearer vision, and is called *Anāgāmi*, a Non-Returner, because when sensuality is rooted out, he cannot be reborn in the realm of sense pleasures (*kāma-loka*) which includes the human world, the lower heavenly worlds and all states of woe. He is reborn in the Brahma worlds.[2]

Through his clear insight he then attains the fourth and the final stage of realization and becomes known as *Arahaṁ* (an Arahat), the Consummate One, the Perfect One. With this attainment the remaining five fetters:[3] (6) lust for form, (7) and for the formless,[4] (8) conceit, (9) restlessness and (10) ignorance are broken. With this final catharsis he reaches the state where dawns for him, in all its fullness, the Light of *Nirvāṇa*, that Calm beyond words, and Unshakable Deliverance of the mind so that the world holds nothing for him any more.

Being freed he knows: 'Destroyed is birth; lived is the life of purity (the noble life); done is what was to be done; there is no more of this to come (meaning there is no more continuity of the aggregates, that is no more becoming or rebirth).'[5]

An Arahat has gone beyond both good and evil.[6] As he is free from karma-producing volitional formations (i.e. *saṁkhāra*, the second proposition, in the theory of Dependent Arising), he ceases to accumulate any fresh *karma*, though he is not exempt from the fruit of his past *karma*. Whatever he does, whether by thought, speech or physical act, creates no fresh *karma* for him, but is 'issueless'. These acts are not conditioned by any passions or latent tendencies. They are mere deeds (*kiriya*) yet they affect others. It is to such perfect saints that the Buddha referred when he said:

1. These five are called the 'lower' (*orambhāgiya*) fetters, because they bind man to the lower worlds known as *kāma-lokas*, or worlds of sense pleasures. See *M.* 6 and 64.

2. See *M.* 6: *S.* v. 61.

3. These five are called the 'higher' (*uddhambhāgiya*) fetters, because they bind man to the higher worlds. See *D.* 33: *S.* 561.

4. This is the desire for form worlds (*rūpa-loka*) and formless worlds (*arūpa-loka*), or the desire for the *rūpa-jhāna* and *arūpa-jhāna*. Though these desires are not so coarse as the desire for carnal pleasures, still they are desires in a subtle way, and therefore hinder higher attainments.

5. *S.* iii. 822.

6. *Dhp.* 39, 412.

'He who has broken human bonds
And transcended those from heaven,
He who from all bonds is free,
Him I call a *Brāhmaṇa*.[1]

He whose lust, hate and pride have fallen
As mustard seed from a needle's point,
Him I call a *Brāhmaṇa*.'[2]

The temperament or character (*carita*) of human beings varies. The *Visuddhi Magga* mentions six main types which include many lesser ones. They are those disposed to lust, hate, infatuation, faith, intellectuality and discursiveness. As temperaments differ, so do the subjects of meditation (*kammaṭṭhāna*).[3] One comes across these subjects scattered in the Pāli texts, especially in the discourses. The *Visuddhimagga*[4] describes forty of them:

Ten Objects called *Kasiṇa* (Skt. *kṛtsṇa*),
Ten Objects of Impurity, *Asubha*,
Ten Recollections, *Anussati*,
Four Sublime States, *Brahmavihāra*,
Four Formless Spheres, *Āruppā*,
One Perception, *Ekā Saññā*,
One Analysis, *Vavatthāna*.

As to suitability it is said that the Ten Impurities and Mindfulness of the body are suitable for one of lustful temperament: the four Sublime States and the four Colour (*vaṇṇa*) *Kasiṇas* for the irritable: mindfulness on in- and out-breathing for the deluded and discursive: the first Six Recollections for the faithful: and for the intellectual Mindfulness of Death, the Recollection of Peace, the Analysis of the Four Primaries and the Perception that Food is Repulsive. The remaining *Kasiṇas* and the Formless Spheres are suitable for all types of temperament.[5]

There is neither room nor need to list the various subjects of

1. *Dhp*. 417. Here the word '*Brāhmaṇa*' is a synonym for the Arahat in the sense of 'One who has put aside evil'—'*Bāhita-pāpa*' cf. *Dhp*. 388.
2. *Sn*. 631.
3. *Vism:* ch. iii or *Path of Purification* by Bhikkhu Ñāṇamoli (Colombo, 1956), ch. iii. para 121.
4. *Vism*, ch. iii.
5. *Vism*, ch. iii.

meditation in this chapter on Right Concentration. Those interested can study them in the *Visuddhimagga*[1] or the *Vimuttimagga*.[2]

As a matter of fact hard and fast rules cannot be laid down with regard to different temperaments and subjects of meditation. In the *Majjhima Nikāya* there are two discourses (Nos. 61, 62) in which the Buddha exhorts the Venerable Rāhula when teaching him the *Dhamma*. They are devoted wholly to instructions on meditation. In the sixty-second it is interesting to note that the Master gives seven types of meditation to young Rāhula who according to the Commentary was only eighteen and a *sāmaṇera* when he received them. Here is an extract from the discourse:

'Develop the meditation on lovingkindness (*mettā*), Rāhula; for by this ill-will is banished.'

'Develop the meditation on compassion (*karuṇā*), Rāhula; for by this cruelty is banished.'

'Develop them editation on sympathetic joy (*muditā*), Rāhula; for by this aversion (to meditation) is banished.

'Develop the meditation on equanimity (*upekkhā*), Rāhula; for by this hatred is banished.

'Develop the meditation on impurity (*asubha*), Rāhula; for by this lust is banished.

'Develop the meditation on the concept of impermanence (*anicca-saññā*), Rāhula; for by this pride of self (*asmi-māna*) is banished.

'Develop the concentration of mindfulness on in- and out-breathing (*ānāpānasati*), Rāhula: in- and out-breathing with mindfulness, Rāhula, developed and frequently practised bears much fruit, is of great advantage.'

One cannot and need not practise all the forty subjects of meditation: what is important is to select the one that suits one best. It helps to seek the guidance of a man who is experienced in meditation, but to start with, the books mentioned above are enough for the earnest meditator. It is, however, most important to recognize honestly what your temperament or character is; for until you have done so you cannot select the suitable subject of meditation. Once you have chosen it, work at it with confidence. If you are engrossed in worldly affairs, in routine work, it may not be easy for you to cut yourself off and sit down in a quiet place for a definite period each

1. *The Path of Purification*, translated by Bhikkhu Ñāṇamoli (Colombo, 1956).
2. *The Path of Freedom*, translated by the Rev. Ehara, Soma Thera, Kheminda Thera (Colombo, 1961).

day for serious meditation: but it can be done and if you are sincere you may well succeed. The meditation must be done regularly at fixed times for a considerable period and you must not expect quick results. Psychological changes come very slowly. It is through training in quiet contemplation that a quiet mind is achieved. Can you also achieve it? Lord Horder's answer is interesting: '... The answer is "Yes". But how? Well, not by doing "some great thing". "Why were the saints saints?" someone asked. And the answer came: "Because they were cheerful when it was difficult to be cheerful and patient when it was difficult to be patient. They pushed on when they wanted to stand still, and kept silent when they wanted to talk." That was all. So simple, but so difficult. A matter of mental hygiene. . . .'[1]

Let us now consider one of the forty subjects of meditation. Mindfulness on in- and out-breathing (*ānāpānasati*) is a well-known meditation liked and practised by many. It was used by the Bodhisatta when striving for Enlightenment under the Bodhi Tree and the Buddha himself was most emphatic on the importance of practising it. Once the Blessed One said: 'Monks, I wish to live in solitude for three months. Let my only visitor be the one who brings me food.' 'Very well, venerable sir,' replied the monks. At the end of the three months the Blessed One addressed the monks thus:

'Monks, if others (those belonging to other faiths) were to ask you: "What meditation did *Samaṇa Gotama* frequently practise during the Rains?" you should say: "The Blessed One spent the Rains frequently practising the meditation of Mindfulness on in- and out-breathing." Herein, monks, mindful I breathe in, mindful I breathe out. . . (as in the discourse above, p. 189). Monks, one who speaks rightly should say mindfulness on in- and out-breathing is the *ariya* (noble) way of life, the *brahma* (sublime) way of life, the *Tathāgata's* way of life.'[2]

The Buddhist canon is full of references to this meditation on *ānāpānasati*, and it is no wonder that the Master when exhorting Rāhula, gave detailed instruction on it. Let us turn again to the sixty-second discourse of the *Majjhima Nikāya*:[3]

1. *The Hygiene of a Quiet Mind*, Trueman Wood Lecture delivered before the Royal Society of Arts, 1938.
2. *S.* v. 326.
3. See also *M.* 118, *Ānāpānasati-sutta* and *Ānāpāna saṁyutta, S.* v. 311.

'A monk, Rāhula, having gone to the forest, the foot of a tree, or a lonely place, sits down cross-legged[1] keeping the body erect, and his mindfulness alert, mindfully he breathes in, mindfully he breathes out. When breathing in a long breath, he knows: "I breathe in a long breath"; when breathing out a long breath, he knows: "I breathe out a long breath"; when breathing in a short breath, he knows: "I breathe in a short breath"; when breathing out a short breath, he knows: "I breathe out a short breath." "Conscious of the entire process[2] I will breathe in," thus he trains himself; "conscious of the entire process I will breathe out," thus he trains himself. "Calming the bodily function (of breathing) I will breathe in," thus he trains himself. "Calming the bodily function (of breathing) I will breathe out," thus he trains himself'; and so on; the discourse proceeds and ends up stating: 'Mindfulness on in- and out-breathing, Rāhula, thus developed and frequently practised is productive of much fruit, of much advantage. When, Rāhula, in- and out-breathing with mindfulness, is thus developed and frequently practised even the last in-breath and out-breath ceases consciously and not unconsciously.'

Here one should note with care the words 'consciously he breathes in and consciously he breathes out', etc. 'Consciously' means 'with awareness'; 'with mindfulness (*sato*).' He is mindful of the breath and not of himself, his one and only aim is to focus the mind on the breath to the exclusion of other thoughts and fix the mind there; for if what is in the 'marginal' zone breaks in upon the 'focal' zone, he cannot concentrate, he becomes discursive.

When you practise concentration on in- and out-breathing, you should fix your attention at the point where the moving air strokes the nostrils and note how your breath goes in and out, but do not follow it. There should not be any holding or stopping of your breath. It should be quite natural without any effort or force on your part. At times it may become so fine that you may no longer notice it. When you go on developing this mindfulness by degrees, and when your mind is fully concentrated on the breath, you will notice that there is only a breath and nothing behind the scenes—no Self, Soul, ego or anything of that nature—that is, the breath and you are not two things, there is only a process. If you can come to that level, your concentration is very high and with this comes rapturous joy, calm and peace of mind, but this may be only for a

1. See p. 189, n. 2. 2. See p. 189, n. 3.

short moment, and your mind may again become discursive, your thoughts may wander and you may find it difficult to concentrate. It does not matter, you should 'onward ever bravely press'. Even if you fail to gain jhānic experience, this meditation will bring many benefits. It will aid clear thinking, deep understanding, mental balance and tranquillity. It will improve your health both physical and mental and keep you fit.

The Buddha says: 'Mindfulness on in- and out-breathing, monks, if developed and frequently practised is productive of much fruit, of much advantage. Mindfulness, on in- and out-breathing, monks, if developed and frequently practised, fulfils the "Four Arousings of Mindfulness";[1] the Four Arousings of Mindfulness, if developed and frequently practised bring to fulfilment the Seven Factors of Enlightenment;[2] the Seven Factors of Enlightenment if developed and frequently practised bring to fulfilment, freedom through knowledge.'[3]

The account of mindfulness on in- and out-breathing given above is far from adequate for a beginner, but it is not possible within the scope of this chapter on *samādhi* to go into greater detail. Those who so wish are referred to the books mentioned above.[4]

Meditation being the heart-beat of his Dispensation, the Buddha often stressed the importance of mental discipline. He urged and encouraged others to gain self mastery, in such words as these:

> 'Irrigators direct the water,
> Fletchers fashion the shaft,
> Carpenters bend the wood,
> The wise control themselves.'[5]

The story connected with this stanza is important from more than one angle. A disciple of the Venerable Sāriputta, Paṇḍita by name, very young and still a novice in the Order, followed the Elder when he entered the village for alms. When they were thus proceeding the novice saw a ditch and asked his teacher:

– Venerable sir, what is that?
– A ditch.
– What do they use it for?

1. See p. 188. 2. See p. 169, n. 1. 3. *M.* 118.
4. See also *Meditation Based on Mindfulness with regard to Breathing* by Kassapa Thera (Colombo, 1962).
5. *Dhp.* 80; *Thg.* 877.

– They use it to direct water to their fields for irrigation.
– Is this water something animate, has it a mind?
– No.
– Then, venerable sir, can they direct this thing which lacks reason, which is inanimate, to any place they like?
– Yes.

Then thought the novice: 'Well, if people can direct an inanimate thing like this wherever they wish, why cannot they who have a mind bring that mind under control and win the fruit of this life, sainthood (arahatship)?'

Proceeding further they saw some arrow-makers fashioning shafts.

– What are these men doing, venerable sir?
– They are fletchers; they straighten the shafts.
– Have these shafts the power of reason?
– No, they lack reason.

Then reflected the novice: 'If these man can fashion these shafts, why cannot man who possesses a mind focus it under control and strive thereby to attain the goal?'

Proceeding still further, they watched some wheelwrights at work.

– What are they doing, venerable sir?
– They bend wood and shape it into cart-wheels.
– Does this wood have a mind?
– No.

Then pondered the novice: 'These men are able to shape this senseless wood into wheels. Why cannot a man who possesses the faculty of reason, control his mind and lead a holy life?'

The novice thus carefully observing these three things said to the Elder: 'Venerable sir, would you please take back your alms bowl and robe, as I want to turn back.'

When the Elder agreed, the novice paid obeisance to him and turned back. He entered the Elder's cell and sat there in meditation. Developing contemplation on his own body, riveting and centering his thoughts on it he gained Insight-meditation and attained Arahatship. Thus did a *sāmaṇera* on the eighth day of his ordination, though young in age, but mature in meditation, awaken to Reality by controlling his mind.[1]

1. *Dhp. Com.* ii. 141.

The Buddha, referring to such saints, said:

> 'The monk who has entered a lonely cell,
> Whose mind is calmed and who sees the *Dhamma*,
> The Truth, with Insight, to him there comes
> Rapturous joy transcending that of men.'
>
> 'Whenever he reflects upon
> The rise and fall of Aggregates
> He obtains joy and rapture,
> Deathless is that to the wise.'[1]

1. *Dhp.* 373, 374.

15

CONCLUSION

IT SHOULD now be clear that the Four Noble Truths are the central concept of Buddhism. What the Buddha taught during his ministry of forty-five years embraces these Truths, namely: *Dukkha*, suffering or unsatisfactoriness, its arising, its cessation and the way out of this unsatisfactory state. One who thinks deeply will interpret these Truths as man and his goal, his final deliverance; that is the sum total of the Four Truths. What we call man, in the ultimate sense, is a combination of mind and body, or the five aggregates of clinging. On the human plane *dukkha* does not and cannot exist independently of man, his mind and body. It therefore becomes clear that *dukkha* is nothing else but man himself. As the Buddha himself said: 'the five aggregates of clinging are *dukkha*'.[1] Then we know that the second truth is *taṇhā*, Craving or 'Thirst' which is the arising, of *dukkha*. Now where does this craving arise? Where the five aggregates of clinging are, there this craving arises. The third is the stilling, the cessation of this Craving, *Nirvāṇa*—the final deliverance. This, too, is not external to man. The last and the fourth Truth is the Way out of this unsatisfactory state, this repeated existence, *saṁsāra*.

Now on close analysis we come to understand that the attempt here is to point out *saṁsāra* and its cause; *Nirvāṇa* and the way to it. *Saṁsāra* is only a succession of the mental and bodily aggregates of clinging; in other words, repeated existence, and not the physical world with its sun and moon, rivers and seas, rocks and trees. In this sense *saṁsāra* is another name for man who consists of the aggregates of clinging. This is the first Truth. In the second Truth we see the cause and condition of *saṁsāra*. In the third we see the stilling, the cessation of *saṁsāra* which is supreme security from bondage—*Nirvāṇa*. In this connection it may be noted that in the Theravāda, *saṁsāra* is diametrically opposed to *Nirvāṇa*; for we

1. See above, p. 44.

see that *saṁsāra* is the continuity of the aggregates of clinging whereas *Nirvāṇa* is the cessation of this clinging. In this life the man who enjoys pleasures of the senses is not liberated from *saṁsāra*. As long as his craving and attachment are not extinguished, he clings to the aggregates and to things pertaining to them. The liberated one, however, experiences *Nirvāṇic* bliss here and now; for he does not cling to sense objects; his craving and attachment have ceased and therefore, for him, there is no more continuity of aggregates, no more repeated existence, *saṁsāra*.

The last and the fourth Truth is the Noble Eightfold Path. In the Four Noble Truths, as you may have now realized, the Eightfold Path is the only aspect which deals with practice. Whatever there is to be practised, to be cultivated, in Buddhism, comes within the scope of the Eightfold Path. It is the A B C and the X Y Z of the Buddha's way of life. The Path is a summary of the means that enable us to get out of this tangle of *saṁsāra*, and realize *Nirvāṇa* which is the only unconditioned *dhamma* in Buddhism. Hence it is necessary to bear in mind that the Path does not function as the cause and condition of *Nirvāṇa*. It is only a means to it.

As this Noble Eightfold Path is the only aspect[1] of the Buddha's teaching which deals with practice, we have to focus all our attention on this practical teaching; for theories and speculations are of no avail to one genuinely bent on practising the *Dhamma*.

There are no short-cuts to real peace and happiness. As the Buddha has pointed out in many a sermon this is the only path which leads to the summit of the good life, which goes from lower to higher levels of the mental realm. It is a gradual training, a training in speech, deed and thought which brings about true wisdom culminating in full enlightenment and the realization of *Nirvāṇa*. It is a path for all, irrespective of race, class or creed, a path to be cultivated every moment of our waking life.

The one and only aim of the Buddha in pointing out this Noble Path, is stated in these words: 'Enlightened is the Blessed One, he teaches the *Dhamma* for enlightenment; tamed is the Blessed One, he teaches the *Dhamma* for taming; calmed is the Blessed One, he teaches the *Dhamma* for calming; crossed over has the Blessed One, he teaches the *Dhamma* for crossing over; attained to *Nibbāna* has the Blessed One, he teaches the *Dhamma* for attainment of *Nibbāna*.'[2]

If this is the purpose for which the Blessed One teaches the *Dhamma* and points out a path, it is obvious that the aim of the

1. See p. 40.　　2. *M*. 35; *D*. 25.

listener or the follower of that path should also be the same, and not anything else. The aim, for instance, of a merciful and understanding physician should be to cure the patients that come to him for succour, and the patient's one and only aim, we know, is to get himself cured as quickly as possible. That is the only aim for a sick man.

We should also understand that though there is guidance, warning and instruction, the actual practice of the *Dhamma*, the treading of the Path, is left to us. We should proceed with undiminished vigour surmounting all obstacles and watching our steps along the right Path—the Very Path trodden and pointed out by the Buddhas of all ages.[1]

To explain the idea of crossing over, the Buddha used the simile of a raft.[2] Let us listen to him:

'Using the simile of a raft, monks, I teach the *Dhamma* designed for crossing over and not for retaining. Listen and attend carefully to what I say.'

'Even so, venerable sir,' the monks replied. The Blessed One continued:

'Monks, a man sets out on a journey and comes to a vast stretch of water. The near bank is dangerous, the far bank is safe. But no boat goes to the further shore and there is no bridge. He thinks: "Vast indeed is this stretch of water, the near bank is unsafe but the further one is without danger. I had better collect grass, leaves, branches and wood to make a raft and with its aid using my hands and feet ferry myself across to the further shore."

'Then, monks, that man having made a raft, crosses over safely to the further shore striving with his hands and feet. Having crossed he thinks: "This raft has been very useful, for with its aid I have reached the further bank safely: I had better carry it on my head or back and go wherever I want."

'What do you think, monks, if he does this is he acting rightly about the raft? Suppose that man who has crossed over to the further bank should think: "This raft has been very useful, with its aid I have reached the further bank safely: I had better beach it or (let it) float down the vast stretch of water and go wherever I want." If he acts thus, monks, he would be acting rightly about the raft.

1. *S.* ii. 106. 2. *M.* 22.

Even so, monks, using the simile of a raft have I taught the *Dhamma* designed for crossing over, and not for retaining. You, monks, who understand the *Dhamma* taught by using the simile of a raft, have to give up good things (*dhamma*); how much more the evil things (*a-dhamma*).'[1]

One may ask why the Path is called the Noble Eightfold Path, and why the word 'right' (Pāli, *sammā*) is placed before each factor. The plain and simple answer is that there is also a path which is not noble, which is false and the word 'wrong' (Pāli, *micchā*) is placed before each of the eight factors of that wrong path. In two edifying parables the Buddha makes plain the right and the false one.

Addressing Tissa, the Elder, the Master said:

'Suppose, Tissa, there are two men, one unskilled and the other skilled in knowing the way. The unskilled one asks the skilled one the way, and that other replies: "Yes, man, this is the way. Carry on for a while and you will see the road fork. Reject the path to the left but take the one to the right. Proceed for a while and you will see a thick forest . . . then a large marshy pool . . . and a steep precipice. Go a little further and you will see a delightful stretch of level ground."

'I will now, Tissa, illustrate the meaning of my parable:

'By "the man who is unskilled in knowing the way" is meant the worldling. By "the man who is skilled in knowing the way" is meant the Tathāgata, the Arahat, the Supremely Enlightened One. By "the fork" is meant perplexity. The "left-hand path" is the wrong eightfold path, namely wrong understanding, wrong thought, wrong speech, wrong action, wrong livelihood, wrong effort, wrong mindfulness, wrong concentration. The "right-hand path" is the Noble Eightfold Path, namely: right understanding and so forth. The "thick forest" is a name for ignorance; the "large marshy pool" for sense-pleasures; the "steep precipice" for vexation and despair and "the delightful stretch of level ground", Tissa, is a name for *Nibbāna*. Take delight, Tissa (in the monk's life)! Take delight! I shall advise you; I shall teach you.'[2]

The second parable which is somewhat similar to the above is

1. *Dhamma*, here, according to the Commentary, means calmness or concentration of mind (*samatha*) and insight (*vipassanā*). Clinging even to such high mental attainments as these should be given up. Need one speak of the evil things.

2. *S*. iii. 108 (*sutta* 84).

found in the nineteenth discourse of the *Majjhima Nikāya*. Here the Buddha mentions a herd of deer living in a wooded valley where there was a marshy pool. Now a man not desiring their happiness but bent on their destruction comes along. If he were to block the safe road and open up a treacherous one on which he had placed a decoy and tethered a doe as a lure, that great herd of deer would be hurt and dwindle away.

But if another man desiring their happiness and safety were to open up the safe and close the treacherous road, loosing the decoy and the doe, that great herd of deer would grow and increase. The Buddha then explained the meaning of his parable: The marshy pond is another name for sense-pleasures; the great herd of deer for beings; the first comer represents *Māra*, the Evil One; the treacherous road is the eightfold wrong path, namely wrong understanding and so forth; the decoy stands for passionate pleasure; the doe for ignorance; the man desiring the welfare of the deer stands for the Tathāgata, the Arahat, the Supremely Enlightened One; the safe, secure and happy road is the Noble Eightfold Path, namely right understanding and so forth.

'Thus, monks,' the Buddha says, 'I have opened the safe, secure and happy road, closed the treacherous road and loosed the decoy and the lure. Whatever, monks, a compassionate teacher wishing the welfare of the disciples ought to do, that I have done out of compassion for you. Here are trees, here are solitary huts. Meditate, monks, do not be heedless, be not remorseful later. Thus I admonish you.'

The Buddha, the Compassionate Teacher, is no more, but he has left a legacy, the sublime *Dhamma*. The *Dhamma* is not an invention, but a discovery. It is an eternal law; it is everywhere with each man and woman, Buddhist or not Buddhist, Eastern or Western. The *Dhamma* has no labels, it knows no limit of time, space or race. It is for all time. Each person who lives the *Dhamma* brings it to light, sees and experiences it himself. It cannot be communicated to another, for it has to be self-realized. The Buddha Gotama discovered the *Dhamma*, as did his predecessors, the Buddhas of the past. If we wish to see it with our mind's eye as it really is, and not as it is presented in books, we should follow this *Ancient Path*. The Liberated Ones, the Consummate, have spoken in glowing terms of the Path and the final Deliverance in the *Psalms of the Early Buddhists*. Others hearing of their experiences rejoice and are inspired. But mere rejoicing and inspiration cannot lead them to the desired goal. Hence the need to cultivate the Path:

'Be loving and be pitiful
And well controlled in virtue's ways,
Strenuous, bent upon the goal,
And onward ever bravely press.
That danger doth in dalliance lie:
That earnestness is sure and safe:
This when ye see, then cultivate
The Eightfold Path, so shall ye touch,
So make your own,[1] the Deathless Way.'[2]

The *Ancient Path* is open to all. There is no distinction in *Nirvāṇa*. Referring to the Noble Eightfold Path and comparing it to a chariot the Buddha says:

' . . . .
And be it woman, be it man for whom
Such chariot doth wait, by that same car
Into *Nibbāṇa*'s presence shall they come.'[3]

From the foregoing it is clear that he who does not possess this chariot, and he who while possessing it fails to proceed towards the goal as instructed, will not reach his destination. There is an interesting dialogue between the Buddha Gotama and the brahman Ganaka-Moggallāna in the one hundred and seventh discourse of the *Majjhima Nikāya*. Answering a question of the brahman the Buddha explained in detail how he instructed and trained his disciples. The brahman, who listened intently, wished to know if all or only some of the instructed disciples attained the unchanging goal—*nibbāna*.[4] The Buddha's reply was that some on being instructed by him attained the unchanging goal—*nibbāna*, and some did not. The brahman then put this question to the Buddha:

'What is the cause, good Gotama, what the reason why since *nibbāna* does exist, since the way leading to *nibbāna* exists, since the good Gotama exists as adviser, some of the disciples on being instructed attain the unchanging goal—*nibbāna*, but some do not?'

1. 'Touch'—i.e. 'realize', Commentary reading *phusantā*.
2. *Psalms of the Early Buddhists, The Brethren*, P.T.S. 1951, Verses 979, 980.
3. *Kindred Sayings*, i. p. 45.
4. *Accantaniṭṭhaṁ nibbānaṁ*.

'Well, then, brahman, I will question you on this point in reply. You may answer me as you please. What do you think about this, brahman? Are you skilled in the way leading to Rājagaha?'[1]

'Yes, sir, I am skilled in the way leading to Rājagaha.'

'What do you think about this, brahman? A man might come along wanting to go to Rājagaha; having approached you, he might say: "I want to go to Rājagaha, sir; show me the way to this Rājagaha." You might answer: "Yes, my good man, this road goes to Rājagaha; go along it for a while. After a time you will see a village; go along for a while; after a time you will see a market town; go along for a while. After a time you will see Rājagaha with its delightful parks, delightful forests, delightful fields, delightful ponds." But although he has been exhorted and instructed thus by you, he might take the wrong road westwards. Then a second man might come along wanting to go to Rājagaha . . . (as above) . . . " . . . you will see Rājagaha with its delightful . . . ponds". Exhorted and instructed thus by you he might get to Rājagaha safely. What is the cause, brahman, what the reason why, since Rājagaha does exist, since the way leading to Rājagaha exists, since you exist as adviser, the one man, although being exhorted and instructed thus by you, may take the wrong road to the west while the other may get to Rājagaha safely?'

'What can I, good Gotama, do in this matter? A shower of the way, good Gotama, am I.'

'Even so, brahman, *nibbāna* does exist, the way leading to *nibbāna* exists and I exist as adviser. But while some of my disciples on being exhorted and instructed thus by me attain the unchanging goal, *nibbāna*, some do not attain it. What can I, brahman, do in this matter? A shower of the way, brahman, is a Tathāgata.'[2]

Man tends to regard whatever is old as obsolete. Hasty critics may rush to conclusions and say that the Noble Eightfold Path discovered by the Buddha Gotama is twenty-five centuries old and therefore not suitable to modern conditions. But this is shallow, unbalanced thinking. What is important is to know if a thing old or new is practical, whether it can be put to use.

There have been many problems in the world from time immemorial, each period has its own problems and our attitudes to them

1. A large town in India now known as Rājgir. The Buddha spent much of his time in the celebrated Veluvana monastery there. It was in a cave in this town that the First Convocation of the *Dhamma* and *Vinaya* was held three months after the passing away of the Buddha. The cave is still to be seen. (Author's Note.)

2. *Middle Length Sayings*, I. B. Horner (P.T.S., London), iii. pp. 55, 56.

vary; many solutions having been attempted. The Noble Eightfold Path reduces these problems to one which the Buddha called *Dukkha.* He called their origin and cause *Avijjā*, ignorance or misunderstanding and *Taṇhā*, desire or selfish motives. Now the question is, has modern man found a solution to these problems, or have we merely aggravated them? Does man now live in a state of security and happiness or of fear and constant tension? Does he follow a path leading to sanity or to madness?

Now let us see what this *Ancient Path* is. It is composed of eight factors: Right understanding, right thought, right speech, right action, right livelihood, right effort, right mindfulness and right concentration. Which factor can we put aside as obsolete and not conducive to man's material or spiritual progress? Which factor hinders man's development worldly or otherwise? Surely only the muddle-headed can call the Noble Path out of date, for though it is ancient it has a perennial freshness. As mentioned before,[1] all life's solutions can be reduced to one problem, that of *dukkha*, unsatisfactoriness: and the solution put forward by the Buddhas or Enlightened Ones of all ages, is the Noble Eightfold Path. Just as the proof of the pudding is in the eating, so the proof of this solution lies in the practice of it.

'Buddhist or not Buddhist, I have examined every one of the great religious systems of the world, and in none of them have I found anything to surpass in beauty and comprehensiveness, the Noble Eightfold Path of the Buddha. I am content to shape my life according to that Path.'[2]

In conclusion I consider it no exaggeration to say that the Buddha's greatness still shines today like a sun that blots out the glory of lesser lights, and his *Ancient Path*, still beckons the weary pilgrim to the haven of *Nirvāna*'s Security and Peace.

And as the old saying goes: 'Some run swiftly; some walk; some creep painfully; but all who keep on will reach the goal.'

MAY ALL LIVING BEINGS BE WELL AND HAPPY!

1. See p. 41.
2. Professor T. W. Rhys Davids, Founder President of the Pāli Text Society of London.

ABBREVIATIONS

A. BOOKS

All references to Pāli texts are to the editions of the PTS.

A: *Anguttara-nikāya* (number of the volume and page marked against).
Bv: *Buddhavaṁsa*.
D: *Dīgha-nikāya* (number of the sutta marked against).
DA: *Dīgha-nikāyaṭṭhakathā*, *Sumaṅgalavilāsinī*.
Dhp: *Dhammapada* (number of the verse marked against).
Iti: *Itivuttaka*.
Jat: *Jātaka*.
M: *Majjhima-nikāya* (number of the sutta marked against).
Ma: *Majjhima-nikāyaṭṭhakathā*, *Papañcasūdanī*.
Mhvg: *Mahāvagga* (of the Vinaya).
S: *Saṁyutta-nikāya* (number of the volume and page marked against).
Sn. : *Suttanipāta* (number of the verse marked against).
Sv: *Sammohavinodanī*.
Ud: *Udāna*.
Vbh: *Vibhaṅga*.
Vin: *Vinaya*.
Vism: *Visuddhimagga*.
Thg: *Theragāthā* (number of the verse marked against).
Therig: *Therīgāthā* (number of the verse marked against).

B. TERMS

Ch: Chapter.
Com: Commentary.
Gr: Greek.
Lit: Literal.
Nikāya: A collection of *suttas* in Pāli.
n: Foot Note.
PTS: Pāli Text Society of London.
Skt: Sanskrit.
Sutta: A sermon or discourse of the Buddha or his disciples recorded in the Canonical Texts.

INDICES

I PROPER NAMES

II. ENGLISH AND PĀLI

Reprinted and Donated by
The Corporate Body of the Buddha Educational Foundation
11th Floor, 55, Hang Chow S. Rd. Sec 1,Taipei,Taiwan R.O.C.
TEL:(02)3951198・FAX:(02)3913415
Printed in Taiwan (This book is not to be sold.)
FOR FREE DISTRIBUTION
1995, APR 25,000 COPIES

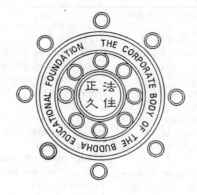